Change is the only
constant: **Berenberg.**

Change is the only
constant: Berenberg.

A history
of one of the world's
oldest banks

Hanser

1590

The year 1590 is on the Berenberg logo, and we display it with pride. Whenever a company can look back on 425 years of history, it does so with great respect for the service of all those who have gone before and worked with so much dedication and commitment. From trainees to employees, right up to management, everyone has contributed and continues to contribute to the success of the whole. However, my special thanks go to our clients and business partners, some of whom have been with us for generations.

In the over 400 years of its existence, Berenberg has had just 38 personally liable partners. This is a testament to the unique continuity at the top of the company. But such continuity, marked by success, is only possible if the people know the needs of their clients and put them at the heart of their actions and if they react quickly and flexibly to changing market conditions and constantly realign the company. This willingness to embrace change and the courage to always question one's own actions to create new things is what upholds such a long tradition like the one Berenberg knows today.

Over the last 20 years, our company has managed the transition from a private Hamburg bank working predominantly in the credit business to an internationally operating consultancy that focuses on securities. Today, there are 1,250 employees at 19 locations – three-and-a-half times as many as before the turn of the century.

Successful companies are characterised by the fact that they shape the future in a vibrant way against the backdrop of their own history while maintaining a steady eye on the future. In this vein, tradition and change are synonymous for us. We operate between these two poles on a daily basis.

At this point, I would like to express my thanks to everyone who has worked on writing this book. Clarita (née von Berenberg-Gossler) and Hartwig Gräfin and Graf von Bernstorff wrote the history of the family from the 16th century to the middle of the 20th century and relied on material from Professor Dr Manfred Pohl. Emanuel Eckardt wrote the more recent history right up the anniversary year 2015.

I am delighted that you are interested in Germany's oldest private bank and hope you enjoy reading about our company history.

Dr Hans-Walter Peters
Spokesman for the Managing Partners

THE BERENBERG FAMILY BEFORE 1590

THE COMPANY IN HAMBURG 1590–1769

JOH. BERENBERG, GOSSLER & CO. 1769–1914

IN THE SHADOW OF WARS AND CRISES
CORNELIUS VON BERENBERG-GOSSLER 1874–1953

The history of the Berenberg family can be traced back to the end of the 15th century. It was a time of major discoveries that led to the economic reorientation of Europe, and, yet, it was a time of bloody religious conflicts. Like many other early bourgeois families, the Berenbergs were searching amidst the turmoil for a place which offered a promising future for its trade dealings and for its new religion. They ultimately found this place in Hamburg.

The Berenberg family originally came from the Bergisches Land region in North Rhine-Westphalia. Around 1465, Thillmann Berenberg was born near Gummersbach on the "Groß-Berenberg" estate, from which the family took its name. According to tradition, the patriarch was engaged in the cloth trade, which remained the main activity of the family for several generations.

His son Jan first went to Cologne, which was one of the most important strongholds of the Hanseatic League, but as early as 1515, *Thillmans zon de Coelenaere* (Thillman's son from Cologne) became a citizen of the city of Lier, which was situated just a few kilometres away from the gates of Antwerp. Jan's oldest son, Jasper, continued the father's business there while younger brother Paul I worked as a cloth-maker and merchant in Antwerp beginning in 1582.

With his translation of the Bible, Martin Luther (1483–1546) laid the cornerstone for the Reformation (Portrait by Lucas Cranach the Elder, 1528)

Antwerp

In the middle of the 16th century, Antwerp was Europe's richest and busiest city. With the discovery of America by Christopher Columbus in 1492, the voyages of Amerigo Vespucci, the discovery of the passage to the East Indies by Vasco da Gama, the first circumnavigation by Magellan and subsequent colonisation, trade increasingly shifted from the Mediterranean area with Venice to the Atlantic. The cities that profited from this development included Lisbon, Seville, Amsterdam and, later, Hamburg. For a few decades, Antwerp with its protected Schelde Port, became the most important trading centre of all.

"The view of Antwerp made me sad," wrote a Venetian envoy around 1550, "as I saw how it put Venice in the shade". Up to 500 ships lowered and raised their anchor here. The city was already home to a stock market, which was dedicated *ad usum mercatorum cuiusque gentis ac linguae* (to the benefit of merchants of all countries and languages), and low import and export duties attracted merchants from many trading countries. Although the Netherlands

Antwerp Stock Exchange, 1567

Their discoveries and daring ex-
peditions across the Atlantic
helped to establish trading routes
(from the left):
Amerigo Vespucci (1454–1512),
Vasco da Gama (1469–1524),
Ferdinand Magellan (1480–1521)

First contacts with the
Merchant Adventurers

was ruled by the catholic Habsburgs, various religions existed side-by-side, and thus religious reasons certainly also motivated Paul Berenberg to move to Antwerp. A protestant community was located there, which in 1566 – according to the author and priest Flacius Illyricus – had around 30,000 believers.

In Antwerp, Paul Berenberg I established contacts to the Right Worshipful Company of Merchant Adventurers, an English trading group which had the privilege of selling linens on the continent including cloths made from English wool, which were then treated and dyed by skilful Dutchmen. The close ties to the Merchant Adventurers shaped the trading operations of the Berenbergs for many generations, and when the family finally had to leave the Netherlands, it followed the English and made its new home in Hamburg.

The time of tolerance for the Netherlands soon came to an end. The attempt to maintain religious independence and to defend the privileges of the nobility and bourgeoisie against the Spanish rule turned into the Dutch Revolt in 1568.

The Dutch Revolt

Until 1566, William of Orange, as burgrave of Antwerp, succeeded in stemming the attacks by the population with prudence and circumspection and in appeasing the anger of the Spanish governess Margaret of Parma, a half-sister of Philipp II of Spain. However, on 20 August 1566, an iconoclastic event occurred in Antwerp, which led not only to the destruction of numerous valuable pieces of art, but which also provoked the deployment of Spanish troops to Antwerp. On 13 March 1567, the *Geusen*, as the Dutch noblemen called themselves, were defeated in Antwerp by the Spanish. William of Orange and the "most noble merchants" of Antwerp and Lier fled the city. By way of brutal executions, Margaret of Parma laid the way for the introduction of the Duke of Alba, who had been granted special Inquisition authority by Philipp II, and launched his reign of terror that same year.

Paul Berenberg held out with his sons and survived lootings and fires, methods the Spanish used in an attempt to break the Dutch resistance. In 1581, the northern provinces broke away from Spain, and for the next four years Reformed preachers pursued their religious duties relatively undisturbed. However, the peace was short lived. William of Orange was murdered by a catholic fanatic in 1584, and Alexander Farnese, who had been governor of the catholic southern provinces since 1578, began immediately to recapture the north.

The Berenbergs Leave the Netherlands

The second wave of refugees saw thousands of Protestants fleeing the Netherlands, primarily craftsmen and smaller trades people who could count on finding work anywhere. Yet when Alexander Farnese gave Protestants the ultimate choice in 1585 of either converting to Catholicism, or leaving Antwerp within the next four years, most of the merchants decided to look for a new home. Within this four-year period, they were granted the right to take their wealth with them. This marked the end of Antwerp's heyday.

The Merchant Adventurers had already moved their headquarters to Hamburg in 1567; later they went to Wismar and then finally to Stade in 1587. Berenberg senior now advised his sons to build up their own trading operations in the footsteps of the English. He chose to stay behind in Antwerp.

Cornelius, the youngest, went to Cologne, where he died before establishing a company. In 1587, Paul II became a deputy to his father in Stade, where he managed business ties to the Merchant Adventurers. Hans, the oldest, initially followed the Merchant Adventurers to Wismar, where he married

Port scene, 16th century: a merchant-man discharges its cargo

Hans Berenberg relocates to Hamburg

Anna Schnelling; his brother, Paul, married her sister, Francina, five years later. The Schnelling family gave them excellent contacts to Livorno, Venice and Seville.

In 1588, when Hans finally relocated to Hamburg, he saw his father again. Paul I had made the trip to marry his daughter to Augustin Vossenholt, a merchant from Brabant. The decision to have Hamburg as the base for the Berenberg family's commercial activities must have been made at this family reunion. Hans was to pursue the business in Hamburg, and younger brother

Paul was to do the groundwork for the Merchant Adventurers just a few kilometres away in Stade, where their stockyard was located.

With their father based in Antwerp, the close contact to the Merchant Adventurers and the good ties to southern Europe, the Berenberg brothers had a solid business network. When the father returned to Antwerp in 1589, the foundation had been laid for the opening of the business in Hamburg in 1590.

The "Founding Years" 1590–1618

Hans Berenberg moved to Hamburg in 1588. That same year, the destruction of the Spanish Armada by the English in the English Channel led to a geopolitical change. With the Spanish weakened, the English and the Dutch were able to break the Spanish monopoly in overseas trade. From now on, the north of Europe took on much greater significance.

Hamburg profited from the changes. The city had already become increasingly important as a commercial hub over the course of the 16th century. Given its favourable free access to the ocean and the waterways that led to the interior as well as the shift in trade to Western Europe and the opening of the Hamburg-Silesia and Hamburg-Austria-Hungary-Bohemia trade routes, Hamburg took on a pivotal role for "east-west" relations.

At this time the Hanseatic League was forced increasingly out of trade with England and its main position, the London steelyard. Hamburg, unlike previous dominant Baltic cities, had adjusted early on to the changed con-

The new crane and city scales in the Port of Hamburg (ca. 1650), painting by Elias Galli

The goal was to overthrow the "Virgin Queen" Elizabeth I, but the winds proved unfavourable for Alexander Farnese in 1588: English naval victory over the Spanish Armada in the English Channel

For the Berenbergs, the textile trade was the family's chief source of income for several generations

ditions. The Hamburg clothiers had begun setting up their own processing industry in the first half of the 16th century, and when the Merchant Adventurers began trading (especially with cloth) via Stade and Hamburg, an experienced local cloth industry was in place, which was in a position to have the raw English products imported directly. Hamburg experienced a boom, which a contemporary commented on at the end of the 17th century with the words *florentissimum emporium totius Germaniae.*

The boom started with the goods trade. Hamburg had been home to a stock market since 1558, incidentally, the first stock market on German soil, and as of 1603 a formal exchange law. When the Hamburger Bank was founded in 1619, Paul II and Hans Berenberg were involved.

The Hamburger Bank viewed maintaining monetary stability as one of its main tasks; this had suffered from an increasing deterioration of coinage. Only those who deposited full-fledged Thaler, special coins with a specified silver content, were permitted to open an account. The pioneering adherence to the silver standard allowed the "Mark Banco" to become one of the strongest and longer-standing currencies in Europe. This made life easier for merchants who could now deposit from one account to another; it was the start of the clearing system in Hamburg. Later, the deposits were used as credit for refinancing purposes in return for security.

The Dutch in Hamburg

Hamburg's boom was primarily boosted by the entrepreneurial energy of the Dutch refugees. Moreover, numerous Spanish and Portuguese Jews who had also flown to Hamburg shared in this as well.

Hans and Paul Berenberg launch their company

When the Berenbergs founded their Hamburg-based company in 1590, around 1,000 Dutch people were living in the city. Some had arrived with the first wave of refugees and provided tremendous support to newly arriving families. In addition to the many trades people who invigorated local business, it was experienced merchants such as the van Uffelen, Bodeck, Amsinck, de Hertoghe, Verpoorten, Groenendal, van Duyveland, van Haesdonck families, who stimulated trade and financing. A Dutch builder constructed the first stock exchange building, the Hamburger Bank was founded in 1619, and the maritime insurance and the exchange law were also organised according to the Dutch model.

In 1619, 42 Hamburg-based companies had turnovers in excess of 100,000 marks; 32 of them were of Dutch origin. The Berenberg brothers were ranked fifteenth and sixteenth, and by 1622, Paul had climbed to sixth in the rankings.

But the ranking is deceiving as these figures only include the transactions done through the Hamburger Bank; a considerable amount of trade was still handled through direct payments.

Goods Trade and Other Business Dealings

In keeping with family tradition, Paul II and Hans Berenberg traded mainly with cloth in the early years and, thus, took advantage of their good ties to the Company of Merchant Adventurers. Up until 1605 one of the brothers lived at the stockyard of the Merchant Adventurers in Stade. Later on, they hired a representative.

The merchants of Hamburg supplied the English with *Nestauer Röte*, fustian from upper Germany, indigo and gauze and in addition on to cloth, imported luxury items, including ingredients to dye fine materials and spices. Salt came from Lisbon and rye from Arkhangelsk. The Berenberg brothers focussed on the trade with silk and fustian, a flannel-like material made of cotton. A large number of other locally available goods were also traded.

Trading with silk, fustian and other textiles

In 1597, the Hanseatic League threatened to abolish the British staple in Stade. Almost immediately there was a run on available linen, which the Berenbergs took advantage of as a business letter from Hamburg documents: "Everyone has Jettender linens, who never had the notion prior to trade them. Berenberg and another Dutchman, Lieven van der Eggen, bought over 200 fine linens for 200 pounds to 60 pounds with a view to reselling them all here. If we are no longer allowed to bring linens to Germany, they will reap great

Silver sovereigns from Hamburg

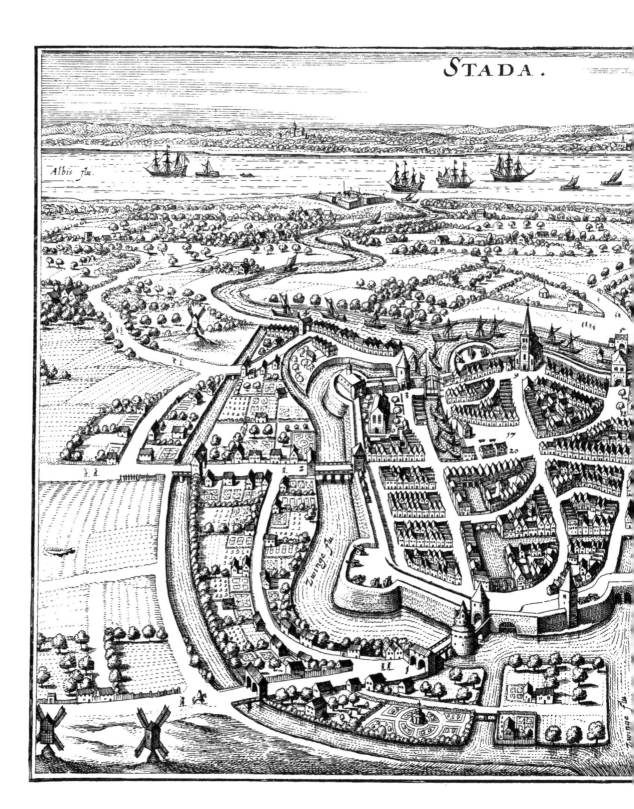

STADA.

Albis flu.

Zwinge flu.

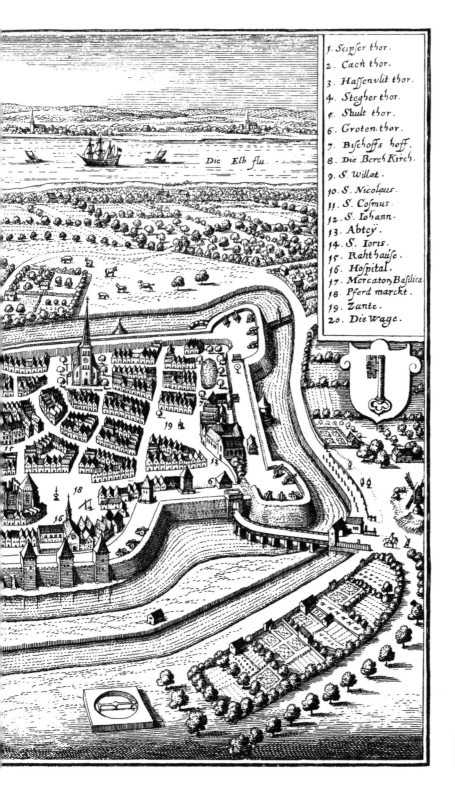

Die Elb flu.

Just outside Hamburg: the city of Stade, an engraving by Matthäus Merian the Elder from 1653

The steelyard in London served Hanseatic merchants as a residence and workplace in England

Expansion of operations into the Baltic region, Arkhangelsk and Italy

profits; otherwise I don't believe it. But there are others who are always prepared to buy fine linens."

The English government reacted by closing the steelyard in London and threatened the Hanseatic League with other restrictions in England whereupon Hamburg relented and lifted the ban on the company of Merchant Adventurers in Stade. The Berenberg brothers sat on their linens and were not successful at "reaping great profits", but they sold the "200 linens" "to others".

The constant uncertainty of the location of the "Court of Merchant Adventurers" in Stade or in Hamburg prompted the brothers to expand their company's business base. The import and export business with the Iberian Peninsula was an option, which also entailed an expansion of their business to the Baltic, Arkhangelsk and to Italy. Conversely, the ties to the Merchant Adventurers saved the Berenbergs from losses if trade with Spain or Portugal was not going well.

Whether the Berenbergs were active in financial transactions at this point remains unclear. On 4 March 1597, Paul Berenberg started out for Frankfurt am Main to take part in the spring trade fair as his father had done in the past. He took advantage of links to the Dutchman Johann von Bodeck, who had settled in the city on the Main in 1585 and had become one of the leading merchants and bankers.

In addition to the goods trade, the broker business in Hamburg grew quickly due to the strong trade activity with foreign markets. And here, too, the Dutch were the main driving force. Around 1605, there were 31 sworn brokers in Hamburg; the majority of them Dutch.

The same applied to the insurance branch, which primarily became important to cover damages incurred at sea and with the loss of ships. The first mention of this type of insurance in Hamburg was in 1588.

Integration Problems

The ties to the Merchant Adventurers in Stade formed the basis and focus of the Berenberg company. Yet there was another reason why the company's location proved to be advantageous. Trade restrictions could be circumvented in Stade which the Dutch were subject to in Hamburg. The citizens of Hamburg initially resisted the successful foreigners, quite in contrast to the Hamburg Council, which kept pointing out the potential harm to the customs duty, the common good and the citizens, if the foreigners "were turned away."

Trade in Hamburg was subject to strict regulations, which were only relaxed gradually. Foreigners were forbidden to have business dealings with other foreigners within the city. As a result, many of the Dutch who had immigrated in the second half of the 16th century became citizens of the city such as Wilhelm Amsinck and Cornelius de Hertoghe. Paul and Hans Berenberg decided not to take this step.

In 1604, the Council finally issued a new mandate, which regulated the interests of foreigners. The new trade regulation attempted to give advantages to the citizens of Hamburg without ruining the foreigners' business base. As a result, city citizens were still the only ones allowed to trade in products of the city and the environs. This included products such as hemp, pitch, tar, linen, woollen linen, ammunition, lead, iron, grain, bread, butter, cheese, herring, flatfish and kippers as well as salt.

Free goods were essentially new and rare luxury goods, which Hans and Paul Berenberg also traded, and included Rhenish wines, Hungarian copper, gemstones, pearls, cochineal, indigo and other valuable dyes, ebony and basilwood, elephant tusks, sugar, spices such as pepper, cloves, nutmeg and ginger, salt, velvet and silk, white English cloths, Silesian canvas, madder, wax, flax and Nuremberg goods. In Hamburg, the Berenbergs traded in goods which were off-limits to them in Stade.

Just one year later, in 1605, a ten-year agreement put the Dutch almost on equal footing with the citizens of Hamburg. They were allowed to purchase houses and property, assume common honorary offices and, should they leave the city, they were permitted to take their wealth with them without paying the tithe. The agreement was extended in March 1615 for another

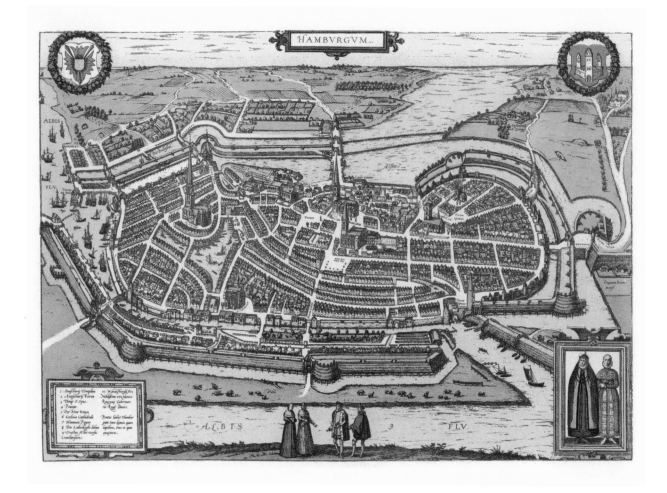

Outline map of the city of Hamburg before 1600 with the port entrance at Baumwall and "Kehrwieder" (Turnaround) Point at the left margin, as depicted by the engraver Franz Hogenberg

15 years. An extension in 1630 was initially rejected by the citizens, but in 1639 a third 15-year extension was concluded. A fourth agreement was unnecessary since most of the immigrated Dutch, with the exception of the Berenbergs, had already become citizens of Hamburg.

As evident from the first agreements, Hans and Paul Berenberg II did not intend on becoming citizens of Hamburg. Upon conclusion of the third agreement in 1639, only Paul Berenberg II was still alive, and he signed the agreement. Even the sons of Hans and Paul II refused to become citizens of Hamburg. They preferred to reach an agreement in person with the Senate about their rights and duties. Cornelius Berenberg (1634–1711), a member of the third generation of Berenbergs in Hamburg, became a citizen of Hamburg in 1684.

The growing prosperity of Dutch families in Hamburg can be illustrated by comparing the dues which they as newcomers had to pay to the city in 1605 and in 1639, 34 years later. In 1605, 130 families paid 5,721 marks; in 1639, 160 families paid 14,980 marks. On average, in 1605 the individual family had to pay 44 marks, in 1639, 93.60 marks. Roughly one-quarter of the entire wealth of all inhabitants at this time was said to be in the hands of the Dutch and newcomers to Hamburg.

Welfare: the Dutch Relief Fund for the Poor

Among the Dutch who had settled in Hamburg there were, of course, not just successful merchants. Many of the fleeing families were poor and required assistance. The affluent merchants Wilhelm Amsinck and Gillis de Greve were compelled by this fact to set up the "Dutch Relief Fund for the Poor" in 1585. Hans and Paul Berenberg became involved in the activities of the fund soon after they had relocated to Hamburg. De Greve came to Hamburg from Antwerp in 1568, and Amsinck came from Deventer in 1576. Both ran businesses that were similar to the Berenbergs, and the families became closer when Wilhelm Amsinck's son, Arnold, married Hans Berenberg's daughter, Francina, in June 1609.

Initially, money was simply collected in a box in the old part of the city. To this end, two well regarded Dutchmen had to go door-to-door once a week in the parishes of St Peter, St Nicholas, St Catherine and St James. Later, the districts expanded to include the new part of the city. The money collected was given to the administrator, who noted the sums and the names of the bearers in his accounting book. Donations were another source of funds and allowed people to buy themselves out of the irksome task of going around with the collection box. Moreover, donations were made on special occasions, such as in the event of favourable business results, or the return of a ship that was thought to be long gone.

Money collected in this way benefited the registered Dutch poor, who were helped with a regular donation for the rest of their lives as long as they had no other sources of income. Later, people also started supporting widowed surviving dependents and "the deserving poor". In addition, a fund was

Hans and Paul Berenberg collected and donated money for the "Dutch Relief Fund for the Poor", which was founded in 1585

made ready for all Dutch people to provide financial relief in the event of a sudden emergency.

Hans and Paul Berenberg took part in the collection box rounds, made donations and, beginning in 1607, were also part of the management of the Dutch Relief Fund for the Poor. Hans Berenberg senior held the position of administrator in 1607/08; brother Paul assumed the role in 1622/23. Upon his death in 1626, Hans Berenberg left 1,000 marks to the relief fund.

The Berenberg brothers were moreover involved in other charitable establishments, including an orphanage, which grew out of an initiative by Gillis de Greve, for orphans of the 1596/97 plague, but also in a more or less charitable prison, which Wilhelm Amsinck initiated in 1615/16. Here, beggars still capable of work were guided to a meaningful job, and the building also served as accommodation for convicts. The money to build the institution came from the first ever lottery to be organised in Hamburg in 1616 in keeping with the Dutch model. The lottery generated so much money that the construction costs were covered for the most part.

Everyday Life, Family and Religion

Hans Berenberg senior owned a house in the St Nicholas' parish whose value upon his death in 1626 was pegged at 15,000 Thaler (roughly 45,000 marks). Brother Paul had been living in St Peter's parish since 1605 and later moved to the parish of St Catherine, the preferred residential area of the Dutch. The old Dutch merchant quarter with the streets Holländischer Brook, Alter and Neuer Wandrahm, Hüxter and Cremon had to give way in the 19th century to Speicherstadt, the warehouse district of the free port of Hamburg. Aside from houses, people had a garden in front of the then Dammtor gate, such as in the area of today's Großen Bleichen and the Fuhlentwiete.

In the beginning, the Berenbergs led a comparatively frugal life. In 1629, the household costs for Hans Berenberg junior's family came to 2,606 marks, which appears to be a small amount considering that a house back then cost 720 marks in rent per year, a groom received 40 marks in wages a year and that "two horses with carriage" cost 615 marks. Just a few years later, the household expenses had increased to almost 6,000 marks, to the level of a well-off Hamburg-based merchant family.

The Dutch immigrants were Protestants, but their Reformist, Calvinistic faith incurred the ill will of the church authority because Hamburg was Lutheran. The conflicts between the faiths went on outside of Hamburg with similar intensity akin to the struggle between Protestantism and Catholicism. Melanchthon called the religious hate of his time *rabies theologorum*, and this "raving madness" was soon to trigger the Thirty Years' War. Hamburg was fortunately rather moderate in this respect meaning that the Reformists were not forced to change faiths. However, they were prohibited from establishing their own religious communities. In 1588, they founded a Walloon congregation in Stade, and the Merchant Adventurers offered advice and assistance. Baptisms, marriages and funerals had to be held outside the city until 1602 when the Reformed Church in nearby Altona was given construction permission.

Swiss reformer John Calvin (1509–1564)

At the beginning of the 17th century, before the turmoil of the Thirty Years' War, Hans senior and Paul II Berenberg integrated into Dutch communities and were prosperous and renowned. Their children married into the Amsinck, de Hertoghe, Ruhlant, Janssen van Duyveland, van Haensdonck and van Uffelen families, whose ties to Spain, Portugal, Italy and North America subsequently would prove useful time and again. The brothers had demonstrated business acumen and were involved in the founding of the Hamburger Bank and various other social institutions. In so doing, they laid a business and social foundation upon which their descendents could successfully build.

Hans Berenberg senior (1561–1626) died eight years after the outbreak of the Thirty Years' War at the age of 65. Both his sons, Hans junior (1593–1640) and Andreas (1595–1661), had long since started to follow in the footsteps of their father. Together with their Uncle Paul II (1566–1645) and his son, Paul III, they carried on business dealings through initially very troubled times.

A pivotal event in Central European history: the Battle of White Mountain near Prague, 1620

Thirty Years' War 1618–1648

The Thirty Years' War began in 1618 as a local conflict between Bohemian Protestants and the catholic emperor. In 1619, the Bohemian Diet proclaimed the Calvinist Elector Palatine Friedrich to be its king although Emperor Ferdinand II was rightfully entitled to the throne. Johann T'Serclaes Tilly's victory over the emperor in the Battle of White Mountain near Prague ended the "Bohemian phase" of the war in 1620. Bohemia was brutally reconverted to Catholicism, the Palatine fell to Bavaria, and the catholic states received the majority in the German Imperial Diet.

By now, the conflict had escalated to a European war, which saw the involvement of all European powers except England and Turkey. The extent of the catholic victory was unsettling for the protestant potentates as well as for the Catholics: the German princes saw their freedoms threatened by the growing power of the Emperor, and the Pope sympathised with the French view that the Habsburgs were becoming too powerful for France and the freedom of the papacy. Thus, he turned a blind eye when Cardinal Richelieu taxed the French Catholics to help German Protestants and later the King of Sweden against a catholic emperor. The individuals Gustav Adolphus of Sweden and Wallenstein represented both sides of the struggle in historical memory.

The war devastated almost all of Germany and terrible losses were suffered. The Spanish advanced to the Rhine, the Danes into northern Germany and the Swedes via the Baltic Sea. When France intervened, an international war broke out, and the imperial estates were no longer in a position to manage the development that had been set in motion. The warlike actions were arbitrarily protracted by the armies. According to rather conservative estimates, the population in Germany and Austria was reduced from 21 million to 13.5 million during the Thirty Years' War.

The Peace of Westphalia, which was finally adopted in Münster in 1648, by the emperor, France and Sweden along with their respective allies, led to a reorganisation of Europe. In addition, numerous unresolved religious issues were regulated and Protestantism was saved. The German principalities confirmed their pre-war freedoms vis-à-vis the Emperor, the Empire remained torn, its economic power faded. The Habsburg Spanish finally had to acknowledge the independence of the northern Netherlands. France benefited and was able to expand its borders, and the Bourbons replaced the Habsburgs as the dominant power in Europe.

Neutrality and Business

Amidst the chaos of war, Hamburg tried with varying degrees of success to hold a course of neutrality. Fortunately, it was one of the best fortified cities and due to the insistence of the Dutch merchants, Council had arranged for the Dutch fortress builder Johan van Valckenburgh to come to the city to restore the fortifications between 1616 and 1625. The fortification encircled large portions of the newer part of the city and left room for future expansion possibilities. In the years of war that followed, its 24 bastions proved to be a strong argument against the enemies of Hamburg's neutrality.

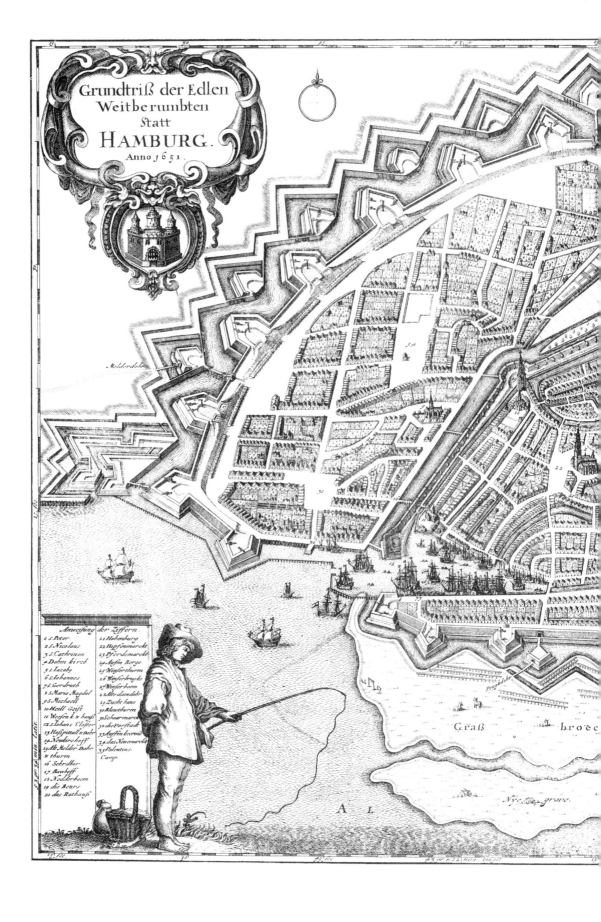

Grundtriß der Edlen Weitberumbten Statt HAMBURG.

Anno 1651.

Melderdohr

Anweisung der Ziffern.

1 S. Peter	21 Hohenburg
2 S. Nicolaus	22 Hopfenmarckt
3 S. Cathrinen	23 Pferdemarckt
4 Dohm kirch	24 Auf'm Berge
5 S. Jacob	25 Winserthurm
6 S. Johannes	26 Winserbruck:
7 S. Gertruth	27 Winserboom
8 S. Maria Magdal	28 Alte Landohr
9 S. Michaell	29 Zuchthaus
10 Heill Geist	30 Blaweturm
11 Weesen k. u. hauß	31 Schaarmarckt
12 Johans Closter	32 die Vorstadt
13 Hoßpittall u. dohr	33 Auf'm teerwik
14 Newkirchoff	34 das Newenmarckt
15 Alt. Melder Dohr	35 Palentins.
& thurm	Camp.
16 Schrdhor	
17 Bawhoff	
18 Nedderboom	
19 die Beurs	
20 das Rathauß	

Graß broec

Nye grave.

A L

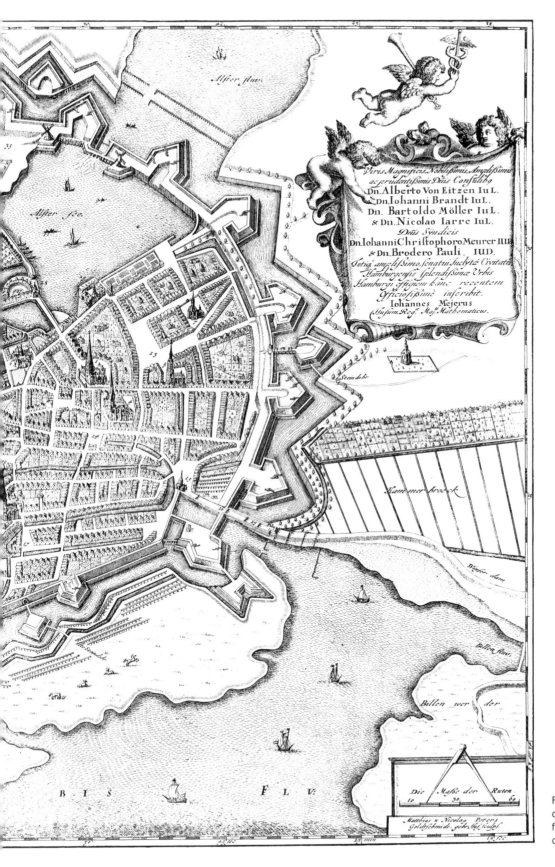

Featured in the engraving by the cartographer Johannes Mejer from 1651: the new fortifications of Hamburg

One of the biggest threats to this policy was posed by the Danish King Christian IV. The affluent city of Hamburg, with its favourable location, had been a thorn in his side for a long time, and he attempted on several occasions to bring the Elbe-Weser Triangle under his control. In 1617, he founded Glückstadt as a competing location and equipped it with numerous privileges.

Two years later, Denmark occupied Stade and, in 1621, forced Hamburg with the Steinburg Treaty into a subservient relationship; however, the Danish interpretation that Hamburg was now subservient was quickly contested by Hamburg.

The conflicts with Denmark continued during the entire war and led to unpredictable fluctuations in trade dealings. Hamburg had signed treaties in 1606 with Spain and France and had flourishing trade dealings, but between 1625 and 1633, dealings with both countries dropped 7 percent as the Netherlands, Denmark and England had concluded a treaty in 1625 against Emperor Ferdinand II and Philipp IV, the King of Spain.

Philipp IV attempted to persuade the emperor to establish a joint shipping company with the Hanseatic cities, the so-called Admiralty. In 1627, the emperor entered into negotiations with the Hanseatic cities with a view to establishing the German-Spanish trading company under imperial protection and imperial maritime power. The goal was to eliminate Dutch trade at sea, and, together with the Hanseatic cities, bring the Baltic Sea trade under control. In return, Hamburg was promised unimpeded shipping along the Elbe River. Without its permission, no fortification was to be built on the Elbe, no duties were to be levied and no foreign warship was permitted to travel the river. Although Hamburg entered into the negotiations, it ultimately declined the attractive offer out of fear of Christian IV.

With these tactics, the Hamburg Council had hoped to persuade Denmark to give in. However, this was not to be the case. Even though the city had rejected recruiting Catholics, the Danish king retaliated by levying such an oppressive customs duty in Glückstadt that Hamburg made an attempt in April 1630 – with Sweden's encouragement – to conquer Glückstadt. By September of the same year, Christian IV had chased them away again. Yet he never dared to venture into Hamburg.

Under constant Danish pressure, Hamburg signed a treaty in 1632 with Gustav Adolphus of Sweden, which was to guarantee the city trade protection on all routes. In return, the city granted Swedish advertising and financed

PRÆLIUM NAVALE INTER SUECOS ET DANOS. A: 1644

In his drawing, Peter Lotichius listed the ships engaged in the naval battle between Sweden and Denmark in October 1644

parts of the Swedish army, which constituted a clear breach of the neutrality policy. Following the treaty with Sweden, the trade turnover with Iberia and France increased again. For Paul Berenberg II, it went from 13,287 Mark Banco in 1632 to a temporary high of 37,600 Mark Banco in 1634.

In 1633, when Emperor Ferdinand II saw himself forced to grant the Danish king the Elbe customs duty for four years, the turnover in trade with Iberia dropped with a certain delay to 19,940 Mark Banco in 1637, but recovered because Hamburg was returned the Elbe privilege, something that was once again expressly confirmed by the new emperor, Ferdinand III.

Christian IV was at it again in 1643: The city had to once again renounce its sovereignty over the Elbe River, acknowledge the Glückstadt customs duty and subservience, hand over Danish ships and goods and pay a considerable amount of money.

In 1645, Denmark was finally defeated by Sweden with the help of the Netherlands and had to renounce the Glückstadt customs duty once and for all as part of the Peace of Brömsebro. Hamburg and Bremen concluded a trade agreement in the same year with the Dutch, which guaranteed both cities trade protection along the Elbe-Weser waterway.

Hamburg made constant tactical moves during the war and went back and forth between Sweden, the German Emperor and Denmark without ever reaching long-term solutions. Yet, the policy of neutrality was, for the most part, adhered to because, apparently, even the fiercest opponents were all of the same opinion that Hamburg was essential as a bastion of neutrality. The city supplied friend and foe and had become a packaging and storage centre, banking centre and gathering place within Europe. Despite numerous contributions, the city's wealth had grown steadily, and the population had almost doubled.

The Dutch colony in Hamburg was flexible enough to adapt to the changing conditions and difficulties; in these risky times, the merchants engaged more often in different business dealings together.

During the war, grain was an important commodity in all of Europe, and it goes without saying that this applied in even greater measure for Germany, which had been heavily destroyed. Together with the Amsinck family, Hans junior and Andreas Berenberg took part in this flourishing trade. Danzig was the hub of the grain trade at this time, supplying not only the German hinterland, but also Spain and Portugal via Hamburg.

In the years that followed 1632, the accounting books of the Authority for Business and Transportation, founded in 1623, the so-called "Admiralty", noted for Hans and Andreas Berenberg the following commercial goods: sugar and cinnamon from Lisbon; verdigris (for dyeing) and almonds from Marseille; ginger, indigo and olives from Sanlúcar; wool, wine and raisins from Malaga; silk from Venice, "blue" (for dyeing) from Cadiz; flax to Lisbon, wax to Genoa, Sanlúcar and San Sebastian; rye to Lisbon, timber to Malaga, metal, lead, copper wire and oats to Rouen as well as cinnamon, ginger and cloth to Nuremberg. Records in a notebook belonging to Hans Berenberg junior indicate that close business ties with the Netherlands and Danzig can also be inferred.

As a result of the Peace of Westphalia in 1648, the situation became consolidated around Hamburg. Sweden received the Archdiocese of Bremen as an imperial lien, which encircled Stade and went up to the gates of Hamburg. In the north and the west, Hamburg bordered on the imperial Danish section of

Hamburg supplied friend and foe – the Berenbergs traded in grain

Holstein, to which Altona belonged, and in the north and northeast on the Duchy of Schleswig-Holstein-Gottorp. In the east, there was the Duchy of Lauenburg and in the south, the Duchy of Lüneburg.

New problems were, however, already foreseeable as Lüneburg, Celle and the Electorate of Brandenburg claimed free access to the Elbe estuary, and the conflict with the Danes had only been temporarily resolved.

Along with Hamburg, Danzig (now Gdansk) was an important seaport and transshipment venue for grain: coloured copper engraving from ca. 1650 showing a view of Danzig from a nearby rise

Diversification and Continuity:
Cornelius Berenberg (1634–1711)

Following the death of Hans Berenberg junior in 1640, sons Rudolf and Johann continued to run the business, working closely with their uncle Andreas. When their younger half-brother Cornelius began working in the company after completing his merchant training, he soon proved himself to be an outstanding personality so much so that he would shape the company for half a century right up until 1711.

Cornelius Berenberg becomes a citizen of Hamburg

Without denying his Dutch background, Cornelius Berenberg felt he was first and foremost a Hamburg merchant. He emphasised the company's founding by his grandfather as well as the ties to the city of Hamburg and its merchants, thereby being the first Berenberg to establish a sense of family tradition in Hamburg. By taking the Burgher Oath, he became a burgher of the Hanseatic city on 20 June 1684 and thus opened up the possibility for subsequent generations to work in all the city's public offices. Unlike the large cities most notably in southern Germany, there was no aristocracy in Hamburg; government business was not restricted to the old dynasties and families. Instead, immigrant families were able to advance comparatively quickly to assume official roles if they possessed wealth and owned an inherited house.

Competition

As a result of Dutch supremacy on the world seas, Hamburg was long denied overseas shipping. Dutch merchants were advancing in almost every part of the world, dominating the Levant trade in India and America. In trade between England and the continent, the Dutch supplied colonial goods. Hamburg was restricted to trade with the Iberian Peninsula, France and the German hinterland, and even then a large part of the trade went through the Netherlands. In 1647/48, 956 of the 1,773 ships that left the Hanseatic city went to the Netherlands. Hamburg tried repeatedly to free itself of these tight restrictions to its trading options.

One possibility to circumvent the restrictions was the Greenland route. At the end of the Thirty Years' War, lucrative whaling attracted whalers to Greenland, and as of 1663, Christian V of Denmark let Hamburg partake in

this exceedingly promising business. A Dutchman based in Hamburg founded the first *Societas Gronlandiae* (Greenland Society), the first to be granted privileges by the Danish king. Thus, in 1670 Hamburg sent a total of 40 ships to Greenland that were equipped especially for whaling. Cornelius Berenberg was commercially involved in these trips. But here, too, the Dutch had a head start; they had got involved sooner and more intensely; in the same year they set sail in 148 ships. Whaling led to a strong revival of Hamburg's fish oil distilleries, which primarily supplied the German hinterland, but the rest of the market continued to be dominated by the Dutch.

The Dutch were not the only ones causing trouble. Since the end of the Thirty Year's War, the Dukes of Brunswick-Lüneburg (originally from Celle) who had been ruling Harburg since 1642, had been trying to expand the city to compete with Hamburg. Harburg did not have a single seagoing vessel. The Elector of Brandenburg, who found the Hamburg custom duties too high, supported the dukes' efforts. He concluded a treaty with Brunswick to build up Harburg to become a trading centre for grain and timber from the Märkish region. And when the Duke of Brunswick-Lüneburg had an armed sconce built before the fork in the river near Bullenhausen, Hamburg's staple right was noticeably shaken. Hamburg eventually reacted by lowering duties, and Brandenburg soon lost interest in Harburg.

More dangerous for Hamburg was the strengthening of Altona. In 1664, the Danish king, Christian V, had bestowed city rights on this downstream location, and he built up Altona as planned to be the counterpart to Hamburg. Inevitably, the old conflicts with the Danes resurfaced again in the decades that followed.

Despite these rivals, Hamburg's trade developed positively and with the opening of the *Müllroser* or Frederick William Canal, as of 1668 there was a much improved connection to the eastern hinterland. Frederick William, Elector of Brandenburg had this canal built between the Oder River and Spree River in an effort to ship primarily grain and timber to the trading centre, where the commodities made their way down the Spree River and Elbe River to Hamburg. The canal also created a connection to Silesia (which mainly shipped its sought-after linen) and to Bohemia.

Goods Trade

At this time, the wine trade proved to be an important commodity for the Berenbergs as, due to the favourable treaties with France, Hamburg had become an important trading centre for French wines and colonial goods.

Yet, in keeping with tradition, Cornelius Berenberg chose to focus on trade with Iberia. As a large number of shipments did not even go through Hamburg's port but went directly to their destination, thorough planning and arrangement became essential.

Hamburg-based merchants often organised foreign trade with the help of befriended Dutch families or members of their own family who acted as agents and factors, or as forwarding agents.

When it came to trade with the colonies, to bypass navigation codes such as when trading with Brazil, subsidiaries of Hamburg-based merchants in Lisbon had to sign as the ship owner, or Hamburg merchants became associated with English ships as they could not send their own.

Beginning in 1663, trade with England also grew in importance for the Berenbergs despite Cromwell's Navigation Act, which had been adopted in 1651 as a means against the Dutch trade rivals and prohibited foreign ships from entering England. Hamburg now re-obtained the right to enter English ports with its own ships and own crew and also to trade with countries which were enemies of England in war times.

Trading with England grows in importance

New Lines of Business

Although the goods trade was not yielding great profits, Cornelius Berenberg was very successful during this time as he was also involved in other lines of business.

Like most merchants, he was also involved in maritime insurance. Those looking for insurance were connected with merchants who, with their signature, declared their willingness to compensate certain damages in return for the payment of a premium. This type of insurance brings to mind Lloyd's of London.

Maritime underwriting

As a result of the engagement in the Greenland trips, dealings now also involved the shipping business. As a so-called ship owner, partner Cornelius Berenberg not only had shares in the whaling and freighter trips, but he was also among the buyers and distributors of fish oil, which he had processed at his own expense with a view to exporting the finished product.

In 1675, he sent off two ships. The 120-Last (240 tons) *Wynbarg* under Greenland commander Johann Dittmers brought home 667 Quardeelen (approximately 6,700 kg) of blubber from 15 captured whales, the 130-Last *Johann Baptist* under commander Peter Klasen 320 Quardeelen in barrels from five whales. The blubber was boiled and purified and then used as lubricating and illuminating oil, to manufacture soap and pomades and for medical purposes. The enormous bones of the whales were used to decorate doorposts and to make all sorts of instruments and equipment. Baleen plates from the baleen whale found buyers mainly in the clothing trade.

Cornelius was the first Berenberg who verifiably worked as a merchant banker. Since all the trade transactions had to be financed by the merchants themselves, merchants often extended credit to others who were temporarily short on liquid assets. Cornelius intensified these financing transactions. He also devoted a considerable portion of his work to mortgage dealings. At a time when stocks did not yet exist, the mortgage was almost the only option to invest money not required in trade dealings, or to borrow money to boost liquidity. In all of these dealings, great confidence was placed in Cornelius Berenberg, a fact that is reflected in the numerous wills he executed and in curatorships.

In 1665 the Commercial Deputation, a forerunner of the chamber of commerce, was founded by Hamburg merchants involved in maritime trade; representation of a crane, scales, stock exchange and the old city hall, dating from ca. 1735

Cornelius Berenberg concludes initial banking transactions

Hamburg's Domestic Policy – The Citizens strengthen

While the family-run company experienced a time of continuity and stabilisation with Cornelius, the city of Hamburg was experiencing far-reaching changes.

The flourishing merchant life in Hamburg necessitated more and more associations for administration, and, increasingly, these were established by merchants on their own.

The *Hamburg Assecurateure* (Hamburg insurers) formed an association in an effort to better enforce their goals. Uniform terms were drawn up which were binding for all members and which reduced the liability for the insurer and increased the obligations of the insured. Paul Berenberg, a son of Andreas, was one of the deputies of the *Hamburg Assecurateure* in 1687.

In 1665, the association of merchants trading at sea founded the Commercial Deputation out of which later grew the chamber of commerce. The goal of the Commercial Deputation was to do everything that would help Hamburg's trade succeed, and this also included protecting ships from pirates and from the constant attacks from warring nations. The responsibility for the safety of maritime transport lay officially with the city's "Admiralty", but it was financed by merchants. Since 1662, the merchants of the city had been paying "convoy money" with which special escort ships were to be built. When the completion of the much anticipated frigates was dragged out by the city, the merchants lost lots of money and, ultimately, their patience. With the Commercial Deputation, they had a well-organised interest group that was capable of taking action and which did not shy away from harsh disputes. The merchants trading at sea from among whose ranks deputies were elected now called themselves an "honourable merchant" – a clear provocation to the "honourable council". The latter was not impressed and attempted to ignore the Commercial Deputation as a factor in trade policy. Even after it was officially acknowledged in 1674, when it was gaining increasing influence in administration, any control over the use of the convoy money was denied and a perennial conflict was the result.

The Immigrants

Between 1600 and 1680 the population doubled to 80,000. Although Hamburg was ranked behind London, Paris, Antwerp and Amsterdam, it had become the second-largest city on German soil after Vienna. Immigration brought new ethnic groups to Hamburg, which gradually pushed back the influence of the Dutch. While Dutch merchants still wrote in Dutch in their accounting books, the new affluent class spoke French.

The majority of the immigrants from the time of the Thirty Years' War and the years following settled in the new part of town in the parish of St Michael's. The three-nave church received its Baroque bell tower in 1668. In 1682, St George was populated and integrated into the fortification, the sconce was built as protection from enemies from the west and St Paul's Church was built, which would later lend this suburb its name. The town hall and the stock market building were extended, the port was expanded and the first wood bridge was erected over the Alster River, which was named Lombard Bridge after the Lombard (pawnshop) situated on the right bank.

Unser Sünden folgen Gottes Strafen
Aescherten den Tempel ein. —
Doch er will nicht immer strafen.
Will auch wieder gnädig seyn

Darum ward durch Seine Gnade
Und durch guter Menschen milde Gabe
Dieser Tempel Schöner hergestellt /—
Bittet, das auch Ihm dies Werck gefällt

In 1750, lightning struck the "Michel" (St Michael's), Hamburg's most famous church, which was built by Christoph Corbinus beginning in 1661. Hamburg merchants contributed to its repair and renovation

"The Darn Opulence"

With growing prosperity, the rather Puritan lifestyles changed. For the first time within the walls of Hamburg there was the advancement of art and science. Lawyers and physicians came together to form professional associations. *Sprachgesellschaften* (language associations) were formed to maintain mother tongues. In 1678, the curtain rose on the first regular opera on Gänsemarkt, and that same year, numerous coffee houses opened their doors to what was soon to become a flourishing business. By filling in the Reesendamm, a promenade was created which was soon given the name *Jungfernstieg* on account of the many wenches who strolled along there. The Council felt obliged to call for moderation: One shouldn't wear any diamonds, pearls and gemstones and one should do without golden and silver lace, sable mufflers, long trains, such were the regular and apparently ineffective appeals. "The darn opulence", sighed Mayor Johann Schulte in a letter to his son, referring to the ever increasing "splendour of clothes, eateries and other things".

Even members of the Berenberg family turned against the general moral decline. In 1680/81, Cornelius' cousin, Paul Berenberg, the son of Andreas, in his capacity as administrator of the Dutch Relief Fund for the Poor ensured that annual dinners which were at risk of running late into the night were stopped, and that instead the annual administrator in question had to give 50 marks to the poor. At his instigation, it was also adopted that the poor who were healthy enough to support themselves were no longer given bread and beer. In the report, it justifies this move by saying that increasingly "all sorts of noise and hardship" had resulted.

The directors of the Dutch Relief Fund for the Poor were obliged to visit the poor once or twice a year to get a first-hand look at their living conditions and to convince themselves of their neediness and, above all, of their worthiness. In 1689, the directors began distributing copies of the New Testament to those who could read and during the annual visits, gave tests on Christianity. Those who failed, or who no longer had the precious book, ran the risk of being crossed off the list of those worthy of welfare.

Clerical Squabbling

The Berenberg family felt closely affiliated with the Pietism that spread throughout Germany. The Pietists turned against the rigid orthodoxy of the Lutheran church. They rejected the outer organisational forms of faith and, instead, focussed on a purely spiritual church, a "Christianity of the heart" and on personal piety. In the process, the hope of the Coming of Christ and the dawn of millenarianism gave their faith an enthusiastic ardour. More significance was attributed to the personal relationship to God rather than to the acquisition of knowledge and its practical use, and to an appreciation of the individual, to personal responsibility and to welfare, which definitely applied to the Age of Rationalism and to the ambitious bourgeoisie.

Another cousin of Cornelius was active in church life and made sure that after the appointment of Anton Reiser to head pastor at St James, another Pietist was appointed pastor of St Michael's. Yet, this seemingly innocuous move ingnited conflicts that were not as harmless as they seemed.

The Hamburg church authority accused the Pietists of infatuation and dangerous sectarianism, which is why the clerical squabbling became increas-

Construction of Hamburg's opera house began at Gänsemarkt in 1677. A mere 80 years later, it was torn down again

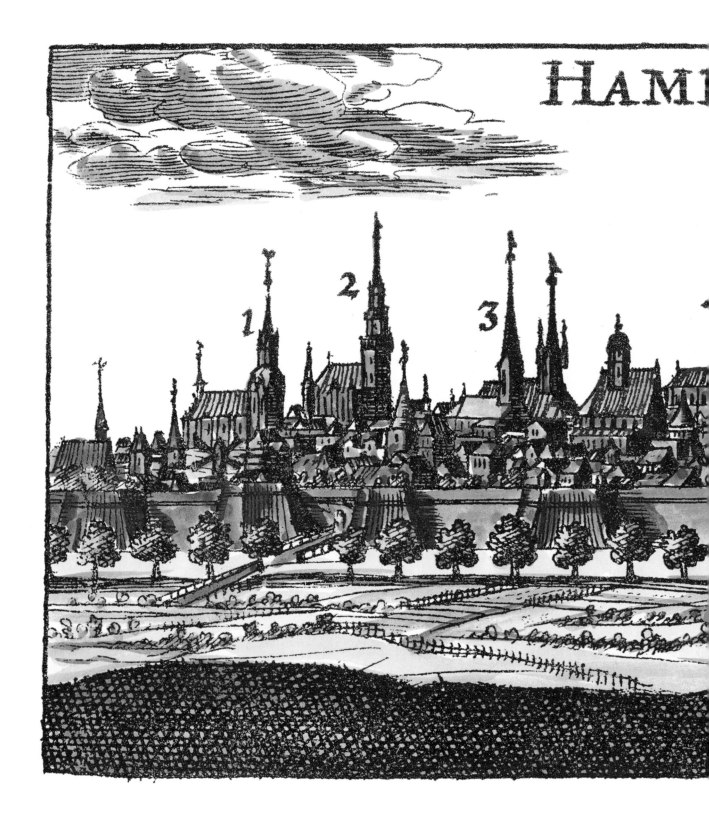

URG.

5

6

Hamburg's churches around 1686:
1. St Gertrude's, 2. St James',
3. St Peter's, 4. St Catherine's,
5. St Nicholas', 6. St Michael's

ingly more serious. Residents of the richer St Nicholas parish started to cancel their mortgages in the neighbouring parish of St Michael's, carpenters engaged in street brawls with brewery workers. Even on the stock exchange, there were said to be scuffles among "honorable merchants" because of the Pietist issue.

Domestic Policy Disputes: the Constitution of 1712

Soon, things were brewing everywhere in the city, given that the self-confidence of the bourgeoisie had grown. Citizen representatives roundly doubted the honesty of the Council, accused it of nepotism in the administration of public funds and demanded more rights. Finally, they came together without being convened by the Council: The citizens met in the large hall at city hall "under the crown", in an effort to no longer be separated by parishes but to consult together and vote by heads. As part of this process, non-residents who had no political rights and even non-citizens were granted access to the meetings.

As a result of all of the disputes, the position of the *Oberalten*, political representatives of the parishes, was weakened in such a way that the majority of the Council under Mayor Meurer requested assistance from the emperor in 1686. The civic Popular Party under the leadership of merchant Jeronimo Snitger and ship owner Cord Jastram looked for backing from Hamburg's archenemy, Denmark. They had the support of one of the other three mayors and of a minority of the Council. A third group which made an effort to mediate turned to Brandenburg.

King Christian V of Denmark recognised his opportunity, appeared before the walls of Hamburg with 10,000 men, 2,500 horsemen as well as heavy artillery and demanded not to help the Popular Party but instead, the start of Danish occupation, an oath of allegiance and a payment of 400,000 Thaler.

This impertinence brought Hamburg to its senses albeit temporarily; the people unified and, with the help of the Duke of Lüneburg-Celle, defeated the Danes at the sconce. Christian V headed back home, his claims abandoned. The Elector of Brandenburg arrived after the battle with his troops.

Meurer had won, the leaders of the Popular Party, Jastram and Snitger, were brutally tortured and beheaded in 1686 for treason. From now on, the city and its citizens had to bow to Meurer's dictatorial rule until his death in 1690.

Merchant Hieronymus Snitger (left) and ship owner Cord Jastram (right) were beheaded in Hamburg in 1686

But the deathly calm did not last for long. After Meurer's death, the conflicts flared up again, but now the emperor wanted to put an ultimate end to the anarchy in Hamburg. In 1708, he sent Count Hugo Damian von Schönborn with such a superior army that any sort of resistance would have been useless and under this outside pressure, Hamburg finally agreed after four years of negotiation to the Constitution of 1712, the so-called *Hauptrezess*. The constitution remained in force until 1860 and was praised by contemporaries as being exemplary: "Neither entirely aristocratic, nor entirely democratic, nor entirely representative, but all three together" just hamburgesque.

The Integration of the Berenberg Family into Hamburg's Political Life: Johann and Rudolf Berenberg

Cornelius Berenberg would not live to experience this historic agreement. He died in 1711 at the age of 77, leaving the company to his sons, Johann (1674–1749) and Rudolf (1680–1746). The initial phase of their commercial activity after their father's death was hard for the brothers. Even though the Constitu-

Johann and Rudolf Berenberg take over the company

tion of 1712 had brought order to the heart of the city again, Hamburg did not calm down.

During the Nordic War, which saw Russia, Poland-Saxony and Denmark pitted against Sweden (1700–1721), Swedish Stade had to surrender to the Danes in September 1712 after intense shelling, whereupon Sweden destroyed Altona in 1713. The Vierlande, an area in Hamburg, was occupied by the Danes, as well as the suburbs known today as Bergedorf, Barmbek, Hamm and Horn. Hamburg was surrounded by the Danes and blackmailed. Next, the plague broke out, and by March 1714, around 10,000 people had died. Ships from Hamburg were turned away from foreign ports for fear of infection and trade almost collapsed entirely.

The Peace of Stockholm concluded in 1719/20 finally ended the Nordic War. Sweden had to relinquish Bremen and Verden to Hanover, which had been associated with England since 1714 in a personal union. Stettin and large parts of West Pommerania fell to Prussia; the Baltic provinces fell to Russia in the Treaty of Nystad, which, at the expense of Sweden, entered the realm of European superpowers.

In an effort to ward off competition from the ports of Harburg and Altona, Hamburg finally became a *porto transito* in 1727, and almost completely waived transit duties. The medieval staple policy was abandoned primarily on the insistence of the Commercial Deputation and from then on Hamburg was a free port open to all regions.

That was of particular importance in light of the mercantilist policy of Frederick II of Prussia. Starting in 1740, he built up Swinemünde, Stettin and Magdeburg to become rivals of Hamburg as well as to direct Prussian trade via the Oder River and the Baltic Sea. Hamburg was literally left high and dry, and in 1742 at the end of the first Silesian War, which saw Frederick take Silesia, Hamburg's trade dealings suffered a considerable decline notably in Silesian linen, a fact which also affected Rudolf and Johann Berenberg.

A rough idea of the Berenberg's maritime import and export trade business after the Nordic War can be gleaned from the duty lists of the Admirality dated 1729 to 1733. At the top of the list, well ahead of all the other imported goods was, surprisingly, currants, which predominantly went to customers located inland. Next was cane sugar, which was processed in Hamburg's sugar cane processing factories for forwarding, followed by coffee, indigo, drugs and

In August 1700, Charles XII of Sweden stormed the Danish coast

In 1712, the plague befell Hamburg, raging for two years and leaving over 10,000 dead

silk. Among exported goods, metals and metalware dominated, closely followed by linen, which was mainly forwarded to overseas colonies.

In addition to the goods trade, the extremely risky maritime insurance business occupied an important position due to the many pirates and the always unpredictable weather. The plan from 1720 to open an insurance company in Hamburg founded on stocks had failed although 160 respected merchants, including Johann and Rudolf Berenberg, were in favour of it. Bogus gambling on the stock market in Paris, London and Amsterdam eroded confidence in stocks. The collapse of the "Law'schen Aktiengesellschaft" in Paris and a run on shares in Hamburg, which did not yet exist, prompted the Council to decline. Thus, private insurance remained in Hamburg, where Rudolf Berenberg worked successfully.

Plan to establish a stock-based insurance company fails; the private enterprise is successful

Positions and Duties

Johann and Rudolf Berenberg became citizens of Hamburg on 8 April 1707. They paid the required amount, proved ownership of a musket and their father was the guarantor.

...ung HH: H: Erb: regerirend, wie auch
HH: Deputirten Moniren zu
neiren, welche Selbe Hn: als
da wegen zufälligen contra=
Winde, die Zeit von einer Ab=
dorten zu kurtz, zu roeßig
daß den Bier Wochen nach
kunfft des Schiffes in Jahr=
bewegnehmen, wegen es
weiter redressirt werden ...

Morauf S. Erb: Kaufm:
Schluß dahin erging, daß ...

Daß S. Jochen: Rath von Commer=
cien der neuen König: und
E. H: Hannoverischen Verord=
zu Brauschauen, Dienst und
Danten und gebüß zu repl=
Meil es dorten mit den Ab...
en den Wochen in den Schiff
innerhalb deren Davien
den Bier Wochen impractical
weil keine Zeit in den Trac...
oder Recess von A° 1691 auf...
als S. Jochen: Rath geriehnen
den Termin der Bier Wochen
Anlauß des Schiffs in Ham...
außzurichten.   Danen

2. Daß alle bißherwangegebnen Gra=
mina, wegen der Brauschau
Zollen beijgebracht, S. Jochen ...
übergeben, und denselben erf...

S: Erb: R:
Schluß auf
den Han=
noverschen
Brauß
und
Neuen
Verord=
nung

In 1722, Johann Berenberg was elected president of the Commercial Deputation. Three other Berenbergs followed him as heads of the Commercial Deputation and chamber of commerce

For Johann and Rudolf Berenberg, becoming burghers of Hamburg and the intertwining of the Berenbergs in Hamburg's merchant life soon meant the appointment to numerous public, religious and non-profit offices and tasks. They had a career that was typical for affluent citizens who engaged in trade. The following list of offices provides an idea of the amount of work which is performed by organised authorities and state institutions today and which back then was done on a volunteer basis, and the extent to which the Berenbergs were already integrated into Hamburg's society.

Even when his father was still alive, Johann Berenberg was elected to the office of *aufn Mehlkauf*. It was created in 1651 to allow the city's poor to buy flour at lower prices. The city subsidized the purchase of flour annually with 10,000 Mark Banco.

In 1713, Johann became *Fortifikationsbürger* (fortification citizen) and was responsible for maintaining the ramparts and bastions. As *Bürger auf dem Admiralitätszoll* (citizen of the Admiralty duty) from 1714 to 1716, he made sure that arriving and departing ships paid the required duties, and as *Deputierter des löblichen Niedergerichts* (a deputy of the lower court) he ruled for two years in civil and criminal cases which were tried there in the first instance.

In 1717, Johann was named *Deputierter bei der Feuerkasse*, (deputy of the fire fund) and soon thereafter *Kriegskommissar* (war commissioner) with the infantry and the dragoons and finally *Artilleriebürger* (artillery citizen) who not only had to ensure safe keeping of the gun powder and good condition of the weapons and cannons, but also had to select and name various ranks. As the *Bauhofbürger* (construction citizen), he oversaw public buildings, and beginning in 1726 as the *Banco Bürger*, he was a member of the administrative body of the Hamburger Bank. He became commercial deputy and as such he sat simultaneously on the Düpe Commission, which was responsible for the fairway depth on the Elbe River and in the port, and was active in a special *Sanitätskollegium* (sanitation council), established in 1720 when the plague broke out in Marseille, which, fortunately, was disbanded three years later.

His brother, Rudolf, held almost the same offices. On 22 February 1735, he was elected to the Council of the Hanseatic City, which was the highest honour a citizen of Hamburg could receive. "Lord" Rudolf Berenberg appeared from then on in a "habit" with black coat, white ruff collar and pointed hat.

Johann Berenberg leaves the company

The brothers now operated as "Johann and Lord Rudolf Berenberg", which took into account the special position of Rudolf as city councilman as the office was not only associated with a myriad of other offices and duties, but also with special solvency and creditworthiness.

In 1738, the brothers decided to go separate ways in business. Johann founded his own companies, which were soon given up by his sons. Rudolf Berenberg managed the operations Berenberg & Co. as well as Lord Rudolf Berenberg.

The final balance sheet for Councilman Berenberg from 1746 showed assets amounting to 134,000 Mark Banco. With that, Rudolf Berenberg belonged to the affluent – if not rich – citizens of the Hanseatic city. He owned two properties, each with construction authorisation on Gröninger Street, had one-eighth of a share in the ship *De gonde Wallross*, worked as a private insurer and traded in various goods, of which the following are listed in the duty lists of the Admiralty: cotton, oil, coffee, drugs, gall bladders, soap, indigo, pepper, ginger, linen, sugar, tea, capers, Javanese pepper, shellac, camphor and Senegal gum. Trading partners were located in England, France, Spain, Portugal, Italy, Holland, Ghent and Copenhagen.

"On 9 December 1746," as it reads in the Amsinck city chronicle, "Lord Rudolf Berenberg, a councilman, died after a brief respiratory illness. He had only just been at the town hall on 7 December. He was also the oldest *praetor* and was buried on the 15th in St Catherine's with a very large funeral procession formed by 317 good citizen couples."

The Hamburg Senate's book of heraldry includes the coat of arms of Senator Rudolf Berenberg, the co-owner of the company from 1715 to 1764

Mother and Sons

The first woman to head the company: Anna Elisabeth Berenberg

After the senator's death in 1746, his widow, Anna Elisabeth (neé Amsinck) (1690–1748), at first ran the company alone and then together with her youngest sons, Paul (1716–1768) and Johann (1718–1772).

Paul and Johann had six siblings. The oldest brother, Rudolf junior (1712–1761), had gone into business for himself before the death of his father. Cornelius (1714–1773), the second oldest, had moved to Livorno in 1735, where he was a partner first at Bouwer und Berenberg, then at Berenberg and Spreckelsen and finally at Berenberg & Co. The youngest son, Johann, had completed his apprenticeship in the same company. Cornelius never married and remained in Italy until his death. Johann soon returned to Hamburg, where from 1747 onwards he was part of the family business "Rudolf Berenberg Witwe und Söhne" (Rudolf Berenberg Widow and Sons) together with older brother Paul and mother Anna. Rudolf, Cornelius and the four sisters were paid out, and the remaining capital totalled around 160,000 Mark Banco for the business, half of which was made up of loaned money, such as deposits from family members and relatives.

Johann Berenberg headed the company together with his mother, Anna Elisabeth, and his brother Paul

On 1 March 1747, the mother concluded a detailed agreement (retroactive to January of the same year) with both Paul and Johann. And although this agreement was only valid for a short time, it is of interest because the document is typical for its time. It reveals that prudence in business and Protestant tradition were still very closely intertwined.

"Let the affectionate God grant divine success and rich blessings and remain merciful in the face of all adverse circumstances." This was written in the preamble of the two-year agreement, which permitted the mother to withdraw her share in the business at the end of 1749; she maintained a say in business affairs without, however, being involved in company management. Profits and losses fell four-eighths to the mother and three-twelfths to the sons respectively. The widow assumed any losses and benefits deriving from any goods transactions which the father had initiated and which were still ongoing. She also assumed any debts that existed prior to the agreement. Both sons received 6,000 Mark Banco each as an endowment to invest in the business. She provided capital amounting to 20,000 Mark Banco, and for the additional deposit of 20,000 marks, she received 4 percent. The sons also received the same percentage for deposits which exceeded 6,000 marks. Rent for storage rooms, such as packaging buildings, attics, and cellars was borne by the company even if they were located in family buildings. Anna received 300 marks the first year and 400 marks the next, but goods were also stored at the sons' places. To ensure that the company would continue to be run by the sons undivided, they had to commit to refrain from concluding separate business transactions. Decisions to act as guarantor and grant credit required the approval of all three partners.

With regard to the insurance business, "The parties are permitted to continue to be in the insurance business in expectation of God's blessing" but the sum to insure a ship should remain limited to 2,000 and to a maximum of 2,500 Mark Banco. And the sons were also ensured a decent life with this agreement. The annual expenses of Paul, who was 31 after all, and Johann, 29, were not to exceed 1,000 Mark Courant, with each having to pay their mother 300 marks for room and board and clean laundry. They paid for "clothes and important paraphernalia" on their own, "… they pledged to lead a proper way of life save all unnecessary expenses."

Signed and sealed in triplicate, Anna's brother, Senator Zimbert Amsinck, as curator of the widow's estate added his weighty name to the agreement, which, as it turned out, was not even going to be in effect for a year. In February of the following year, Anna Elisabeth Berenberg (neé Amsinck) died. Her sons continued business dealings in a different manner.

The contract between the widowed Anna Elisabeth Berenberg, née Amsinck, and sons Paul and Johann from 1747. The widow's brother, Zimbert Amsinck, had to sign on her behalf

From an Operation to a Company 1748–1768:
Paul und Johann Berenberg

Enlightenment in Hamburg

The emerging intellectual reorientation of the Berenberg family was indicative of the change which Hamburg was undergoing in the first half of the 18th century, and which from 1750 onwards was to lead to a cultural and economic boom for the city. While Anna Elisabeth Berenberg was still a devout Pietist, the sons looked ahead to the future and raised their children in the spirit of the enlightenment that had its own Hamburg flair.

When Anna Elisabeth married in 1709, special mention was made of the fact that she had been raised in accordance with Pietism. Above all, her "chastity, friendliness and fear of God" were praised and importance was attached to the same virtues at the marriage of her brother-in-law, Johann Berenberg with Elisabeth Brommer (1688–1761) in 1708.

However, the educated Hamburg merchants, including the Berenbergs, encountered the ideas of the English Enlightenment. In England, several moral weeklies appeared, such as the *The Tatler* (from 1709 onwards), *The Spectator* (1711) and *The Guardian* (1713). Hamburg merchants became familiar with these publications during their visits to England and brought them to the city on the EIbe.

Along the lines of these weeklies, Johann Mattheson published the moral weekly *Der Vernünfftler* in Hamburg from 1713 to 1714, which was the first of its kind to gain historical prominence. In 1724, the Hamburg poet Barthold Heinrich Brockes (1680–1747) followed the example with the magazine *Der Patriot*.

The primarily patriarchal bourgeoisie of the Hanseatic city showed reluctance to abstract ideas. As a practical expression of reason, they appreciated the

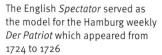

The English *Spectator* served as the model for the Hamburg weekly *Der Patriot* which appeared from 1724 to 1726

Mark Banco, the "symbol of calculating reason". The Constitution of 1712 and the free port status were Hamburg's symbols of the new period, which helped the city spread its wings intellectually and in terms of material goods. Practical liberalism broke the confines of the old order and dispelled the religious resignation to fate of earlier generations. The success of Hamburg as a trading centre depended on the pragmatism and the cosmopolitan attitude of its merchant bourgeoisie. In 1735, the Commercial Library opened, which today is the oldest library in the world specialising in business and economics – a typical Hamburg pairing of culture and commerce.

And the intellectual change was also noticeable in Hamburg's parlours. Above all, it was the women in the Berenberg family who took part; they were talented and educated, kept diaries and wrote poems. The writings of Barthold Heinrich Brockes (1680–1747), Friedrich von Hagedorn (1708–1754) and later notably of Friedrich Gottlieb Klopstock (1724–1803) were also among the favorites of the Berenbergs. And even if these authors cannot be described as writers of the Enlightenment in a rationalistic sense, they helped spread Enlightenment thought.

Brockes was probably the most popular poet Hamburg ever laid to rest. In 1720, he was appointed to the Council and knew how to combine the roles of a respected politician and a recognised poet known throughout Germany. His sensuous poems combined intimate contemplation of nature, liberality and bourgeois utilitarian thinking. Even in the tiniest elements of nature, his poetry celebrated God's beautiful and sensible work, whose wisdom even revealed itself in the horns of the chamois, as these were splendidly suited for walking sticks. Without any irony he proclaimed in a poem: "True wisdom starts in business." And in the newspaper *Der Patriot* he imparted interesting facts from many areas. He advocated very emphatically and with a modern outlook for raising sons and daughters equally, something which Anna Elisabeth's son, Johann Berenberg, would take to heart.

Zum Preise Gottes, blühen Gärten und in derselben Anmuth scheint. die Symmetrie mit Form und Farben, ja recht Natur und Kunst vereint.

Between 1721 and 1748, Barthold Heinrich Brockes (1680–1747) wrote innumerable poems that were published in the compilation *Irdisches Vergnügen in Gott* (Earthly Pleasure in God)

Hagedorn, a friend of Brockes, was close to the Berenbergs for the mere reason that he was also a Hamburg merchant. In his poetry of small forms, he identified himself as a comfortable and elegant man of the world, who extolled the Epicurean worldly wisdom and expressed a refined sensuousness. He became one of the most popular poets of his time and the even greater Klopstock, idolised some of his work.

Klopstock was, after all, the physical and spiritual embodiment of a man of letters – primarily of northern Germany – and the Berenbergs knew him personally. Especially with regard to Pietism, Klopstock's compositions unfurled a force of relaxing emotions, which gave words to the inner world, which had previously been silent and intensely Puritan. The people in Hamburg loved this enlightenment poet who shed light on inner life; the aggressive rationalism of Gotthold Ephraim Lessing remained foreign to them.

When Lessing was appointed to the newly founded National Theatre in Hamburg in 1767, his failure was foreseeable. In the years that followed, he wrote the highly influential and pioneering *Hamburgische Dramaturgie*, according to which tragedy was to encourage the "virtuous skills" of people. But the audience preferred entertainment and remained indifferent towards the notion of the stage as a moral institution. Theatres had to be profitable and to adjust to popular taste. For financial reasons, Lessing withdrew from Hamburg, but highlighted the sophistication and liberality of the city: "Oh to only have been able to stay in this city!"

Business Counts!

After their mother's death in 1748, Paul and Johann immediately set about drawing up a new agreement. Profit and loss were to be shared and any capital brought in by wives was to be integrated into the company. Business transactions for one's own account were forbidden and violations to this were reprimanded by donating 100 Reichsthaler to the orphanage or a foundation.

However, the initial situation of the brothers was very different and the agreement presumably never came into effect: As a result of his marriage to Anna-Maria Lastrop (1723–1761), Johann was able to contribute a dowry of 26,500 marks, which by 1752 had more than doubled. The older brother, Paul, on the other hand, took over the parents' house upon the death of his mother, which meant that after the siblings had been paid out, hardly any liquid assets remained. In 1748, he had a debt of 900 marks. Apparently, the brothers were unable to agree on several transactions and processed them for their own account. In the duty lists of the Admiralty, apart from records referring to the company "Paul & Johann Berenberg", the companies "Paul Berenberg" and "Paul Berenberg & Co." were mentioned. Paul proved to be especially enterprising as by 1760 he was able to half the difference to Johann's share of the equity in the joint company. From then onwards, the brothers worked together. In 1760, "Paul & Johann Berenberg" imported goods valuing 82,920 Mark Banco, but "Paul Berenberg & Co." hardly recorded any transactions.

From 1747 to 1768 the range of goods expanded considerably, and Paul and Johann Berenberg intensified foreign trade. New trade relations developed with Russia, especially Arkhangelsk. The ties with England, France, Spain, Italy, the Baltic region and the Netherlands continued and when cousin Johann Peter Berenberg settled in Gothenburg, the business the company had carefully maintained with Scandinavia – and still maintains today – was expanded.

But there were also slumps. As a result of the mercantilist economic policy of Frederick the Great, the goods trade with the important eastern hinterland became less important for Hamburg-based trading companies. Prussian economic strategists chose to promote primarily the local textile and armament industries with import duties and export premiums and only processed exports through their own ports. The significant export of Silesian linen, for instance, dropped by the middle of the 1850s and became insignificant. In 1747, the balance sheet of "Rudolf Berenberg Witwe und Söhne" (Rudolf Berenberg Widow and Sons) showed linen exports totalling 28,200 marks; however, by 1754 it had fallen to 5,990 marks. Even the export of metals and metalware dropped noticeably in Hamburg. Thus, Johann and Paul Berenberg focussed increasingly on other lines of business.

Rudolf Berenberg entered the insurance business with the utmost caution, and his widow had also compelled the sons to exercise restraint. But just one year after the death of their mother, the insurance account of the brothers was 11,000 Mark Banco and increased each year peaking at 35,000 Mark Banco in 1763.

The ship owning partnership was now showing signs of growth. Whereas their father had had a one-eighth share in a ship, his venturesome

Transactions involving insurance, ships and candles

sons continually increased their share of one-eighth in three ships in 1750 to a share of 21,000 Mark Banco in 12 ships in 1762.

A new line of business was added in 1761 when the oldest brother, Rudolf Berenberg, who was just 49, died. He ran a wax bleaching business with candle production in Altona. He left it to Paul, and in 1762 it appeared in the company books with 33,219 marks. As a manufacturing operation, wax bleaching was a combination of industry and trade and thus a typical company for the time. The Berenberg's customers for candles and other wax products spanned from Lübeck to Stade and from Stralsund to Iserlohn. Spain bought large amounts, and the Berenbergs even supplied several private and public customers in Hamburg and Altona.

A major change was looming from 1750 onwards in the area of financial transactions. Up until the middle of the 18th century, merchants had mostly financed their own trade transactions and on this basis, depending on capital strength, those of other merchants as well.

Financing of commodities

However, beginning in 1756, the financing of the entire foreign trade in all of its possible manifestations moved into the spotlight. Above all, the financing of commodity transactions in various currencies had to be contained. In London, people stocked up on English pounds, and from London, remittances went in Mark Banco to Hamburg and so on. Guarantee loans, which took on a revolving character given longer loan periods, took on more importance as a source of revenue. The context for this development was the extremely favourable economic situation in Hamburg during the Seven Years' War (1756–1763) and in the English-French colonial war. Banking transactions, notably the exchange business, became more profitable than mere trading transactions. Yet, over the next decade, the risks involved with concentrating on financial transactions became clear when, on the heels of the boom experienced during the Seven Years' War, a hitherto unprecedented and nationwide financial crisis arose.

War and Crisis

The Seven Years' War got underway in 1756 – initially it was about Silesia. In the First and Second Silesian War, Frederick II of Prussia had attempted to liberate the rich province from the Habsburg monarchy and to incorporate it into his own kingdom. Austrian Empress Maria Theresia had been weakened by the numerous conflicts over her succession, and in the Peace of Aachen, Silesia fell to Prussia in 1748. However, the following eight years were rather a phase of recovery and military build-up than a time of peace. In 1756, war broke out again. Prussia was pitted against almost the whole of Europe with the exception of England, Hanover, Denmark, the Netherlands, Switzerland, Turkey and Hesse-Kassel; more than 700,000 people lost their lives on the continent.

In the end, Prussia was victorious thanks to the support it received from its English allies. Although the impact of the war for Prussia was disastrous, and, in terms of territory, merely pre-war status was restored, with the Peace of Hubertusburg in 1763 a course was set for German history. The power of the Habsburgs diminished while that of the Hohenzollerns grew.

Yet, another momentous conflict with major historical ramifications was being carried out not in Europe, but on the Atlantic, in North America and in India. While Frederick II was fighting against France with English financial support thereby consuming French powers on the continent, England deployed its superior navy in the English-French colonial wars and almost stripped France of all its colonies: The rise of the British Empire had begun.

Frederick II (1712–1786), King of Prussia from 1772

For Hamburg's economy, these wars initially came with considerable advantages. They promoted the goods trade as well as the lending business, and almost all Hamburg-based companies posted respectable profits. As a result of the growing demand for money by the warring powers, a tremendous circulation of money was actuated, and high commissions also tempted trading companies in Amsterdam and Hamburg to speculate in financial transactions. The subsidy payments made by the English to Prussia, the business of supplying warring armies, the deterioration of coins and the issuing of large masses of paper money by the Swedish government were the most important factors that led to a hardly manageable bill jobbing. Discount rates of 10 to 15 percent enticed numerous people in Hamburg to invest their liquid funds and savings in kite-flying.

The Große Grasbrook area around 1790: the Port of Hamburg expands

Bank crash

At the end of the war, not only did the demand for goods decline abruptly, but soon the exchange business also collapsed. Frederick II had new coins minted and promptly removed the increasingly devalued money used for war financing from circulation. Since Prussia and other nations had incurred considerable debt abroad, several Dutch banks collapsed. "A general crash" was the result. In Hamburg alone, 63 companies went bankrupt; in previous years, the figure had been around 24 to 50.

By establishing a loan office, the Council was able to drum up 245,000 Mark Banco at short notice, which was basically to assist healthy companies in times of temporary illiquidity in return for pledged goods. Paul and Johann Berenberg's company was among those especially hard hit, and it was provided with roughly one-seventh of the entire sum. As security, the following items were given: 1,000 sacks of ginger, 75 boxes of soap, linen with a value of 17,700 Mark Banco, wax for 5,300 marks and 20 three-quarters Oxhoft coffee (Oxhoft at 200–240 litres). In addition, relatives and acquaintances helped out with considerable sums. The borrowed funds of 58,400 in 1762 therefore increased to 140,600 Mark Banco in 1763, but by the end of 1764, a large portion of the debt had been paid off. The reputation of the company obviously suffered no harm: four years later, Paul Berenberg was elected to the Council of the Hanseatic city.

A New Era Is Ushered in

For almost 180 years the descendants of Hans Berenberg senior had been running the company down the family line. In 1748, a new phase of business development arose when the business dealings were diversified by Paul and Johann Berenberg. The company now rested on five pillars: goods trade, insurance transactions, ship owning partnership, wax bleaching, and the banking business was beginning to emerge. However, in 1768 and with the approaching end of the fifth generation of Berenbergs in Hamburg, the continued existence of the company as a family-run company appeared suddenly threatened. On 3 April "the dignified Lord Paul Berenberg died in St Catherine's church during the midday sermon at 12 pm amidst singing. God takes delight in his soul in front of his throne and his dear wife replaces this most painful loss with much joy." This, the Herrenschenk Johann Eybert Gossler the Elder wrote in his diary. Margaretha-Elisabeth Berenberg (neé Geertz), the "dearest wife", survived her husband until her death in 1804. Their marriage remained childless.

Rudolf, the only son of Johann and Anna-Maria Berenberg, succumbed to tropical fever in Surinam in 1768. The sole remaining child and beneficiary was their daughter Elisabeth (1749–1822). Johann Berenberg was about 50 at the time. To ensure the continuity of the family company and Elisabeth's part of the inheritance, a successor, who was associated with the family, had to be identified.

That same year, Johann Hinrich Gossler proposed to their daughter, and the parents happily gave their approval. The marriage, which produced ten children, was not just exceedingly prosperous for Elisabeth and Johann Hinrich, but the company also experienced an enormous boom.

Five pillars: commodities, insurance, shipping lines, wax bleaching, banking

The Trend towards Financial Transactions:
Johann Hinrich Gossler 1769–1790

Records show that the Gossler family had been in Hamburg since the 13th century. Whether Johann Hinrich's grandfather, Claus Gossler, who took the oath of a Hamburg burgher on 2 May 1656, is a descendant of this old Hamburg family, cannot be clearly established.

The old Gosslers were *Caffamacher*, which meant that they manufactured a velvet-like material called caffa from pure wool or camel hair. Johann Eybert Gossler, Johann Hinrich's father, a bookkeeper, took the oath of a Hamburg burgher on 15 October 1739, and on 28 October 1739 bought the *Raths-Schenken Dienst* for 10,600 marks, which he seldom performed himself. He took minutes at the Council meetings and provided courier services for the Council and the high court.

Johann Hinrich, his son, attended the Johanneum and in 1752 began his apprenticeship with a Hamburg merchant,

Johann Hinrich Gossler (1738–1790), a company partner from 1769 to 1790

A partner from outside the family

who had to file for bankruptcy a short time later. Thus, his father concluded a seven-year apprenticeship agreement for Johann Hinrich with Paul and Johann Berenberg on 28 May 1754. After the apprenticeship, Johann Hinrich took a job in 1761 at de Somer, van Rechem & Co. in Cádiz and worked for them in Spain and Portugal. In 1766, the company also went bankrupt. Gossler, who had kept in contact by letter with his former patrons in Hamburg, stayed for two more years in France before returning to Hamburg in 1768 as a man of the world, who spoke fluent English, Spanish and French. Immediately upon his return, he visited his former masters and soon became son-in-law and partner. The company was now called Joh. Berenberg & Gossler.

In the permanent partner agreement dated on 1 January 1769, Johann Berenberg and Johann Hinrich Gossler agreed in keeping with family tradition, to not do business dealings for their own account, to share profit and loss, to not take money from the company without the knowledge of the other and to not act as guarantor nor do business transactions without consulting with the other partner. If one of the partners died, it was determined that the beneficiaries would be able to remove the capital "in a reasonable

The Nicolai quarter was one of the first parts of the old town to be almost completely destroyed by the great fire of May 1842

The Spanish port of Cádiz in the 17th century

period of time", "because it would be unreasonable to take the remaining individual by surprise." Any differences were to be resolved by the arbitrators' award "between known virtuous good men". When the agreement was signed, Johann Berenberg's share was around 65,000 marks and that of Johann Hinrich Gossler 5,000 marks.

Johann Hinrich Gossler had already increased his share in the company nine-fold when father Berenberg died in 1772. Elisabeth's part of the inheritance, which amounted to 85,000 marks, remained in the company, and a few years later, the company's capital account was four times the amount it was in 1772.

Merchant Banking

Under the auspices of Johann Hinrich Gossler, a new era began in the history of the company. The business activity was broadened considerably and merchant banking pushed the goods trade from the dominant position it had held up to that point, and merchants became merchant bankers. Up to the middle

The Berenberg merchants become merchant bankers

of the 18th century, it was difficult to distinguish between major merchants and merchant bankers in Hamburg as the financing of one's own trade was still very much in the foreground. However, in favourable economic times, such as during the Seven Years' War, banking transactions were often more lucrative than the straight goods trade. Hamburg merchant bankers borrowed money, gave customers credit or acted as brokers, allowed clients to draw bills on them or gave them a bill of acceptance. This typical way to finance the import and export business had now become one of their main tasks.

With the founding of Parish & Co. in 1756 at the start of the Seven Years' War, Hamburg experienced the emergence of a wave of new companies whose main activity was merchant banking. It continued in three intervals until it peaked at the end of the century: the conditions for the trend were conceivably good. The Seven Years' War had required considerable financial means, the American War of Independence opened an enormous market and the French Revolution with Napoleon's subsequent seizure of power made Hamburg the leading banking and insurance centre in Europe.

An important prerequisite was the Hamburger Bank. The currency which was based on the silver unit of account, the Mark Banco, had the advantage over coin money in that its value did not fluctuate, but was based alone on the purity of the silver. This stable unit of account made crisis-proof clearing transactions possible.

During the Seven Years' War, the Hamburger Bank began working as a clearinghouse not only for Hanseatic merchants, but soon also for European and British bankers. The payments of France to America and those of England to its confederates went via Hamburg. Between 1772 and 1799, the bank funds increased from 3.5 million to 38.5 million marks. Hamburg had finally taken the place of Amsterdam following the revolutionary wars and the incorporation of Holland by the French in 1794/95.

In the bill of exchange lists for Joh. Berenberg & Gossler, there were copies of all the bills of exchange that went through the company, whether the company drew them, gave a bill of acceptance, discounted them or drew them as the endorsee. The sums were in Mark Courant, Mark Banco, Reichsthaler, Sterling, Gulden, Franken and Peso, and when it came to the place of issue, the names of all the important centres of the trading world at the time appeared, which all converged at the Hamburg stock market in its role as one of the main banking centres.

Companies founded by Hamburg's merchant bankers:

1756	Parish & Co.
1757	Johannes Schuback & Söhne
1767	Christ. Math. Schröder & Co.
1779	Siemssen & Co.
1780	Isaac Hesse, later: Hesse, Newman & Co.
1781	prior to 1781: Voght & Co., from 1788: Voght & Sieveking
1788	Jacques de Chapeaurouge
1790	Martin Josef Haller, later Haller, Söhle & Co.
1791	de Chapeaurouge & Urqullu
1795	J. H. & G. F. Baur, Altona
1797	Heckscher & Co., since 1818: Salomon Heine
1798	M. M. Warburg & Co. Conrad Hinrich Donner, Altona
1799	H. J. Merck & Co. (already in 1794: Heiner. Joh. Merck)
1800	L. Behrens & Söhne

The current street name *An der Alten Börse* (At the Old Stock Exchange) recalls the private exchange on what was then Bohnenstrasse

In addition to mere commercial bills, the bill of acceptance was a credit resource. Those who, like Johann Hinrich Gossler, had an account with the Hamburger Bank also made deposits using bills of exchange instead of in silver and could have the required sums paid out again in bills of exchange. The procedure of cashless payment and the granting of credit worked smoothly to the satisfaction of everyone involved.

The main item on the balance sheets of Joh. Berenberg & Gossler was the commission account where the profits from financing and brokering transactions were recorded. From 1780 onwards, the *Cambiokonto* (exchange account), which recorded the results of the bills of exchange transactions, was noted separately. The "interest" account showed the interest income from granted credit, shareholdings and mortgages. Another item was the "bad debts", which in 1781 alone for Boedecker in Nuremberg, a relative of Gossler's mother, amounted to 4,000 Mark Banco, but the situation was obviously never too dire because after 20 years, the profit from financial transactions was around 413,000 Mark Banco.

Hidden Partner

The company grew steadily, and Johann Hinrich Gossler needed assistance. In Franz Friedrich Kruckenberg (1746–1819) he found an exceptionally competent business partner, who had already been working for the company for years and who, moreover, was related to the Gossler family.

Johann Hinrich Gossler had one real brother and five half siblings, whom he and Elisabeth looked after with great care. After the death of Johann Hinrich's mother, Catharina Lucretia Boedecker, his father entered a second (but not final) marriage with Friederike Natorp, a daughter of the *Oberalten* Johann Friedrich Natorp. She gave him three children, one of whom, Margaretha-Katharina, married (in her second marriage) the merchant Franz Friedrich Kruckenberg. He began working for the company in 1769 as a bar attendent on account of the agreement Johann Hinrich Gossler concluded with Johann Berenberg, and Gossler came to appreciate him more and more in the years that followed.

In 1774, Johann Hinrich wrote to his brother-in-law at work: "Continue to operate in the best interest of my company and of my activities and in doing so to make up for that which you lack in your understanding, namely, a knowledge of foreign languages and so rest assured that I am endeavoured after a few years to do my best to help increase your happiness provided you don't find resources in other ways." Gossler promised an increasing salary for the following two years and held out the prospect of further opportunities "... To demonstrate a new how realistically I think and how happy I am to keep my word, I want to conclude a formal agreement with you after the above-mentioned two years [1776/1777] that lasts for five to six years and gives you, instead of a salary, a share amounting to one-eighth of all of my business dealings ... If God blesses us, you will earn more, otherwise one would have to manage things."

The tone of the letter was cooperative, but Johann Hinrich insisted on one condition: everything had to "be hid-

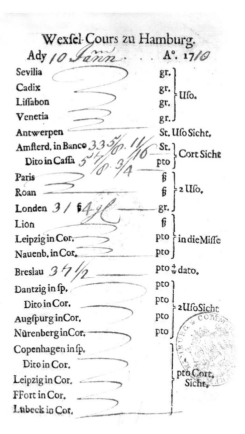

Excerpt from Hamburg's bill register of 1710

den, like with Süberkrupp and the deceased Rowohl, because I am by no means comfortable having a public companion." Obviously, Gossler had other partners before but the continuity of the company name was regarded as going hand-in-hand with a sign of solidity and with maintaining old business ties.

It was an offer that Kruckenberg could hardly decline. Johann Hinrich went on to write: "I doubt very much that there are many bar attendents in Hamburg who can boast the same when they don't have exceptional foreign language skills, which, given the present times, are the main thing. Ask yourself if our dealings would be so respectable if the many French, Spanish, Italian and other commissions were to leave because of this?"

In 1777, Kruckenberg became a partner in Joh. Berenberg & Gossler, and the partnership proved to be an extraordinary stroke of luck for both parties. In the following years, the company's balance sheets recorded continually rising profits even though various crises shook business life in the Hanseatic city. Companies that were most impacted were focussing on financial transactions, while the goods trade at Joh. Berenberg & Gossler was not neglected. This line of business remained a mainstay of the company right up into the second half of the next century because in times of crisis, merchant banking repeatedly declined. It was not until 1929 that Joh. Berenberg, Gossler & Co. sold its last warehouse in the port.

Commodities play supporting role

Goods Trade

Johann Hinrich Gossler more than doubled the amount of goods imported in the two decades of his partnership. He died in 1790. During this time, the people of Hamburg profited from the dealings which Denmark, Spain and France had been gradually liberalising with their respective colonies since the 1760s.

In 1764, the Danes declared St Thomas and St Jean free ports and, from 1767 onwards, all other nations were permitted to travel there albeit with a clear preference for the Danish flag. Denmark had been weakened by the Nordic War and was heavily in debt to Hamburg, and the Danish chancellor, Johann von Bernstorff, had urged time and again for his country to put an end to the detrimental squabble with Hamburg. In the Treaty of Gottorp of 1768, the ongoing feud of more than a century was finally laid to rest and an era of good-neighbourly relations and vibrant trade contacts began. Debts were cancelled in the course of Hamburg's territorial adjustments, which brought the city recognition as a free imperial city and the concession of the most-favoured-nation clause in trade with Denmark and Norway.

More than anything, the American War of Independence (1775–1783), which was also a war between England and France, led to an expansion of trade for the neutral countries. Hamburg merchants were active in supplying the warring powers and, in addition to direct war material, also delivered timber, leather, copper, manufactured goods, horses, harnesses as well as grain and other supplies. Trade with the West Indies was also expanded in wartimes. In 1781, five ships arrived from and travelled to there; in 1782, 35 ships came from there and 26 left Hamburg for port cities in the West Indies.

After the war ended in 1783, the North American continent opened to all trading nations and with the freedom to engage in transatlantic trade, a huge market was now accessible. Hamburg was one of the first to congratulate the United States of America and offered trade relations, which only really gained momentum in the 1790s.

The duration of the ship voyages and the constant rise of the imported and exported goods increased the risk. To counteract the problem, Hamburg merchants preferred to distribute their goods amongst different ships with the goods being increasingly insured. In addition, Johann Hinrich Gossler became involved as a ship-owning partner and an insurer.

Ship Owning Partnership …

The amount of capital which Johann Hinrich Gossler invested in ships exceeded the amounts of his predecessors. Merchants saw the shares in ships either as a simple investment, or they had a say in the ships which transported their own goods.

From 1779 to 1787, Gossler operated the *De fru Agnetha* (a 150-Last barque, roughly 320 gross register tonnes), in which he had a one-eighth share. The ship was used for trading with Arkhangelsk, but mainly with London. And as business dealings with London in the 1780s were on the up and up, Gossler began using the *Hamburger Commercium* in 1782, a barque of 110-Last, for the London trip. Moreover, he had shares in the *De Peter* and in the frigate *De bloyende Hoop*, which he bought for 9,525 Mark Courant from the Hamburg-Altona ship-owning partnerships under the aegis of Willink & Co. *De bloyende Hoop* had a crew of 40 and was used for seal culling and whaling.

Johann Hinrich Gossler had shares in numerous other ships, the majority of which were sent to London as "constant traders". Between both ports, there was at least one direct connection per week, as the Hamburg merchants imported English colonial goods from London, which were sought-after on the continent, as well as an increasing number of products from industrial production. Here, they were in free competition with the British sailors. The risk was high; the ship's shares had to be insured.

… and the Insurance Business

In 1765, the Hamburg Council finally approved the establishment of insurance companies on the basis of shares influenced perhaps by the effects of the 1763 crisis. As "co-operatives for mutual assistance" on the basis of the British "underwriter" system, six insurance companies were established by 1782. Several companies joined forces, and for the founding of the "First Insurance Company", together raised share capital amounting to 500,000 Thaler and for 20 percent cash payments issued up to 500 shares – once they were appropriately convinced of the financial wherewithal of the shareholders. The same risk was covered up to 30,000 Thaler, a sum which private insurers never could have come up with. Profit and loss were divided among the shareholders respectively. According to legislation, the duration of the transactions was limited to 10 years; thereafter they were to be liquidated if the shareholders did not agree to extend for another decade.

Johann Hinrich Gossler was a member of the "Sixth Insurance Company", which was founded in 1781, and he was its honorary chairman until 1784. That same year, he had the honour "to speak with lots of understanding merchants" who knew "that business dealings have not just fortunate but also unfortunate periods and that these alternate with each other". The company had just weathered a rather unfortunate period. The naval war, which accompanied the American War of Independence, had not only brought momentum, but also dangers, which meant that insurance dealings were quite unsettled.

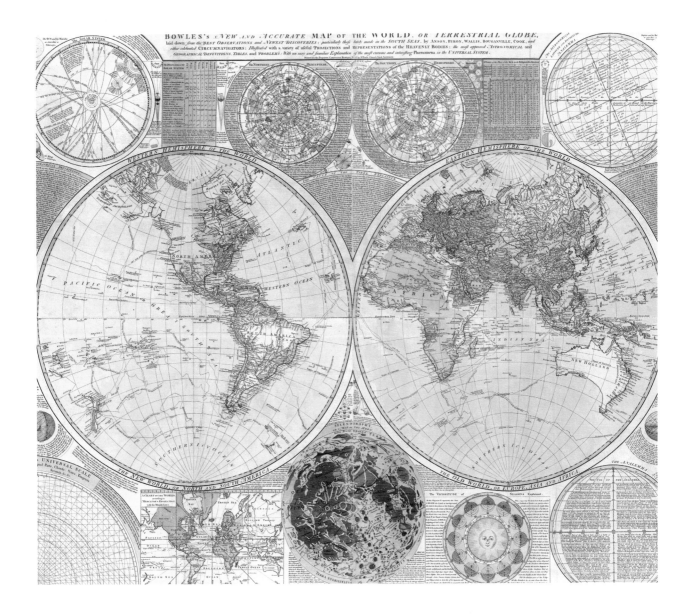

The Continental Congress of all North American colonies (except Georgia) had stopped trading with the mother country in 1774, a situation which Anglophobes and neutral countries knew how to leverage. England reacted with privateering in an effort to stop supplies from reaching America. As a result, the neutral powers of Russia, Denmark and Sweden formed the "First League of Armed Neutrality" in 1780 to protect trade, which Prussia and Austria joined in 1781, and Portugal joined in 1782. But when the Dutch wanted to join the league, England immediately declared war and the Battle of Dogger Bank broke out.

Map of the world, 1780

Celebrations in Philadelphia: On 4 July 1776, 13 colonies declared their independence from England and formed the United States of America

Unpredictable events were not the only source of considerable hassle for Hamburg insurers: "The false confidence in the armed neutrality, false neutralisations, scams on trips to foreign destinations, bad ships, which on top of that were poorly manned, insolvencies, competition from Bremen and Lübeck-based insurers, partial payment of freight which immediately resulted in greater damages – all of this … cost all the insurance companies, and the 'Sixth' too, lots of money." In Bremen, Lübeck, Glückstadt and other locations, companies had been established, and of these, three in Bremen alone folded the following year.

But in the Peace of Versailles in 1783, England acknowledged the independence of the 13 "United States of America". In a speech he gave in 1784, Johann Hinrich Gossler noted that the outlook for the insurance business was positive. He tried to discourage the shareholders from dissolving the "Sixth Insurance Company" prematurely. He went on to say that the losses were not as high as the audience assumed and that especially now in light of diminishing competition there would be an opportunity for good business. He added that the "Sixth Insurance Company" ought to listen to its own appeals to stand firm because soon after there would be profits to work with.

From 1769 to 1778, the wax bleaching operation made good profits; however, substantial funds were tied up. Then business slowed down and in 1788, when Spain ceased to be the main buyer of candles, the company began recording losses. In 1805, the operation was sold.

A New Lifestyle …

Not only was Joh. Berenberg & Gossler flourishing superbly, but so was the growing number of children born to Johann Hinrich and Elisabeth. Both business and family needed room.

The office had been on Gröninger Straße until 1769, but the storage room was no longer sufficient. Johann Hinrich bought a house on Kleinen Reichenstraße for 46,500 marks; he paid 7,500 marks in cash and financed the rest with a mortgage between 3 percent and 4 percent. In the beginning, the attic, storage area and cellar were rented in part, but things got too tight here as well even though a third storey was added in 1778. Johann Hinrich and Elisabeth now had ten children. On 22 September 1788, the Gosslers bought a house on Alter Wandrahm for 60,000 marks. And here too, calculations revealed that a mortgage with an annual interest rate of 3.6 percent was more advantageous than withdrawing capital from the company.

The house had been built in 1621 by jewellery dealers Hans and Jacob Moers and was therefore named *Moershaus* or *Mortzenhaus*. It had a magnificent Renaissance façade and was so spacious that with the growing number of servants, ultimately 20 people lived there. There was also a stable and behind it to the canal, there was a six-storey, half-timbered house, which was used as a warehouse. From here, the port and the stock market were easy to access. *Mortzenhaus* no longer exists since Alter Wandrahm had to give way to build the free port at the end of the 19th century.

Until its sale, the wax bleaching served as an excursion destination and summer retreat. Where today traffic flows on Stresemannstraße, the family enjoyed fresh air. In the very elegant garden house, which was situated next to

In 1788, Johann Hinrich Berenberg
purchased the house at Alter Wandrahm
21. The palatial building is also known
as *Mortzenhaus*

The magnificent Comédie-Française theatre in Paris

the manufacturing building, there was a piano and a billiard table. Not only were friends hosted here, but lavish meals were arranged for business partners. The Gosslers hosted dinners in the city. The meals were obviously good and plentiful and each year, Johann Hinrich ordered large amounts of Bordeaux and Rhine wine.

In Paris, Johann Hinrich not only learned French, but also came to appreciate the French savoir-vivre and visited operas. He loved music: in the *Mortzenhaus* there was a harpsichord, two pianos, three violins and a cello, which the children played. In 1769 alone, Johann Hinrich and Elisabeth went to eight public concerts. They were also invited to the home of banker friend H. J. Stresow, the home of scholar and distinguished pianist Christoph Daniel Ebeling and the home of Johann Georg Büsch, the founder of the *Handlungs Akademie*, (similar to an English Dissenting Academy) where they listened to private concerts. At the Büsch home, Carl Philipp Emanuel Bach, who had been the choirmaster and music director in Hamburg since 1767, introduced his pieces, and pianist Thomas Augustine Arne introduced Hamburg to the music of Handel.

… and a New Spirit

Elisabeth Gossler (neé Berenberg) came from a traditionally Pietist home, but she had been raised entirely in the new spirit of the Age of Enlightenment. In addition to the Latin classics, she also read French and English philosophy and poems in their original versions and in the process, she learned about ideas with which her grandmother, Anna-Elisabeth, would have hardly been in agreement.

It has been historically documented that Elisabeth read John Locke (1632–1704), the English Enlightenment philosopher, who interpreted people's own senses to be the starting point of all knowledge and declared non-sensual "items" such as the immortality of the human soul and the freedom of will, cornerstones for the Christian tradition, to be an issue of individual faith. In Locke's Theory of the State, he advocates the right of revolution, a constitution government, guaranteed freedom and rights for everyone and the separation of powers.

In this way, Elisabeth Berenberg arguably became familiar with the ideas of the Enlightenment and their interpretation of the bourgeois-liberal state thinking. But she must have been suspicious of the over-evaluation of reason because the Gosslers read less of Lessing and Voltaire than of Gellert, Klopstock and Rousseau, whose books were delivered individually to the home from 1782 onwards.

Jean Jacques Rousseau's critique of culture and civilisation, in which he emphasised the natural freedom of each person, presumably resonated more with Elisabeth than the theory of the sovereignty of the people, which was to inspire French revolutionaries. Along with Klopstock, whom the Gosslers knew personally and appreciated, people in Hamburg shared a general feeling of happiness over the outbreak of the great revolution, but were just as shocked by the bloody consequences of the unleashed "sovereignty" of the people, as was the poet of the *The Messiah* and of *The Odes*. Klopstock loved reason – but as the thought of God, as it was revealed to us in moments of personal emotion. This is definitely a Pietist legacy and it should have reconciled Elisabeth with the spiritual tradition of her ancestors, for all the talk of the Enlightenment.

In England, America and France, the Enlightenment helped the bourgeoisie on the road to success. On the American continent, the struggle for independence from England had already been decided; in France, the great revolution was looming and the emancipated English bourgeoisie were embarking on the Industrial Revolution.

Hamburg's hinterland, on the other hand, was ruled by monarchs in the 1770s and 1780s, who essentially felt obligated to enlightened absolutism. The new thought did not serve the revolution, but strengthened the power of the state instead.

Leading figures of the Enlightenment
(from top left to bottom right):
Dramatist Gotthold Ephraim Lessing (1729–1781)
Philosopher Jean-Jacques Rousseau (1712–1778)
Poet Friedrich Gottlieb Klopstock (1724–1803)
Poet Christian Fürchtegott Gellert (1715–1769)

Frederick the Great, the "first servant of his state", gave the Enlightenment a certain importance in the Prussian state structure: the "General state laws for Prussian states", for instance, defined a few fundamental rights for individuals independent of status or religion, schools went from being in church hands to being in state hands, and the universities were "democratised". He summoned Voltaire to his court from 1750 to 1752 and even granted radical materialist Julien Offray de La Mettrie shelter. But the principle of "everything for the people and nothing through the people" continued to apply. The nobility was privileged, serfdom was maintained and the bourgeoisie was kept in leading-strings – the industrial progress so longed for was reserved to the English for the moment.

While much of Germany's policy and business stayed the same, the country experienced an unprecedented blooming in the humanities, poetry and music.

In 1733, there were said to be 3,000 German authors, in 1778, 6,000. Lessing, the father of the German Enlightenment, was presumably one of the few who could eke out a living from writing. In 1771/73, the young Johann

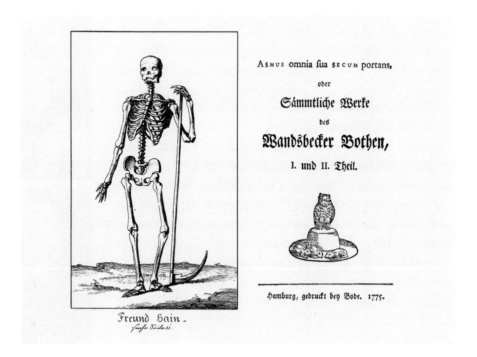

Matthias Claudius was the man behind the newspaper *Wandsbecker Bothe*, which was published until 1775

Wolfgang von Goethe (1749–1832) had been shoved into the spotlight of literary life with his *Götz von Berlichingen* (*Götz of the Iron Hand*) and even more with the *Die Leiden des jungen Werthers* (*The Sorrows of Young Werther*) in 1774. The exaggerated sensitivity of the young Werther expresses the sentimentality of these decades, which we also find in Hamburg. The young Goethe bundled the intellectual movement of his time, which was enthusiastic about Rousseau and Shakespeare, yet inclined to Pietism.

The second half of the 18th century marked the beginning of the Classic and Romantic literary period, whose works were to become required reading in the education of the nation. The same applied to music with Handel, Haydn, Mozart, Beethoven, and to philosophy with Kant and Fichte. Kant succeeded in blending the experience-oriented English and the rational German Enlightenment philosophy. With his definition of the Enlightenment as "The liberation of man from his self-imposed immaturity" in 1784, he subsequently left his mark on the age. However, the practical sciences remained comparatively underdeveloped in German; they were still in the grips of philosophy.

German philosopher Immanuel Kant (1742–1804)

In Hamburg, the intellectual and political climate was full of excitement but peaceful. The independence of America and the French Revolution were welcomed, but the spark did not turn into fire: the bourgeoisie, elsewhere supporters of the revolution, made political decisions here anyway. The city had an unprecedented liberal press at the time. Newspapers such as the *Staats- und Gelehrte Zeitung des Hamburgischen unpartheyischen Correspondenten*, the *Hamburger Relations-Courier* and the *Hamburger Neue Zeitung* had as many as 30,000 copies in circulation. *The Patriot*, which was mentioned earlier, was reprinted as a book a total of four times by 1765, and renowned authors of the time published in the *Hamburgischen Neuen Zeitung. Wandsbecker Bothe* achieved literary prominence in 1771. Its editor, Matthias Claudius, published his own writings and was also able to secure Klopstock, Lessing, Herder, Voß and Goethe as authors. Moreover, the first German Masonic Lodge was founded in 1737, and the *Patriotische Gesellschaft* (Patriotic Society) endeavoured to spread Humanist thought. In Hamburg, Lessing's *Minna von Barnhelm* had its German première in 1767, and in 1771, Klopstock's popular *Sammlung neuer Oden* was published. Johann Heinrich Voß achieved prominence in German-speaking areas with his translations of *Homer*, which appeared in Hamburg beginning in 1781.

Johann Heinrich Gossler and his wife, Elisabeth, often visited performances at the Hamburg Theatre after the well-known theatre director Friedrich Ludwig Schröder took over. The audience loved Shakespeare's major plays, but also Goethe's *Götz von Berlichingen*, Lessing's *Emilia Galotti* and in 1787, the German premiere of Schiller's *Don Karlos*.

Elisabeth Gossler and Partners 1790–1800

Johann Hinrich Gossler's rising pharmacy bills and intake of Pyrmont water indicated that he had become ill by 1788. He died on 31 August 1790 "of dropsy at an age of 52 years … God rejoice in his soul after he spent almost two years here sick. Blessed be the Lord that He put an end to his suffering," noted his brother, Johann Eibert, in his diary. That same year, Elisabeth lost her two youngest children.

Johann Hinrich had made provisions for the continuation of the company. In 1775, the actor couple Seyler had enrolled their 17-year-old son, Ludwig Erdwin, with Johann Berenberg & Gossler for an apprenticeship. In his apprenticeship agreement, he was obligated to serve initially for six years "faithfully and honestly and untiringly" and for every year not served, he was to pay 1,000 Species to the orphanage. After the apprenticeship, Seyler committed to working as a *Comptoir-Bursche* (bar lad) for an "annual salary of 200/300/400 and 500 marks Hamburger Courant respectively."

After another three years, the Gosslers were willing to welcome him into the family and the company. On 20 May 1788, he married the oldest daughter, Anna Henriette (1771–1836), who was just 16, and he signed a ten-year partner agreement retroactive to 1 January. Three months prior to his death, Johann Hinrich Gossler concluded a new agreement with Kruckenberg and Seyler on 29 May 1790. We only know from the agreement that the partnerships were to continue to remain "hidden".

His widow broke with common practice in the new agreement dated 1 January 1791, in which Section Two specified the company name "Johann Berenberg, Gossler & Co."; soon, the abbreviated form "Joh. Berenberg, Gossler & Co." applied. Elisabeth

Ludwig Erdwin Seyler (1758–1836), president of the Commerce Deputation and, from 1788 to 1836, joint owner of the Berenberg Bank

committed herself to continuing the "well established operation" in her own name and in that of her children, with whom she shared joint property, and to allow the company's assets "of her blessed husband … for the benefit and best interest of the partnership to circulate in the company." With Seyler and Kruckenberg, who were increasingly more in charge of the company, an agreement was reached whereby they wanted "to relieve each other but also the widow Gossler of the burden of running the company by working industriously in the *Comptoir* (bar)." Seyler was responsible for the cash desk while Kruckenberg had to keep "a watchful eye" on the "diligent and exact account" of the company books. Profit and loss were distributed four-sixths to the widow Gossler and one-sixth respectively to both partners.

Moreover, the agreement also provided that "one of the two oldest sons, either Johann Nicolaus (1774–1848), or Johann Hinrich Gossler (1775–1842) should be able to enter the company," provided this was their wish and they had an "impeccable nature" and their character was "serious and dignified and they were inclined to diligence and work." If both sons declined, or if they were not suitable to head up a company, "Messrs. Kruckenberg and Seyler would not be obliged to take on another of the Gossler family as a co-partner."

The oldest son, Johann Nicolaus, initially declined going into the company. After he had completed his apprenticeship at Rücker & Wortmann, one of the most distinguished companies in Hamburg, he moved to London for Joh. Berenberg, Gossler & Co. in 1797 "for business of the *Societäts-Handlung*", where, upon his return, he was to be remunerated 20,000 Mark Banco, "for his personal efforts and for the deferred start with the company".

In May 1797, Elisabeth Gossler waived one-twelfth of her share of the profit and loss in favour of Seyler because she "realises completely just how much I have to thank Mr Seyler for the attention, care and his untiring diligence every day and his understanding management over the past few years for the extensive … for the operation of Joh. Berenberg, Gossler & Co." Both adult sons and the three new sons-in-law agreed with the provision, and even partner and brother-in-law Kruckenberg gave his approval, "with renunciation of an improvement for himself."

In 1798, the second-oldest son finally joined the company: Johann Hinrich II, who had been writing his name in High German, was Johann Heinrich by the turn of the century.

Ludwig Erdwin Seyler rises through the ranks

The Big Boom ...

Johann Hinrich Gossler I died too early to fully experience the pioneering merits of his business policy. It was not until the 1790s that Hamburg saw a boom in the goods business, which was attributed to the now flourishing trade with America, the French Revolution and the closing of the Rheinstraße, and the equally big boom in the insurance and banking businesses after the occupation of the Netherlands by the French and the flight of the insurers and investors to Hamburg.

The initial years of the French Revolution (which began in 1789) brought Hamburg considerable profits as large quantities of wheat went to France. Yet the price drop of the Assignats and the exodus of capital from France and the Netherlands to Hamburg were the first sure signs for Hamburg merchants that a storm was looming. Prussia and the Empire demanded that Hamburg soon banish the French ambassador, who, fortunately, left the city freely – otherwise Leopold II would have imposed a trading ban with France. The years 1792–1797 were marked by the War of the First Coalition of the European powers against France, followed by the Netherlands' annexation by the French in 1794/95 and the Rheinstraße was blocked to traffic.

This meant double the luck for Hamburg albeit for a brief period. First, the Netherlands ceased to be active on the diverse trading routes which meant that almost the entire trade on the continent with colonial goods and English manufactured goods went through Hamburg only, and second, Dutch exchange and insurance businesses relocated to the Hanseatic city.

Thus, Hamburg rose to become the most important trading city in Europe. It was home not only to the largest warehouse, but also became the leading European banking and exchange centre and the largest international insurance centre. At the start of the 1790s, Joh. Berenberg, Gossler & Co. had shares in all six Hamburg-based insurance companies and in the Glückstädter Compagnie. When the "Seventh Insurance Company" was founded, the company had a leading financial interest in the new insurance company. Despite enormous competition – by the start of the Napoleonic Wars, there were at times 30 insurance companies in Hamburg – the Compagnie posted considerable profits in the first ten years. Hamburg had reaped the benefits in the insurance sector which Amsterdam had lost.

Interests in investment companies

From 1790 to 1800 alone, seven renowned merchant banking instututions and numerous exchange offices were opened, and as a result of the increasing number of discount brokers, the turnover of goods picked up substantially more speed. In the area of goods trade, America was the main reason for this development. In 1791, the company received its first shipment of goods directly from the the new country – rice from Charleston; the first import from Philadelphia is registered in 1794. Other places of origin mentioned include New York, Boston and Wilmington. But Philadelphia soon accounted for the lion's share of the trade with America. In 1797 alone, the year in which imports for

The painting by Eugène Delacroix "Liberty Leading The People" (1830) symbolises the spirit of the French Revolution (1789–1799)

Joh. Berenberg, Gossler & Co. and other Hamburg
entrepreneurs protest against their ships being
held in Danish ports during 1796

Joh. Berenberg, Gossler & Co. hit a record high of 8.5 million marks, goods with a value of 575,400 marks from Philadelphia. Here is a breakdown:

52,500 marks for coffee
38,700 marks for sugar
8,900 marks for cotton
7,300 marks for cochineal

Export to Philadelphia by contrast, at 20,220 marks, remained far below the import figures:

10,500 marks for camphor
5,550 marks for hemp
3,420 marks for iron
650 marks for bottles
50 marks for coffee grinders
50 marks for smoked meat

A Frenchman in America: Stephen Girard (1750–1831) was an important trading partner für Joh. Berenberg, Gossler & Co. in Philadelphia

The company had a very reliable trading partner in Stephen Girard, a somewhat adventurous self-made man from Bordeaux, who, within a very short period of time, had built up a respectable trading company and a merchant fleet in Philadelphia. His right hand was a Frenchman by the name of Roberjeot, who had completed his merchant training in Hamburg. Girard had earned his ship captain's license and made sure that the best sailors were on his ships. On his ships, which he never insured: given a 10 to 20 percent insurance premium on the value of the ships and low losses, he saved considerable amounts of money. He was doing business with Hamburg by 1791 at the latest, and so it can be assumed that Johann Hinrich Gossler I established contact. Joh. Berenberg, Gossler & Co. became the correspondent firm of Girard's in Hamburg. Starting in 1795, as can be gathered from "Girard's papers", the correspondent firm invoiced over five to eight arriving or departing shiploads annually with him; he repeatedly took the opportunity to praise the excellent reputation, the exceptional payment practice as well as the care and correctness of the business dealings with his Hamburg-based partner.

Likely due to Girard's efforts, extensive trade was underway with Calcutta in 1794, and the company also did business with Manila.

The balance sheet totals at the end of December:

1790	2,820,163 marks
1799	2,524,638 marks
1800	2,052,418 marks
1801	2,452,065 marks
1802	2,684,259 marks

In trade within Europe, London was the most important hub. England's fleet was unchallenged in its dominance of overseas trade, and the colonial goods trade with the mainland was done through Hamburg. Joh. Berenberg, Gossler & Co. had a large share in these transactions. In 1797 alone, it imported goods from England valuing 1,933,250 marks. In keeping with tradition, trade with Iberia and Italy continued to be maintained while business with France declined due to unstable political conditions.

… and the Big Crisis of 1798/99

The unlimited demand for money in the 1790s – Hamburg was not yet acquainted with future transactions – opened the door to goods purchased on speculation.

In the winter of 1798/99, when prices suddenly went up significantly, people bought all the goods they could manage, mostly on bills of exchange. But the sales so hoped for stagnated, prices fell, and the wait for better times, given increasing storage rents and an increasing discount rate, was accompanied by hectic kite-flying. When the European market was suddenly inundated with goods from overseas in the summer, the crisis came to a head. Those who had not sold in time, ran into payment difficulties. Over a six-week period in the fall of 1799, 136 Hamburg companies went bankrupt with a debt totalling 37 million Mark Banco.

The owners of Joh. Berenberg, Gossler & Co. wisely enough did not take part in the kite-flying, which was so commonplace during the crisis of 1799; however, they were still impacted. Since the Elbe froze in the winter of 1798/99, there were no contacts notably to Livorno and London. The ice had barely melted when the longed-for sailing ship expected from London sank. The bills of exchange drawn on Ruben Brothers, A. Goldsmith Sons, D. Eliasson and Louis Sack were dishonoured. Moreover, the balance sheet of 1801 listed non-recoverable debts totalling 190,586 marks. The claims appeared in the balance sheet right up to 1808 until finally 105,000 Mark Banco had to be written off.

The losses the company suffered were, however, comparatively small. Although the company's recovery did stagnate for a short while, things picked up again in 1801/02.

Depression and Internationalisation:
Johann Heinrich Gossler II (1775–1842)

The partner agreement Elisabeth Gossler had concluded with Kruckenberg and Seyler ended on 31 December 1800. Elisabeth was 51 and decided to withdraw from the company to "spend the rest of my days in peace." This "rest" was to be another 20 years, in which she remained the energetic and loving core of her large family. On her estate in Groß-Borstel, her children and grandchildren found refuge in difficult times.

From 1798 the Hamburg Senator Johann Heinrich Gossler (1775–1842) was co-owner of Joh. Berenberg, Gossler & Co. together with his brother-in-law, Ludwig Edwin Seyler

On 22 August 1800, a new company partnership agreement was concluded. Elisabeth's capital stayed in the company at an interest rate of 4 percent. After her death, the heirs were to be permitted to withdraw their share from the company – at the earliest – one year later and then in five instalments, "each running from twelve to twelve months". Johann Heinrich's older brother, Johann Nicolaus, who had returned from London, joined the three partners. As the oldest son, he received, like Seyler, a one-third share in profits and losses, Johann Heinrich and Kruckenberg, by contrast, one-sixth respectively. Johann Nicolaus was his mother's favourite, but also her problem child. He was not really considered to be a realist and only lasted nine years in the company. In 1809, he had his share of the inheritance – amounting to 80,000 Mark Banco – paid out in an effort to try and engage in his own business dealings – to little avail.

Johann Heinrich II, on the other hand, saw his business influence increasing and would head up the company for 45 years. Upon joining the company in 1798, he married the beautiful Marianne Schramm (1777–1824), daughter of the *Oberalten* – and partner in a fashion business – Johann Gottfried Schramm (1780–1827), and gave birth to eight children in rapid succession. He also got off to a good start in the company and experienced prosperous times despite major difficulties; the English temporarily blocked the Elbe estuary. Up until 1808, the balance sheet continued to register around 2.5 million Mark Banco. The figures were the highest recorded in the history of the company – and yet Hamburg was still unaware of the hard times looming on the horizon.

Napoleon Comes Closer – the Wars of Coalition

While Hamburg was content to maintain its foreign trade, aristocratic Europe was trying to resist the expansion of France and an export of the Revolution during the Wars of Coalition.

In the War of the First Coalition, from 1792 to 1797, Prussia and Austria were first involved and were later joined by England, the Netherlands, Italy and the German Empire against the French Republic. But in the end, France formed a Batavian Republic in the Netherlands, which annexed the left bank of the Rhine and turned Northern Italy into a Cisalpine and Ligurian Republic based on the French model. The Swiss Confederation was declared the Helvetic Republic that same year. And the rise of Napoleon had begun. In 1793, he had advanced from artillery captain to brigadier general in the Republican Army in one year; in 1796, he was named supreme commander of the Italian Army and returned from the Italian expedition as a national hero.

In the War of the Second Coalition, from 1799 to 1802, the English, Austrians, Russians and Turks joined forces against France; Prussia remained neutral. Meanwhile, as a result of a *coup d'état*, Napoleon became first consul in 1799. His reconciliation with the church was a prerequisite for the internal peace of the country, and the Napoleonic Code consolidated the new social order. In 1802, Napoleon became Consul for life and was entitled to name his successor. This eliminated the Bourbons, and in 1804, the citizen Napoleon Bonaparte crowned himself emperor of the French people.

The War of the Third Coalition got underway in 1805 and saw England join forces with Russia Austria, Sweden and Prussia. At least on the seas, Lord Nelson was able to ensure English dominance in the naval Battle of Trafalgar. However, on land, Napoleon was unstoppable. In December 1805, his troops achieved a brilliant victory in the "Battle of the Three Emperors" in Austerlitz against Franz II of Austria and Alexander I of Russia.

The victory heralded the end of the Holy Roman Empire of the German nation after almost 1,000 years. A total of 16 small southwest German states, among them Bavaria and Württemberg, broke away from the Empire and formed the Confederation of the Rhine under French protectorate. By 1811, another 20 had joined. Franz II abdicated his imperial German crown and then began referring to himself as simply Emperor Franz I of Austria. Hamburg became a "sovereign" state. The end of the "imperial immediacy" also signalled the end of any protection by the Empire, Hamburg's citizens became "outlawed republicans". However, the situation did not last long. The future of the city was soon to be decided, namely, in Prussia.

Prussia's Defeat and the Occupation of Hamburg in 1806

While under the effect of the Battle of Austerlitz, Prussia concluded an alliance with France in 1805, and not only got Hanover, which was adjacent to Hamburg, but also brought upon itself the declaration of war from England and Sweden and saw the blockade of its ports.

The catastrophic results for Prussia's economy persuaded Frederick William III in 1806 to change sides. In a number of battles, Napoleon put an end to this tactic. In the Battle of Jena and Auerstedt in 1806, and at the Battles of Eylau and Friedland in 1807, Prussia was defeated, and in the Peace of Tilsit, in 1807, disassembled. French troops moved into Berlin, and on 19 November 1806, Hamburg was also occupied. Frederick William III and Queen Luise fled to Memel, while Napoleon now resided in their Berlin chambers. On 21 November, he announced the Continental Blockade whereby all ports of the French Empire were now forbidden from importing British goods; the continent from Danzig to Cadiz (with the exception of Portugal and Stralsund) was subject to a naval blockade.

Hamburg under the French 1806–1814

French occupying forces were not immediately successful at completely stopping Hamburg's trade with England. In fact, the French envoy to Hamburg, Bourienne, is said to have made a fortune in the beginning selling exemptions.

Despite the Continental System, imports predominantly from England jumped considerably. Of particular note are the records for sugar, coffee, indigo, rice, pimento and tea.

But in 1807, the situation became aggravated when the all too enterprising Bourienne was recalled by Napoleon, and Denmark, whose territory extended almost to the gates of Hamburg, sided with Napoleon. Goods which

Hamburg merchants had stored in Altona or in ports in Schleswig-Holstein were immediately confiscated. This meant that Joh. Berenberg, Gossler & Co. lost 582 barrels of sugar. Although the company had provided a security of 114,303 Mark Banco for the value of the goods, the high court in Gottorf refused to surrender the goods with the justification, "that one should keep such a significant quantity for consignment rather than for a company at the risk and account of one single company, particularly during such a critical time." In July 1808, the high court in Glückstadt reacted the same when it had 236 barrels of sugar confiscated, which were in storage in Brunsbüttel for Joh. Berenberg, Gossler & Co.

The Continental Blockade

By 1808 the full brunt of the Continental System was felt. Joh. Berenberg, Gossler & Co. imported English goods valuing just 42,000 marks, and for 1809 and 1810, no more shipments were listed in the duty lists of the Admiralty. British goods were confiscated, some even burned, and the company suffered significant losses. Through it all, Joh. Berenberg, Gossler & Co. still held up remarkably well, given that from 1807 onwards over 180 trading companies suspended their payments. More than 300 ships were rotting in the port, and port workers and sailors lost their jobs. The capital at the Hamburger Bank sank from 42 million to 6.5 million marks in 1808, the silver stock dropped from 33 to 9 million marks. Contribution payments and the upkeep of the occupation troops exacerbated the situation further. During this time, many families lost everything they owned.

However, trade was not entirely crippled. A part of the Hamburg war fleet had escaped prior to the occupation and now travelled from London and Liverpool for the account of their ship owner. A few had organised neutral flags, still others sent their cargo ships to Russia, where they travelled under the Russian flag. Although the French wanted to stop all contact with the outside world, and despite high penalties, people set up cover addresses outside the city and smuggled letters in and out so that the flow of information did not halt entirely. And this was key because as long as there was the possibility of staying in contact with other companies, shipments could be sent from other ports directly to the customers. Payments were made using bills of exchange, which could be traded on the stock market, which was still in operation.

This "drop shipping" prevailed anyhow at Joh. Berenberg, Gossler & Co., and thanks to the broad company base, the business survived the occupation relatively well intact. The old trade relations to Prussia, Russia and Scandinavia now proved to be a valuable replacement for the lack of trade with England. In Lübeck, C. Platzmann Söhne worked for Joh. Berenberg, Gossler & Co. In Russia, Johann Heinrich's brother, Wilhelm, established contacts, then went to London via Berlin, where he reported via smuggle routes about the happenings in the free world.

Since French authorities issued certificates for trade via Neustadt in Mecklenburg and via Schwerin, American – or allegedly American – goods reached Hamburg this way; there would have been many an English shipment among them. But English goods were also smuggled into the city over and over again via Tönning, Altona and Helgoland in cloak-and-dagger operations; French sanctions worked wonders on the creativity of the merchants.

On 16 November 1810 French troops burn British goods at Hamburg's Grasbrook, depicted by Christoffer Suhr

Many activities carried on as usual. A suggestion made by Wilhelm Gossler at the start of a war commission meeting in 1808, "that the feast now common for this organisation be cancelled for the time being on account of the sad times and to request that the departing church community leader, Mr. Schwartze, refrain from giving his farewell dinner", received widespread agreement. However, the Gossler family saw no serious restrictions placed on their personal lives. In the large house on Zuchthausstraße – where today Alstertor and Hermannstraße meet – five children filled the home with noise, for whose care and upbringing nurses, nannies and governesses were hired in addition to domestic workers. And in the summer of 1810, Johann Heinrich and Marianne Gossler took an extended pleasure trip through Germany.

In 1811 Johann Marcus David painted
the "Prospect of the Imperial French
City of Hamburg"

"Une Bonne Ville de l'Empire Français"

On 10 December 1810, Napoleon announced the complete annexation of the Hanseatic towns, Lauenburg and the coastal strip between the Ems and the Elbe Rivers into the French Empire; Hamburg became "a beautiful city in the French Empire." General Davout was the governor, a companion of Napoleon's since the Egyptian Campaign (1798–1801) and who had become Duke of Auerstedt and Prince of Eckmühl, as he had won the battles there for the emperor. With his administrative staff, he assumed all the important functions in the Hanseatic city. The French removed Hamburg's coat of arms from all public buildings and replaced it with the French eagle. The city's militia formed the core of the 127th French line regiment, whose strength grew rapidly with the introduction of compulsory military service.

The senate, parliament and all city offices were dissolved and reorganised on the French model: At the top of the city, was a mayor with several co-ordinated mayors. Instead of a parliament, there was a municipal council, which was to be made up of 30 members, but never actually did so. For the most part, the municipal council was made up of former senators, administrators and respectable citizens, including Johann Heinrich Gossler – who was responsible for the street police – and Seyler's son-in-law, Gerhard von Hoßtrup, who ran the *Börsenhalle*, an institution reminiscent of the English clubs, which enjoyed great popularity. In its entry hall, all the important political and commercial news was posted, and in two reading rooms, there were journals and leaflets, including the *Liste der Börsenhalle*, which based on its literary section, had grown to become one of the leading journals in Germany. Davout now subjected theatres and the press to strict censorship. Newspapers had to appear in two languages so long as they were not forbidden, as was the case with Hoßtrup's *Liste der Börsenhalle*.

Even the Commercial Deputation was placed under French control. Here, Seyler attempted to shed light on the legal jungle, which created additional difficulties after the introduction of the Napoleonic Code. Perhaps unsurprisingly, people found collaboration with the French rather difficult at times, yet hoped they could prevent the situation from getting worse.

And the situation was unpleasant enough. In addition to trade restrictions, French taxes introduced in July 1811 ruined Hamburg's economy. A door tax and a window tax were levied on home owners, a patent tax was

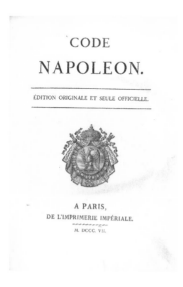

The Napoleonic Code combined
five legal texts in 1804

Hamburg's coat of arms of 1812
prescribed by the French: a cockerel,
imperial crown and three bees

Armes de la Ville d'Hambourg

levied on tradespeople mostly, an *octroi* was levied on food, the *droits réunis* were imposed on tobacco, beverages and playing cards. Napoleon had become so hated that secret organisations formed whose only goal was to topple or murder the emperor.

Foreign trade for Joh. Berenberg, Gossler & Co. had dropped considerably, but in addition to the old ties, which did not operate via trade with England, new paths had been found. In April 1811, for instance, the duty lists for Joh. Berenberg, Gossler & Co. showed indigo and logwood shipments from Altona valuing 24,000 marks.

In 1812, Marianne Gossler's brother, Johann Gottfried Schramm junior, who was married to Johann Heinrich's sister, Johanna Elisabeth, moved to Gothenburg, and so via Sweden, an enemy of Napoleon, a reliable connection to Scandinavia was established once again. For the company, Gothenburg became a pivotal centre for trading foods and the sharing of information for the entire Baltic Sea region, including Russia. As a result of arrangements made by companies in Gothenburg, English goods were smuggled via Stralsund and Wismar to Hamburg. The costs and risks were considerable; in 1812 alone the Hamburg customs court ordered 127 penal orders within 18 days, including a few death sentences. But to save the company in these bad times, every path had to be used. The balance sheet totals illustrate the extent to which the business dealings of Joh. Berenberg, Gossler & Co. had suffered since 1808:

> 1808 2,560,205 Mark Banco
> 1809 1,445,939 Mark Banco
> 1810 1,314,376 Mark Banco

Even equity suffered substantial losses due to the lost compensation and the payments to the French, plummeting from 960,000 in 1798 to 558,567 Mark Banco in 1810.

In 1810, Napoleon was at the peak of his power. In the Treaty of Tilsit in 1807, Prussia lost 49 percent of its former territory and with that loss, it seemed damned to insignificance. In the same treaty, Napoleon and Czar Alexander I mutually agreed that one-half of the continent would be enough for each of them, and as a result of his marriage to the Austrian Archduchess Marie-Luise in 1810 and the birth of a successor in 1811, Austria also seemed tied to Napoleon, and the future of the Bonaparte dynasty guaranteed. The main enemy, England, had come to the end of its tether. The continental blockade had harmed the economy so much that the opposition was calling for peace at any price. However, resistance was steadily building against French rule in Europe.

Prussia Rises like a Phoenix out of the Ashes

Prussia used the humiliating time under Napoleon to reform itself. After the Treaty of Tilsit in 1807, Freiherr vom Stein, with the edict dated 9 October 1807, and then Karl August Fürst von Hardenberg, with the so-called *Regulierungsedikt* in 1811, were able to enforce the liberation of the peasants. It fulfilled one requirement for technical progress and the growth in productivity; farming now became an industry that was accessible to everyone and, subsequently released workers, a fact which benefited the industry.

The changing boundaries of Prussia between 1801 and 1807

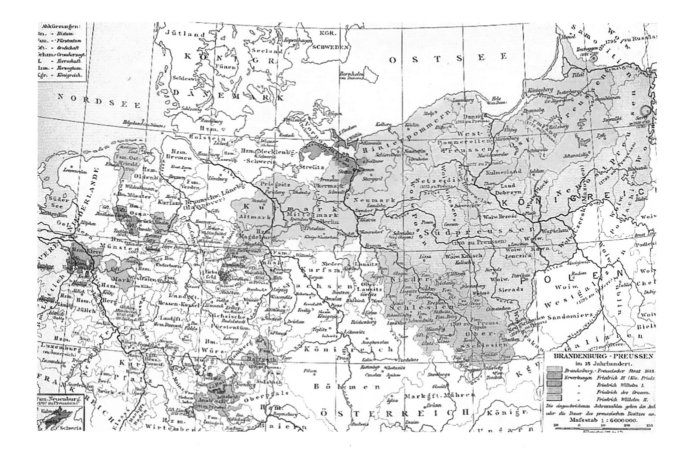

By decree on 19 November 1808, the exemplary self-government of the cities was introduced, "the Magna Carta of the Prussian and German freedom of cities". Public administration was made more effective with the introduction of a uniform state ministry with five department ministers responsible.

In the war ministry, Wilhelm von Scharnhorst and August Neidhardt von Gneisenau were planning the reorganisation and rearmament of the Prussian army. The nobility's prerogative on the officer's career was abolished and compulsory military service was introduced. Napoleon had granted Prussia a standing army with a maximum of 42,000 soldiers. In the course of the reforms, a secret arming was taking place. The official service period was shortened to a month respectively, but the discharged recruits continued to be drilled back in their hometowns. Thus, the standing army maintained itself within the permitted scope, but alongside it, a huge reservist army made up of well-trained soldiers emerged. People were waiting for Napoleon's defeat.

The emancipation of the Jews in 1812, the regulation of taxes and finances, the secularisation of church property and the introduction of free trade were further conditions for the strengthening of Prussia. The founding of the University of Berlin in 1808 by Wilhelm von Humboldt also signalled the dawn of a new intellectual era and new self confidence. Friedrich Schleiermacher, Friedrich Carl von Savigny and Ernst Moritz Arndt all played a role, and it was here that Fichte gave his famous *Speech to the German Nation*.

The bundle of reforms not only laid the way for the liberation war against Napoleon, but it also established important conditions for the future tariff union and the unification of Germany under Prussia's leadership began to emerge.

Napoleon's Russian Campaign

From 1810 onwards, Russia began to distance itself from Napoleon. The czar not only disliked the establishment of a Grand Duchy of Warsaw by Napoleon in 1807, but also his marriage with Marie-Louise of Austria: Napoleon seemed to be aiming at bringing all of Europe under his control despite all agreements. The alliance broke. Alexander I allied himself with Sweden against Denmark, Napoleon's ally, and in May 1812 he concluded an unfavourable peace with Turkey so that he could withdraw his troops from the southern front. The diplomatic preparations were thereby concluded and the fighting could start. Russia's lifting of the continental blockade on 29 May was tantamount to a declaration of war on France.

For his war against Russia, Napoleon ensured the support of the states dependent upon him in Italy and Germany. Moreover, he also succeeded in pulling Austria and Prussia over to his side. For the German states, which were hardly capable of acting independently, one alliance was just as bad as the next: in a clash between Napoleon and Alexander, they would have to fear for their existence regardless of whom their allies were. Yet Hardenberg's and Metternich's diplomatic interventions did not succeed in preventing Napoleon's Russian campaign.

In the spring of 1812, more than half a million soldiers were ready to take on Russia – less than half of them were French. In July, this *Grande Armée*

Founded by Wilhelm von Humboldt in 1809, Berlin's Humboldt University with the equestrian statue of Frederick the Great

7 September 1812 saw the bloody battle of Borodino between Napoleon's *Grande Armée* und Russian troops

crossed the borders of czarist Russia and followed the fighting Russians, who were holding out, right up to Moscow, where the *Grande Armée* planned to reside for the winter. But the Fire of Moscow from 15 to 20 September 1812 annihilated this hope and Napoleon's troops were forced to retreat empty-handed. More than 400,000 soldiers in the *Grande Armée* met their deaths in battles, ice and snow. Among the fallen or missing were Colonel Johann Jacob Gossler (1758–1812), a half-brother of Johann Hinrich, his son, Friedrich Ferdinand, and numerous other members of the 127th French line regiment who had been recruited from Hamburg.

Alexander I was not content to fight off the French army: he followed it beyond the borders of Russia, and initiated, alongside Sweden and Prussia, the so-called liberation of Europe. On 18 March 1813, around 1,400 Russians marched into Hamburg.

A week-long inferno erupted in
Moscow during 1812

Hamburg Rejoices – too soon

For the people of Hamburg, the traumatic French period seemed to have
finally come to an end. With unimagined enthusiasm, they welcomed the Russian "General" Friedrich Karl von Tettenborn (who was actually a colonel)
and his troops, the hated "vultures" were ripped from public buildings and the
Hamburg coat of arms was restored. The senate and parliament reconstituted
themselves. In Hoßtrup's *Börsenhalle* Hamburg merchants celebrated a lavish
party in honour of the coronation of Czar Alexander.

  The business dealings of Joh. Berenberg, Gossler & Co. got off to a
good start soon after the French had withdrawn, but the company retained
the option of processing all transactions through Stralsund in the event of
danger, which proved to be a wise decision because at the end of April, Davout,

In the winter of 1812–13 the French troops began their catastrophic retreat from Russia

who had begun a relief offensive from the Netherlands towards northern Germany, was in Harburg, and soon thereafter, French grenades from the quarter of Veddel reached the area around the church of St Nicholas.

On 29 May 1813, one day before Hamburg was re-occupied by the French, C. Platzmann Söhne in Lübeck reported that wood had arrived for the company. They went on to say that the ship was unloaded but that they were on stand-by to forward the shipment to Stralsund in the event of danger. The same day, a letter came from Johann Gottfried Schramm in Gothenburg announcing that a load of sugar was en route and that ten bales with English twist valuing 1,100 pounds were in Helgoland. In addition, on 22 April, the 86-Last brig, *Der Adler*, had unloaded a batch of bricks valuing 2,350 pounds from Garrique, Girard & Co. He went on to write that the same ship also had a damaged lot of 17 crates with 7,636 pounds of raw sugar "from abroad", ten bundles with 10,000 pounds of sugar from a Swedish refinery and additional bulk cargo on board. Since the shipment could not be forwarded to

Hamburg, it was shipped to Stralsund and from there transported further via sea or land.

On 30 May, Davout entered Hamburg again. With utmost severity, the previous status quo was re-established, but the city was spared mass executions and excessive atrocities, retaliation methods the French had used in other areas: "I prefer to have the people of Hamburg pay; that is the best way to punish merchants," Napoleon is supposed to have said. Davout demanded a punitive payment of 48 million Francs and had 30 renowned merchants, including Seyler, detained in Harburg, in an effort to collect part of the sum. A commission determined amounts to be roughly 10 percent of the assets; Johann Heinrich Gossler paid 4,500 for each of the first two instalments, his mother 15,750 Francs per instalment. Once a sixth of the contribution had been paid, those who had been detained were set free.

Marshal Davout ruled Hamburg with an iron fist in 1813–1814

The Liberation 1813–1814

In August 1813, the allied Russians, Prussians and Swedes finally received support from Austria and inflicted the decisive defeat on Napoleon in the Battle of Leipzig, with numerous troops from the Confederation of the Rhine switching sides.

A short time later, Johann Heinrich's brother, Wilhelm, wrote from London:
"… We can now almost with certainty foresee the day of deliverance and if I am not too mistaken, it is close; because after the French had to retreat close to the Rhine, Hamburg itself – even with a continuation of the alliance with Denmark – remains untenable for them …"

Yet, the worst months were still to come for Hamburg. Davout, one of Napoleon's most capable and stubborn generals, had no intention of retreating, but, instead, tried with all his means to keep Hamburg, Harburg and the Elbe islands. By using women, seniors and children, he had Hamburg refortified and barricaded. Several suburbs, including St Pauli, were levelled to the ground to make room in front of the embankment for a field of fire and leaving the opponent no place to hide. The people of Hamburg had to pay for the work themselves and after the merchants had refused to come up (within 24 hours) with a guarantee of six to seven million francs and a monthly payment of one million francs for the monthly service, Davout seized the Hamburger Bank with all the coins and silver bars valuing 7.5 million marks. Churches, hospitals and private homes, including *Mortzenhouse* on Alter Wandrahm as well as Seyler's home were seized and converted to hospitals. The office of Joh. Berenberg, Gossler & Co. was relocated in early December 1813 to Hoßtrup's previous house, to Neueburg 28.

At Christmas 1813, Davout had more than 20,000 people driven out of the city in freezing weather. In anticipation of a longer siege, the population had been ordered to stock up on food. Those who did not follow the order – and after years of war a large part of the population lived in misery – ran

The invitation or rather »order to attend« issued to Johann Heinrich Gossler for a thanksgiving service celebrating Napoleon's victories in 1813

Monsieur Gossler and Madame

are cordially invited to attend the Te Deum service to be held at the catholic Church at midday 6 June in honour of the victories achieved by His Royal and Imperial Majesty over the combined forces of Russia and Prussia.

The attendees are asked to gather punctually at 11:30 am at the residence of S. A. Monseigneur le Prince, the General Governor, whence the procession will depart directly for the church.

Hamburg, 4 July 1813.

(Please proffer this invitation at the door.)

the risk of becoming a liability to the defenders and were therefore expelled. From a military standpoint, the inhumane approach proved to be a good decision as there were no epidemics nor famine in the besieged city during the winter; however, more than 1.000 died from those who had been expelled.

On 31 March 1814, Russian troops marched into Paris

Johann Heinrich Gossler had moved to Eppendorf to the country estate of his in-laws in the summer of 1813, but even here food was gradually in short supply. On 4 January 1814, the Russians conquered Eppendorf, the Cossaks were accommodated in the Schramm's house, and the close quarters became unbearable. Johann Heinrich then brought his family to his mother's estate in Borstel, where Elisabeth Gossler was already looking after a large number of children, sons and daughters-in-laws, grandchildren and other relatives as well as the Russians who were accommodated there. In March, Gossler and his family went into exile in Lübeck.

On 31 March 1814, the allies marched into Paris. But Hamburg remained fortified. It was not until 30 May – after the abdication of Napoleon, after his grenadiers had been discharged and after he arrived on Elba – that Davout secretly left Hamburg with the last 29,000 men. When the Russians marched in the following day, the senate, the parliament and the *Kollegium der Oberalten* were given back their constitutional rights.

Damage Estimate

The losses incurred by the city of Hamburg as a result of contributions, confiscated goods, destroyed buildings and other strains and financial burdens, were estimated to be 184,308,625 Mark Courant and did not include numerous private assets.

The balance sheet totals for Joh. Berenberg, Gossler & Co. reflected the economic decline. In 1813, the last year of the French occupation, they were just over the half-million mark:

1810 1,314,476 Mark Banco
1811 1,117,056 Mark Banco
1812 1,031,624 Mark Banco
1813   609,780 Mark Banco

It was not until 1835 that the company surpassed the million mark milestone again in its balance sheet totals, and it was not until after 1845 that the company reached the standing it had in 1808.

After the liberation, the immediate concern of the merchants in Hamburg was to re-establish a fund to cover the Banco currency. Effective 31 May, the day the French retreated, the reinstated bankers August Schwalb and Christian Nicolaus Pehmöller, in agreement with the respective senators, cleared the way for interested parties to open a new account by making a deposit. One of the first to do so was Joh. Berenberg, Gossler & Co., which deposited eight silver bars, for which the company was credited 27,350 Mark 3 Schilling Banco. And on 14 July at 4 pm, after the stock market closed, Georg Hillert extended invitations by way of an ad in the *Hamburger Nachrichten*, to enjoy some eel soup in the *Alte Stadt London* – peace had finally come.

After the Congress of Vienna

At the Congress of Vienna in 1814/15, where sovereigns, statesmen and stakeholders from around 200 states, cities, dominions and entities of Europe convened, the European state system was restored for the most part to its basic structure prior to Napoleon's rise to power. The dynasties returned to their lost thrones, many of the constitutional and administrative reforms Napoleon decreed were lifted and thus with that some political, constitutional or economic development possibilities.

In the German territory, the resolutions of the Congress led to a considerable enlargement of Prussia and – as the elected monarchy of the Holy Roman Empire of the German nation had not been restored – to the founding of the German Confederation. In this, 36 sovereign federal states merged on

The Final Resolution of the Congress of Vienna, 1815

The delegates to the Congress of Vienna (18 September 1814 to 9 June 1815) reorganised continental Europe:

1. Arthur Wellesley, 1st Duke of Wellington   2. Joaquim Lobo Silveira, 7th Count of Oriola   3. António de Saldanha da Gama, Count of Porto Santo   4. Count Carl Löwenhielm   5. Jean-Louis-Paul-François, 5th Duke of Noailles   6. Klemens Wenzel, Prince von Metternich   7. André Dupin   8. Count Karl Robert Nesselrode   9. Pedro de Sousa Holstein, 1st Count of Palmela   10. Robert Stewart, Viscount Castlereagh   11. Emmerich Joseph, Duke of Dalberg   12. Baron Johann von Wessenberg   13. Prince Andrey Kirillovich Razumovsky   14. Charles Stewart, 1st Baron Stewart   15. Pedro Gómez Labrador, Marquis of Labrador   16. Richard Le Poer Trench, 2nd Earl of Clancarty   17. Nikolaus von Wacken   18. Friedrich von Gentz   19. Baron Wilhelm von Humboldt   20. William Cathcart, 1st Earl Cathcart   21. Prince Karl August von Hardenberg   22. Charles Maurice de Talleyrand-Périgord   23. Count Gustav Ernst von Stackelberg

the basis of a federal law, the German Federal Act, dated 8 June 1815. In the national parliament in Frankfurt am Main, the assembly of representatives to the national parliament, Austria presided over the negotiation on government affairs. The German Confederation set up a federal army of 300,000 but the "national" independence of the German Confederation, of this highly peculiar entity in terms of constitutional, socio-political and economic issues, was impaired by foreign monarchs: England decided to take Hanover, the Netherlands went for Luxembourg and Denmark for Schleswig-Holstein.

The Uneconomic Development in Europe …

With the resolutions of the Congress of Vienna, the course was also set for Europe's economic development. England was still leading, followed by France and the German Confederation or Prussia. All of the other countries within Europe were far behind.

Since the middle of the 18th century, England had been showing economic and military potential with the Agricultural and Industrial Revolutions, which solidified its dominant economic position in Europe. With its fleet, it dominated the oceans, and with its troops, the colonies and thus the sales markets and suppliers of raw materials for the domestic industry.

Thus, there was England, the emerging industrial and world trade democracy and, in contrast, the so-called peasant democracy in France since the sale of the *biens nationaux*. Although France could, despite its defeat, maintain economic and political influence on the continent, it concentrated on its own agriculture and its agricultural colonies after the monarchy was restored. And in future it was going to be the domestic market and the continent and not the oceans and overseas territories that were going to determine the economic and political life of France. Thus, its economic growth rate and political clout remained behind the English.

… in the German Confederation …

The heterogeneous German Confederation had a poor standing vis-à-vis these nations and markets. There was neither a natural nor politically closed economy, nor an evolved uniform society. In 1816/17, famine struck in the German states despite the fact that for years, cheap, English goods had been flooding the continent; nobody could pay for them.

Only Prussia, with its considerable industrial economic approach in Berlin and Silesia, hinted at significant political and economic development. Aside from the competitor city of Bremen, Hamburg was regarded as the only international trading power of notice on German soil. But Prussia and the Hanseatic cities had become impoverished by Napoleon's looting and thus had nothing to counter Britian's industrial and commercial expansion.

The lack of any political unity was one thing – the national parliament was rather a congress of diplomats as opposed to a parliament – but the economic discord led to an unprecedented customs chaos as well a dependence on outside developments and powers, which must have been a cause for concern for the most convinced particularists. At the same time, the emerging

A special festival to follow the famine: procession of harvest wagons in 1817

On 1 January 1834, the German Customs Union came into effect; its architects were (from the left) Friedrich von Motz, Karl Georg Maassen, Wilhelm Anton von Klewitz, Johann Albrecht and Friedrich von Eichhorn

industrialisation forced the networking of the economic area, the construction of railways, the reduction of custom barriers and ultimately to a uniform "national system", which had long been called for by Freiherr vom Stein and Wilhelm von Humboldt. The most committed advocate was Friedrich List, but that was still a long way off.

Prussia made a first move by passing the Customs Act in 1818. It protected the budding industry with import duties of 10 percent on industrial goods and 20 to 30 percent on luxury goods. In contrast, raw materials were considered duty free. More than any group, the Prussian manufacturers were able to breathe a sigh of relief, as without this introduction of free trade with moderate protective duties, there would not have been any notable industrial progress in Germany. Especially the English industry had the objective of "nipping continental factories in the bud".

Originally, the Customs Act was not intended to serve as a starting point for the German economy, but after many national conflicts and conflicts between groups of states for economic and political supremacy, especially with the states supported by Austria, in 1828 a Bavarian-Wuerttemberg and a Prussian-Hessian agreement were reached. In 1833, there were agreements with Saxony and Thuringia, and finally in 1834, the German Customs Union was established without Austria. In 1836, Baden and Nassau followed; in 1854, the Kingdom of Hanover; in 1867, Schleswig-Holstein and Mecklenburg; in 1872, Alsace-Lorraine and, lastly, in 1888, Hamburg and Bremen.

… in Hamburg …

At the Congress of Vienna, Hamburg was able to maintain its independence within the German Confederation. This acknowledgement by the great powers was a key confirmation for the Hamburg merchants and meant that the city was able to govern and administer itself until 1866. The merchants paid little attention to the political system provided it did not bother them. With a mixture of honest conservatism, civic pride and quiet irony about their own small state, the worldly merchants left most things as they were when it came to their city policy. As for customs policy, they sided clearly with the free traders: there was a tendency to see themselves as being surrounded by the customs union as opposed to being open to the advantages for one's own hinterland, from which they also profited. When Kurhesse joined the customs union, the Commercial Deputation complained, "that there was no more foot of ground left for an unimpeded passage to southern Germany." The conflicts between Prussia and Hamburg lasted over 60 years after their onset in 1818 and focused mainly on the free port and free trade. Thus, Hamburg was forced into an isolated position in Germany lasting many decades.

It took several years for the various nations to agree on a customs union

In addition to the senate commission, Hamburg sent its own representatives to the peace negotiations in Paris to make claims for compensation. At the Paris Convention on 20 November 1815, the city received definite confirmation that it would be adequately compensated. A commission appointed by the Hamburg Council took over in trust for the French government the settlement of the reported damages; finally, sporadic payments were transacted after 1827. Most of the the candidates for compensation received *Liquiditions-abschnitte* as a partial claim to French bonds, and these papers generated such good returns that over the course of 50 years double the original claim rolled in. Joh. Berenberg, Gossler & Co. received the confiscated *Mortzenhaus* back in 1816 and, furthermore, albeit starting in 1842, Danish restitution payments for the sugar confiscated at Tönning.

Yet, recovery for Hamburg business was slow. The French had left a looted city in its wake and there was a lack of capital. It was not until 1840 that

Hamburg had anything approaching the same shipping space as in 1798. The German hinterland was economically weak, trade was accordingly modest. And the city continued to be permanently isolated from the international market as a result of the continental blockade: "Your old ties here have broken away entirely; … London is now more than ever before the centre of all business dealings," wrote Wilhelm Gossler in November 1813 to his brother, Johann Heinrich. The success of the naval blockade and the continental system oppressed not only the Hamburg merchants, but also the entire German foreign trade process for a long time.

… and at Joh. Berenberg, Gossler & Co.

Joh. Berenberg, Gossler & Co. needed serveral decades to replenish lost capital and restore severed business ties. Balance sheet totals after 1815 levelled off around the 1 million mark with a slow upward trend, until finally in 1835 – one year after the establishment of the German Customs Union – the 1 million mark was surpassed again.

In 1819, Kruckenberg died, and Johann Heinrich Gossler II and Seyler continued to manage the business. When Elisabeth Gossler, (née Berenberg) died in 1822 at the age of 73, the company was additionally burdened for the following years by the payout of her capital to her seven heirs, each receiving 81,577 Mark Banco respectively.

Despite the shortage of capital, the company operated without a deficit and occasionally made good net profits as was the case in 1820 when the balance sheet sum was 566,059 Mark Banco; Seyler and Gossler posted a profit of 41,034 Mark Banco.

After 1815, the company focused on goods trade and trade financing. Immediately following the retreat of the French, all measures were undertaken to revive trade. Old ties, notably with Scandinavia, Russia, England, the West Indies and East Asia were revived, and new ones were added.

After 1815, Joh. Berenberg, Gossler & Co. re-established contacts to America. The ties to Stephen Girard in Philadelphia had died out, but in their place, new business connections emerged with New York, Boston, Baltimore, Richmond and New Orleans. The company imported furs, cotton, tobacco, sugar, coffee, whale oil, silk, dyeing wood and many more items and exported

New business associations

quality products in return from Germany's industry and agriculture; pianos and books from Leipzig, toys from Nuremberg, Rhine wine, smoked meat and ham.

The company had sold the wax bleaching business in 1805 and had also retreated from its ship-owning partnerships. This had been made redundant by the improved insurance industry and was replaced by the merchant shipping company, in which the company was not involved, and then by the shareholder shipping companies.

The company continued to be involved in various insurance entities with up to 15,000 Mark Banco; the members of management for the "Dritte Hamburger Versicherungs-Gesellschaft" (Third Hamburg Insurance Society) of 1804, which was rebuilt on a broad base after the liberation, came from the company.

Wisdom und Decisiveness

Johann Heinrich Gossler II was held in high esteem by his fellow citizens, and his business acumen, his historical foresight and his drive made him indispensible in numerous political and economic institutions. In 1821, he became a senator, and other offices followed. Moreover, Johann Heinrich Gossler II was not one of those merchants, for whom, as Jacob Gallois mocked in 1835, "a brilliant book was such a sacred object that they didn't touch it, and who meticulously shunned each person who worked in art and science, because they didn't 'make' in these areas." Gossler was very musical like his father. He had a marked interest in history, notably in those which were concerned with the past of his home city. When the *Verein für Hamburgische Geschichte*, a society that dealt with Hamburg's history, was founded in 1839, Johann Heinrich Gossler was one of its first members.

Johann Heinrich Gossler becomes a senator ...

With all due respect to the past, he set the course for the future of his company. On 9 October 1828, he held a highly acclaimed speech as the customs and excise expert:

... and sets the stage for the future

"Our direct ties with other parts of the world have more than doubled [since 1824], to such an extent that the bulk of our requirements in non-European products is delivered directly to us by the production coun-

A hero for South Americans: Simón Bolívar (1783–1830)

tries; seeing as these imports are not burdened with the costs involved with an interim stop in Europe, that puts us in a position of being able to compete even with England in the export of such goods; as a result, Hamburg's trade has gained in significance and in scope; with these direct transatlantic connections not only do German products have easier access to buying markets, but completely new business sectors have been drawn to here."

And Johann Heinrich Gossler was in the process of leveraging these direct transatlantic ties for his company. While he was in Hamburg speaking in front of the merchants, his son, Johann Heinrich III, was already in – or en route to – Boston, while his nephew, Adolph Schramm (1805–1887), who had been given the necessary start-up capital by his uncle Gossler, was working on setting up a trading company in Brazil, which would soon provide Joh. Berenberg, Gossler & Co. with splendid business dealings on the entire South American continent.

Trade with South and Central America

This development was made favourable by the independence movement across South and Central America. Revolts in Mexico in 1808 and in 1810 were followed in 1813 by the independence of Venezuela from Spain under Simón Bolívar. At the Congress of Tucumán in 1816, the independence of the United Provinces of the Río de la Plata (Argentina) was declared, the independence of Chile followed in 1818. In 1821, Peru won its independence after long struggles against the Spanish (final in 1824), and in the same year, the Brazilian National Assembly declared its independence from the mother land, Portugal.

As early as 1822, Martin Joseph Haller celebrated the fact that after North America, now Central and South America had also become accessible to the world's free trade: "For centuries, all of these countries and parts of the world that have been practically hidden and closed off from us are now open to us and we can say: Hamburg has obtained colonies." Johann Heinrich Gossler II went on to say that while in 1815, 22.5 million pounds of coffee came from England and 6 million from transatlantic countries, in 1827, Hamburg imported 40 million pounds from the latter directly and just 7 million from England.

In 1827, Hamburg concluded a Treaty of Friendship, Trade and Navigation with Brazil; soon thereafter similar agreements with Argentina, Uruguay, Venezuela, Chile, Bolivia, Peru, Ecuador, Columbia and Mexico followed.

Adolph Schramm participated in the negotiations for a German-Brazilian trade agreement in Rio de Janeiro as an interpreter in the position as secretary for the delegation. He knew the language perfectly and was well acquainted with local circumstances when he undertook building up the trading company in Maroim and Pernambuco in 1828 with the financial support from Gossler. This Brazilian company, whose management was transferred a few years later to Adolph's brother, Ernst Schramm (1812–1882), ensured Joh. Berenberg, Gossler & Co. business ties to South America. The company now shifted its focus to bulk commodities and made substantial profits. The goods – which were mainly coffee, sugar, cotton and tobacco – were "floating forward transactions on the stock market or were concluded upon delivery with A. Schramm, Pernambuco-Maroim à meta". Products that continued to be exported came for the most part from German industry, such as hardware,

In 1821 Brazil celebrated its independence from Portugal

In 1893, the US began to limit immigration from Europe

textiles and musical instruments. Export to Latin American countries would continue to multiply in the future.

North America Beckons

In 1827, Hamburg also signed a trade agreement with the United States of America, resulting in the Hanseatic city's trade with North America increasing five-fold between 1830 and 1840. And here, too, Joh. Berenberg, Gossler & Co. reacted quickly. In 1828, Johann Heinrich Gossler's son, who had the same name, was sent to North America to maintain existing ties and to look for new contacts.

The US was worth the trip. In addition to England, France and Prussia, it had the greatest economic momentum of the time. At the turn of the century, the population of the US was roughly four million, but the figure increased rapidly. In and around 1828, roughly 20,000 Europeans each year turned their backs on the old continent and moved to the New World, but between 1847 and 1854, the number of immigrants going to North America jumped from 250,000 to 900,000 per year. Between 1847 and 1856, within just ten years alone, three million Germans had immigrated to the US.

1817 saw construction start on the 363-mile-long Erie Canal, which links the Great Lakes of North America

Although agriculture remained the mainstay for America well into the 19th century, the Industrial Revolution had already begun in 1793 with Eli Whitney's cotton gin: Accounting for 57 percent of total exports, cotton became the leading export of the Americans and supplied the domestic and British cotton industry with raw materials.

Speeding up transportation for mass goods, some of which were perishable, was a key driver for the productivity of the American industry and agriculture. The latest technologies, such as the steamship developed by Boulton and Watt, which took up operations on the Hudson River between New York and Albany in 1807, started opening up the area. The construction of the 550 km-long Erie Canal started in 1817 and the period from 1828 to 1830 saw the emergence of a great interest in railroad building. When the American Civil War (1861–1865) broke out, the entire eastern part of the continent from the coast to Mississippi was already covered with a network of railway connections. The iron deposits required were mainly exploited in Pennsylvania. As a result of improved waterways, the focus of the American cotton industry shifted from South Carolina and Georgia to Alabama and Mississippi. Yet grain and meat production soon increased significantly thanks to the increasing mechanisation of agriculture and meat processing and improved transport routes.

En Route to the Modern Age:
Johann Heinrich Gossler III (1805–1879)

Conquests and Inconveniences

With a letter of recommendation from Baring Brothers & Co. in London in hand, and with letters to business associates and bank correspondents in the New England states, 23-year-old Johann Heinrich III left Hamburg for Boston in 1828. He spoke fluent English, had good manners and few prejudices.

Once in Boston, he immediately contacted Perkins & Sons, whose current account with Joh. Berenberg, Gossler & Co. had amounted to approximately 100,000 Mark Banco dating back to 1822. Next, he visited Guild and Bryant & Sturgis, and established ties that would last for decades.

His achievements were not limited to business. He was able to win over 19-year-old Mary Elizabeth Bray. She came from a respectable and extremely cultivated Boston family; her grandfather, Samuel Eliot, had been president of the National Bank of Massachusetts from 1798 to 1803, the subsequent First National Bank of Boston, one of the most important banks in the US. Her father, Joseph Bray, had been a successful London-born businessman. Mary Elizabeth had lost her parents early, they and her grandmother had left her a considerable inheritance.

On 25 August 1829, they married in Boston. A subsequent honeymoon and business trip took the young couple to New York, Philadelphia and Albany and back to Boston, where they set sail for Liverpool, the main hub for American cotton, and where Johann Heinrich III made new contacts. They next went on to London, where he fostered ties to Baring Brothers & Co. and Fruhling & Göschen, which, in turn, had good ties to companies in Amsterdam. The Gosslers also travelled to Brussels and Antwerp.

Married to the American Mary Elizabeth Gossler (1810–1886), Johann Heinrich Gossler III (1805–1879) was co-owner of the company from 1830 until his death

On 22 December 1829, the couple arrived in Hamburg just in time to spoil the family's Christmas cheer. Although Mary Elizabeth was very beautiful, intelligent, cultivated and rich, she had one major flaw in the minds of many in Hamburg: not only did she come from abroad, which in itself was bad enough, but she was also an "American", and it did not matter whether she was from New England or from the Wild West. She was received in Hamburg with great reservation, sometimes even coldly. At any rate, the reception was unfriendly enough to put a damper on any sort of willingness to adapt that the intelligent and quick-tempered young woman may have had. Understandably, the young couple did not settle at *Mortzenhaus*, but, instead, in 1833 moved into their own – and quite luxurious – house on the Esplanade, whose uniform classic style was regarded back then as not only very elegant, but also – and more importantly – "modern". Mary Elizabeth Gossler lived in Hamburg for more than 50 years, but she remained the "American".

The reception for the business side of the trip to America was far better. At the beginning of 1830, Johann Heinrich Gossler III became a partner at Joh. Berenberg, Gossler & Co.

Gossler & Knorre in Boston

Just how important the North America business had become is evident in the fact that Johann Heinrich III left for a second trip to the US in April 1833, this time with his younger brother, Gustav (1813–1844), who had continued his apprenticeship in England, and joined him in Liverpool.

Operations in Boston

On 23 May 1833, they arrived in New York, and after a four-week trip with stops in Hereford and Philadelphia they arrived in Boston. Here, they were received by Carl (Charles) Knorre, a son of the *Oberalten* Georg Knorre, who had been overseeing the interests of Joh. Berenberg, Gossler & Co. in America. Together, they founded Gossler & Knorre. In a circular dated 1 July 1833 they announced: "… that with the particular support of our friends and near relatives Messrs. John Berenberg, Gossler & Co. of Hamburg we have formed a commercial establishment in this place, under the firm of Gossler & Knorre partly with a view of facilitating the intercourses of the above house with their friends and this country, also for purposes of general commission business." Mentioned as references were: Perkins & Co. as well as

In 1833 Gossler & Knorre was established in the port city of Boston

Byant, Sturgis & Co. / Boston, Fish, Grinnel & Co. / New York, Baring Brothers & Co. / London and D. Crommelin & Sons / Amsterdam.

Johann Heinrich Gossler III, who soon thereafter left for Hamburg, was part of Gossler & Knorre. In Boston, Charles Knorre and Gustav Gossler were to strengthen the American ties of the parent company, add contacts and look after the purchase of goods for Joh. Berenberg, Gossler & Co. as well as be involved in the financing. They arranged trade bills and letters of acceptance and began working with a new means of payment, the letter of credit. The payment method, which London merchants had begun using in 1820, caught on quickly because with the "London Change", the payment could be guaranteed ahead of time.

Up until 1836, business dealings at Gossler & Knorre were going well, but then an economic crisis hit the US, which also affected England. Even top bills of exchange no longer found buyers. When the Bank of England was unable to temporarily sustain the precious metal equivalence, banks from Paris, Amsterdam and Hamburg had to muster up 2.5 million Pounds Sterling to support it.

Joh. Berenberg, Gossler & Co. reacted at the first sign of trouble by establishing a fund to cover any possible losses. Father and son availed the largest part of their profits from 1838, and Johann Heinrich III waived any profits during the next three years from Gossler & Knorre; in 1838, that was, after all, 21,299 and in 1839, 31,394 Mark Banco. Although there was soon a certain degree of calm on the London money market, the situation at Gossler & Knorre remained difficult. In 1841, Charles Knorre left for health reasons, and Albert Kingman, who had been working at the company for four years, was given power of attorney.

An Upward Trend

Back in Hamburg, the partners of Joh. Berenberg, Gossler & Co. had reason to be satisfied as father Gossler's work on establishing transatlantic ties had paid off; they were making profits:

Net profits from 1831–1842

1831	69,326 Mark Banco	1837	94,946 Mark Banco
1832	35,831 Mark Banco	1838	85,996 Mark Banco
1833	65,665 Mark Banco	1839	84,720 Mark Banco
1834	120,000 Mark Banco	1840	111,960 Mark Banco
1835	82,744 Mark Banco	1841	56,520 Mark Banco
1836	53,482 Mark Banco	1842	46,845 Mark Banco

The considerable fluctuations were reported in contemporary trade reports with unusual words: coffee remained sometimes "stagnant"; sugar "still" and tobacco "sluggish". Indian products were at times even entirely "underfoot".

In 1832, Joh. Berenberg, Gossler & Co. had to write off 25,000 Mark Banco in sugar, "partially floating in London, partly bought on the stock exchange." But the next year, Johann Heinrich III wrote: "As a result of the improvement in sugar prices, our sugar stock had a slight edge over the end of last year; and in coffee speculation on the stock exchange roughly 4,000 marks was earned, and we did not keep any stock for our own account." The record profit of 1834 was due mainly to a bank crisis in North America, which was skilfully taken advantage of. In 1836, there were losses in sugar and cotton, but in 1840, there was a considerable profit from an expedition to Mazatlán and with the import of tobacco from New Orleans. The company's capital was constantly increasing.

Much to the pleasure of his family, Johann Heinrich III proved to be exceptionally enterprising. Within five years, he had increased his share of the equity almost four-fold and had surpassed his father.

Sadness and Good Fortune

On 26 October 1836, Ludwig Erdwin Seyler (1758–1836) died, highly esteemed, at the age of 79. He had given 61 years of service to the company. After the early death of Johann Hinrich Gossler I in 1790, company management had lain mainly in his hands. Later, along with Johann Heinrich II, he had been responsible for the course of business. Seyler was generally known to be "very prudent", as well as a "very rare merchant." His capital was divided among his seven children.

After Seyler's death, the fourth son of Johann Heinrich II, Wilhelm Gossler, was appointed partner; he received two-twelfths, while Johann Heinrich II and III had shares amounting to five-twelfths.

From then onwards, Councillor Johann Heinrich Gossler II left the management of the company largely to his sons. He now tended more to his Hanseatic offices and duties. And here, too, he received welcome news: in 1841, when he was councillor to the exchange, the new stock exchange building was opened.

In 1842, in the words of Johann Heinrich III, there was an "unexpected stroke of luck" with the Danish government finally paying the first instalment of 67,000 marks for the sugar it had confiscated in Tönning back in 1807. Over the next two years, Denmark paid further instalments of 60,000 marks, respectively. This money then went to the owners in accordance with their share of the profits and loss: one-third went to the heirs of Seyler and one-sixth to Johann Heinrich II. The one-sixth share of Kruckenberg, who had long since passed away, was also paid to Gossler and the heirs of Seyler's estate as Kruckenberg had considerable tax debts to both of them. The remaining one-third ultimately went to Johann Nicolaus Gossler. For him, this unexpected windfall was very fortunate. He had been living very modestly in

The partners' holdings:
5/12 Johann Heinrich Gossler II
5/12 Johann Heinrich Gossler III
2/12 Wilhelm Gossler

Wilhelm Gossler (1811–1895), joint owner of the Berenberg Bank from 1836 to 1858, launched his own company in 1860

New York and could now return to Hamburg to spend his old age in his home.

However, this good news was soon followed by another loss. On 3 April 1842, Johann Heinrich Gossler II died at the age of 67; he was deeply loved by his children. "After spending eight days sick in bed," reported a printed obituary, "a gentle death led the restlessly active and truly pious man to his eternal home."

Johann Heinrich Gossler II left behind a fortune that was just as large as that of his father back in 1790. The account of his sons in 1842 was almost 600,000 Mark Banco, and excluded private capital which had not been invested in the company. The old level had been more than restored, but the business focus had changed dramatically. Right from the start, the company was involved in trade with North and South America, the company had long stopped dealing with small lots of various items, and instead traded in large lots such as sugar, coffee, cotton, and tobacco. At the same time, the exchange business grew to be quite extensive. Around the middle of the 19th century, Joh. Berenberg, Gossler & Co. stood consolidated and with considerable growth; it was one of the most important merchant banking companies in Hamburg.

The business outlook at Gossler & Co. in Boston was the only one that remained difficult. Gustav Gossler longed for an end to the Opium War in China, which he hoped would coincide with relief for trade. He also planned to return to Hamburg for good because, unlike his older brother, Johann Heinrich III, he did not enjoy living in America. However, just before the planned departure on 2 July 1844, he died as the result of an accident on a business trip to Havana. Albert Kingman, who had been a partner at Gossler & Co. since January 1844, managed the company in Boston together with Carl Heinrich Ferdinand

In 1830, Johann Heinrich Gossler became a citizen of Hamburg

Möring. Johann Heinrich III and his brother Wilhelm set up a realisation account in Hamburg in an effort to protect themselves against any possible losses in Boston.

The year 1847 was particularly successful for Joh. Berenberg, Gossler & Co. After the liquidation of Parish & Co., the company took over the agencies of various English overseas banks, including the Bank of London and the River Plate – later the Bank of London & South America – and the Mercantile Bank of India.

Company assets exceed one million marks in value

When the company assets at Joh. Berenberg, Gossler & Co. surpassed the first million, the Gossler brothers decided to get involved in shipping. Trade with the United States had grown for all companies in Hamburg. Meanwhile, the number of emigrants reached incredible new levels, but the existing shipping capabilities were insufficient in every respect. Thus, Hamburg merchants pulled together under the leadership of Adolph Godeffroy to establish a shipping company based on stocks: the founding capital of the "Hamburg-Amerikanische Packetfahrt-Actien-Gesellschaft" (Hapag) was 300,000 Mark Banco, divided into 60 shares, each valued at 5,000 Mark Banco. Joh. Berenberg, Gossler & Co. bought two shares and took up positions in the board of directors in the new company. The Hapag ships travelled regularly between Hamburg and America, and by 1855, screw steamships were also part of the fleet.

Hapag established

The Big Fire

A few weeks after the death of father Gossler, Hamburg was hit by a catastrophe. On 5 May 1842 a massive fire broke out, which raged until 8 May and reduced almost one-third of the tightly built inner city to ashes. The homes of the Gossler family on Alten Wandrahm and the Esplanade were fortunately spared, but 71 streets with 1,749 homes and 102 storage areas were destroyed, more than 50 people died and 20,000 became homeless. St Nicholas' Church and St Peter's Church succumbed to the flames, St Gertrude's, the town hall, the old stock exchange, the bank, the lower court, Eicke's House with the *Ratskeller* and the building which housed the Patriotic Society were also destroyed. The city lost much of what was precious and dear to the older residents of Hamburg: the old crane, the weigh house, upper and lower mills and the Alster shore burned in addition to the popular *Börsenhalle*. The new stock exchange building, by contrast, was saved. Experts estimated the damage to be at 90 to 95 million Mark Banco, which also included 25 million for burned merchant goods. An unimaginable international relief effort helped alleviate the most immediate consequences.

The Hamburg fire changed the look of the city forever because during the rebuilding phase, thorough consideration was given to the changed traffic and economic requirements of the city, which had sacrificed some of its most beautiful old buildings.

The Great Fire of Hamburg began on 5 May 1842 at Deichstrasse 44

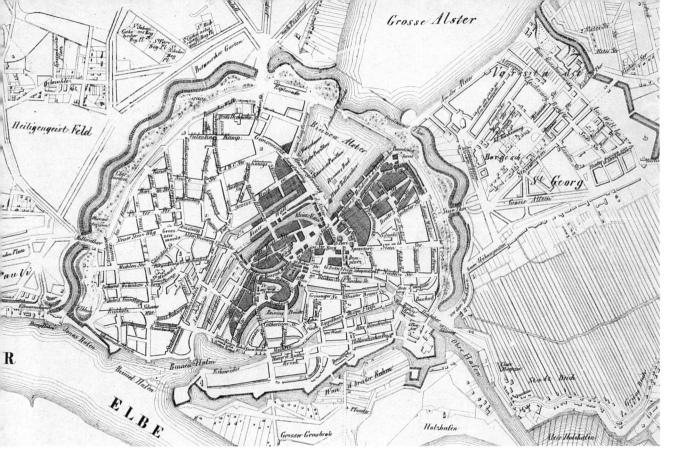

The legacy of the Great Fire of 1842: areas of gutted and demolished buildings are shaded dark on the map

The pre-March

The fire also sparked political discussions, most notably about the Constitution of 1712, which once had been celebrated as progress. The merchants were now uncomfortable with the fact that fellow Jewish citizens paid to support the city but were not permitted to become citizens. This anachronism became particularly embarrassing after the fire. Banker Salomon Heine was most generous in supporting the rebuilding of the city. He was willing to allow every merchant in difficulty to draw a bill of exchange on him up to 15,000 Mark Banco, but he was denied a seat in the Commercial Deputation. The panic and lack of administrative expertise that became apparent during containment of the fire drew more criticism, and, in general, the desire for political independence grew. Thoughts of the French Revolution and the July Revolution in Paris in 1830 were not without consequences in Hamburg.

Reform suggestions were regularly denied by the Council, but criticism could still be clearly expressed in the city, and that was not a matter of course.

The political restoration after the Congress of Vienna under the aegis of Metternich resulted in a Holy Alliance of all Christian monarchs in Europe (except England), which involved the suppression of liberal-national efforts and the maintaining of Christian states based on a "divine right". Hamburg entered the Holy Alliance in 1819, but the notorious Carlsbad Decrees, with their censorship of the press and the subsequent attempts to suppress freedom, were hardly heeded in the Hanseatic city – much to the annoyance of the German Confederation. With the publisher Julius Campe, Hamburg became a centre of *Junges Deutschland*, a group of authors who had been attempting to gain political influence with their literary works since the July Revolution. The works of Heinrich Heine, Karl Gutzkow and Heinrich Laube had been banned in all states of the German Confederation since the *Frankfurt Bundestag* in 1835; Hamburg was the only one which did not abide by the ban. In politics, it was business as usual for the time being.

Publisher Julius Campe (left) and Hamburg banker Salomon Heine (1767–1844)

From 1848 to the German Empire 1871

The Failure of the Bourgeois Revolution

Contrary to all the efforts of the restoration, the Paris Revolution of February 1848 spread quickly to Austria and Germany. By March, Metternich was overthrown, and Friedrich Wilhelm IV of Prussia promised a constitution. On 18 May, the German National Assembly convened with 600 citizen representatives in St Paul's Church in Frankfurt to draw up a constitution for the whole of Germany.

But the attempt to create a German nation state failed. The major monarchist powers Austria and Prussia remained intact. In the National Assembly, there was a division among those in favour of a smaller German solution,

On 18 May 1848, the German National Assembly convened in St Paul's Church, Frankfurt

which entailed an Empire under Prussian leadership without Austria, and a greater German solution, which was in favour of the inclusion German-Austria or of the entire Danube monarchy. Moreover, federalist efforts were pitted against Unitarian ones, and bourgeois liberal groups strove for a constitutional monarchy, while the more radical representatives were demanding the republic. As the individual states continued to exist, the St Paul's Church assembly had no real means of power such as a police force or an army.

After the victory of the Vienna Uprising on 31 October 1848, a constitution was imposed in Prussia under military pressure, which somewhat accommodated liberal thought, but under strict monarchical leadership. And so in April 1849, in a bid to save the German notion of unity, the Frankfurt National Assembly finally elected Frederick William IV of Prussia as the German emperor. But he declined the throne, which he associated with revolution and therefore, metaphorically, described as having a smell of carrion. In May 1849, the last uprisings of Prussian and Union troops were defeated in Baden and in the Palatinate, and so once again an era of restoration began. The attempt by the Prussian king to create the "small unified German Empire" with a German Union with Saxony and Hanover failed due to outside political resistance. Russia and Austria threatened with war, and in the Convention of Olmütz, Prussia had to abandon any solo effort, and the German Confederation of 1815 was restored.

Thus, not only the liberal goals, but also the national goals of the Revolution of 1848 had ultimately failed. It would be later left up to the political finesse of Bismarck to achieve the political unification of Germany from the top down – supported by the nobility and military – once Austria had finally been excluded and following the war against France in 1871.

Industrial and Agricultural Revolution

With the establishment of the German Customs Union in 1834, the economic unity of Germany preceded the political one. The Industrial and Agriculture Revolutions subsequently led to the formation of a large economic region which was about to give the leading industrial nations of England and France some competition.

Between 1835 and 1839, the first German railways were opened; the first one went between Nuremberg and Fürth, followed by a route between Berlin and Potsdam and, finally, one between Leipzig and Dresden. It was just the start of connecting the most important German economic centres: In 1837, August Borsig created an iron foundry and engineering company in Berlin and delivered the first German locomotive as early as 1841. Meanwhile, numerous new technologies and industries were emerging: in the coal and steel sector – as a result of the railway construction the demand for iron and coal increased – the chemical sector and electricity. Cities grew with industrialisation especially on the

In 1838, Potsdam Railway Station marked the end of the line in Berlin

Ruhr and Saar Rivers and in Silesia. By 1850, industrial production in Germany had leapt by roughly six-fold.

The enormous growth would have been unthinkable without the Agricultural Revolution; the farming industry had to ensure that the growing population in the industrial districts had food. Justus von Liebig with his book, *Die organische Chemie in ihrer Anwendung auf Agricultur und Physiologie (Organic Chemistry in its Application to Agriculture and Physiology)* (1840), created possibilities for artificial fertilisation, which led to unparalleled growth in productivity. New ploughs were built for improved cultivation, and in the US, the first harvesters were being developed.

Yet the Industrial Revolution, which was now gaining traction in Germany, also had its downsides. The rapidly growing (heavy) industry needed workers; tens of thousands of people moved from rural areas into the emerging industrial areas, and worked mostly under great hardship: the "social question" arose. The Innere Mission, which endeavoured to improve the social situation for the uprooted workers and their families, was founded in 1848, the same year the *Communist Manifesto* was published by Karl Marx and Friedrich Engels. "In place of the old bourgeois society with its classes and class antagonisms, we shall have an association in which the free development of

Karl Marx (1818–1883, seated) and Friedrich Engels (1820–1895) were the fathers of Marxism. Together, they wrote the *Communist Manifesto*

each is condition for the free development of all", was how they described the final goal of their "Communism."

However, it was not until May 1863 that Ferdinand Lassalle founded the German General Workers' Association. The Social Democratic Workers' Party, founded by August Bebel and Wilhelm Liebknecht in 1869, joined the former and adopted the main points of the Marx/Engel theses in its programme; the "class struggle" was born.

Stock Companies and Private Bankers

The use of new inventions and technologies, the expansion in trade and industry, the development of infrastructure as a result of railways and roads, not to mention the industrial investments to establish the large companies to oversee these developments, demanded so much capital that a new type of company was necessary: the stock company and the joint stock bank.

The pioneers in Germany were mainly the railway companies. The first railway set up based on stocks in northern Germany was opened in 1842 between Hamburg and Bergedorf. In 1843, the Rhenish Railway followed, for which "Bankhaus Oppenheim" paved the way. But the capital requirements of railway companies proved to be endless, and share prices remained volatile. In 1848, the private bank "Bankhaus Schaaffhausen" and indirectly also "Bankhaus Oppenheim" experienced a crisis that threatened to sweep away the majority of Rhenish trading and industrial companies. In response, the Prussian state declared its willingness to finally approve transforming a private bank into a stock company. The newly formed "A. Schaaffhausen'sche Bankverein" owed its new circumstances to a state turnaround measure. This documented fact, however, meant that the absolute power in Berlin would basically no longer be able to avoid concessions to the *grande bourgeoisie*.

By 1850, several outside factors hastened this development. After gold had been discovered in California in 1848, there was a new boom in the industrial and economic opening of North America. At the same time, England was able to access its "own" gold in its colony of Australia, increased its industrial investments and was now less dependent on a continental sales market, exporting mainly to the US. Thus, enormous competitive pressure was lifted from continental industry, and, at the same time, the gold rush also brought the necessary reserves of precious metals to Europe to finance large-scale industry and to stimulate the general demand. In Germany, the Industrial Revolution was preparing to take off. As the financial strength of the private

The "A. Schaaffhausen'sche Bankverein" in Cologne entered a crisis in 1848

Panning for gold in California

bankers was no match for the enormous financial demand, it was now a question of finding more flexible instruments for a comprehensive capital formation.

The solution to this comprehensive economic task came from private bankers. At "Schaaffhausen", it was Abraham Oppenheim, Ludolf Camphausen, Gustav von Mevissen and David Hansemann.

The "Disconto-Gesellschaft", which was also formed by Hansemann in 1851, was transformed into a commercial partnership limited by shares in 1856. With this new legal form – the issuing of shares from a fixed limited liability capital and the distribution of members in general partner, and limited partners – the "Disconto-Gesellschaft" did not need to be authorised by the state, but could still engage in all the typical banking activities, including securities trading.

In 1856, Berlin bankers founded the "Berliner Handelsgesellschaft" based on the same legal form. The specified goal was to run all banking, trading and industrial operations, including the founding, fusing and consolidating of stock corporations and the issuing of stocks and bonds.

While political reasons forced Prussia to make do with the mixed form, as early as 1853, Hesse was permitted a typical joint stock bank based on the Brussels model *Société Génerale des Pays Bas* of 1822 (as of 1830 *Société Génerale pour favoriser l'industrie nationale*) or on the *Credit Mobilier* in Paris. After a franchising in Berlin had failed, Oppenheim, von Mevissen and the Karlsruhe-based private banker Moritz von Haber founded the "Bank für Handel und Industrie" in Darmstadt, the so-called "Darmstädter Bank". Various other joint stock banks followed in this first wave of new banks.

The main benefit of joint stock banks was that there was a possibility through the issuing of shares to mobilise invested capital from broad sections, such as the savings of trades people, merchants, manufacturers, and to supply them to the respective large-scale industry. Meanwhile, a new role was emerging for the modern banker: he now organised the founding of stock corporations, bought and sold shares, made a profit in the process, granted credit in return for securities as collateral, administered the coffers of companies and advanced more often into the supervisory boards of the stock companies.

Senate Puts a Damper on Hamburg

The economic necessity of new banks was also obviously in Hamburg because the turnover of goods had reached great heights. As a result of the rapidly progressing industrialisation, the demand for raw materials had grown, and new sales markets were popping up. The import and export business profited equally, and in addition to North and South America, new economic regions were added. The conquest of Algiers by the French in 1830 once again brought the Mediterranean Sea and the Levant into the focus of Hamburg merchants. In China, the British were practicing their notion of free trade in 1842 when they forced the Chinese with the Opium War to open their ports to world trade. And in 1846, when England finally made the general move to free trade, Hamburg merchants had the option of doing business in parts of the British Empire.

People found creative responses to the Opium War of 1840–1842 between China and Great Britain: they took to smuggling

The far-flung British Empire in the 19th century

From 1845 to 1856, there were occasional attempts made by Hamburg merchants to establish a joint stock company. One great supporter of the new bank was Adolf Soetbeer, a staunch free trader and prominent advocate of German economic liberalism. However, even the *Hamburgischen Correspondenten* printed: "The relationships to money are pushing more and more ... the tremendous facilities which are generated in all areas of the fatherland require more and more currency on a daily basis; we rush with railways, manufacture with steam and remain with the vehicle for this – with our relationship to money – unchanged, as it sufficed for us two centuries ago." The criticism was aimed at the *Hamburger Bank's Bankvaluta*, which was introduced in 1816, whose stubborn defence of the full cover led to the fact that between 20 and

30 million Mark Banco languished in the bank in the form of silver bars and consequently unavailable for monetary transactions. In addition, banking and bureaucratic regulations were clamping down on the circulation of money, which was increasingly unable to cope with the growing turnover generated from the sales of goods.

As a result of the money shortage, Hamburg merchants set about making plans in September 1845 to establish a "Disconto-Bank" which was to be provided with initial capital of 2 million Mark Banco, divided into bearer shares, each worth 1,000 marks. By the middle of January 1846, around 70 shareholders had applied for roughly 1.3 million Mark Banco. Outside buyers hold subscriptions of 0.8 million; Hamburg companies had 0.5 million. Joh. Berenberg, Gossler & Co. were also represented, but their subscriptions did not exceed 25,000 Mark Banco.

Yet resistance to the project came from within their own ranks. The *Altadjungierten*, an advisory board made of seven former deputies, set up a *promemoria* right in the senate. Their misgivings focused on two key points, namely, the establishment of a bank based on shares, and the issuing of unfunded bank notes. For one, the anonymity of the shareholders would favour the infiltration of foreign funds into Hamburg's banking business, for another, paper money would replace Banco money in the long run.

Thus, the senate decided against issuing banknotes, so that the Commercial Deputation in its meeting on 9 February 1846 resolved to disregard the "Disconto-Bank". Indeed, ten years later, the same fear of foreign infiltration and a culture of safety prevented the establishment of a joint stock bank with the authorisation to issue banknotes, and right up to the enactment of the Bank Notes Act by the North German Confederation in 1870, no banknotes were issued in Hamburg. An adherence to tradition and the pride of the Hamburger Bank delayed a modern expansion of the monetary and credit and lending system. Johann Heinrich Gossler III had, after initial hesitation, supported a joint stock bank without the right to issue its own banknotes.

The growing need for money continued to be covered by the merchant bankers, whose business now grew enormously. The balance sheet sums from 1849–1856 provide a good idea of the extent of this growth:

	Balance sheet total	Net profit	
1849	3,052,887	213,492	Mark Banco
1850	3,474,981	142,225	Mark Banco
1851	4,118,607	150,750	Mark Banco
1852	5,593,733	176,354	Mark Banco
1853	5,593,350	225,536	Mark Banco
1854	8,084,329	238,054	Mark Banco
1855	8,709,477	319,722	Mark Banco
1856	9,309,562	375,782	Mark Banco

The First Joint Stock Banks in Hamburg

France and England engaged in the Crimean War together against Russia from 1854 to 1856. France once again became the dominant power on the continent, the anti-French bloc, against which Napoleon I had fought, was defeated for the first time since 1815. During the war, an exceptional amount of money was earned, especially in neutral Hamburg because so many of the transactions, which would have otherwise gone through London, were now handled in Hamburg.

During the boom, a second attempt was made in Hamburg in 1855 to establish a joint stock bank. The committee for the establishment of the "Norddeutsche Bank" included members J. C. Godeffroy & Sohn, Salomon Heine, H. J. Merck & Co., Paul Mendelssohn-Bartholdy, Ferdinand Jacobsen, Robert Kayser, F. J. Tesdorpf & Sohn as well as Ross Vidal & Co. The goal for the new bank was to not only allow it to issue banknotes, but to also have it conduct normal banking transactions, which included bill of exchange trade, the purchase and sale of metals, deposits, the current account and collection business, the granting of loans on securities, metals and goods as well as the authority to trade with government securities, bonds and shares.

After tedious negotiations, the "Norddeutsche Bank" opened for business on 15 October 1856, but the issuing of banknotes was once again prohibited. The share capital was set at 20 million Mark Banco, divided in 40,000 shares at 500 Mark Banco with 8 million marks (only 40 percent) available for public subscription. Within just three days, almost 1.6 billion Mark Banco in shares were subscribed.

Meanwhile, a group of Hamburg merchant banks quietly got together to form the "Vereinsbank" in Hamburg, and since right from the start they refrained from issuing banknotes, there was no problem establishing the bank. In addition to Johann Heinrich Gossler III, the group included Johann Christian Söhle, Wilhelm Amsinck, Rudolph Schröder and Georg Heinrich Kaemmerer Jr. Here as well, the founding capital amounted to 20 million Mark Banco in 100,000 shares at 200 marks. Of this, 15 million were approved for subscription by the public; within one week and 578.5 million Mark Banco later, shares had been overdrawn almost forty-fold.

"Vereinsbank" established

Johann Heinrich Gossler III and other merchant bankers, including Johannes Baur, Eduard L. Behrens, Martin M. Fränckel and Theodor Reincke, took up positions in management and acquired 6,452 of the shares to the tune of 1,290,400 Mark Banco.

The "Vereinsbank" benefited from the close ties of its founders to English banks; it combined the individual knowledge of the foreign markets with the financial strength of a joint stock bank.

For the individual Hamburg merchant banker, a difficult situation arose as a result of the establishment of the two joint stock banks. If he, despite the superiority of the large banks, did not want to walk away the banking business and withdraw to the established goods trade, then the merchant banker had to design his business much more flexibly and also more experimentally than he had done in the past: according to conventional benchmarks, his own equity was no longer able to keep pace with the amount necessitated by the commitment. And over time, history provided some insight into this challenge immediately following the establishment of the first Hamburg joint stock banks.

The Crisis of 1857

The boom during the Crimean War also had a downside. The city was a hub of world trade and with the circulation of money struggling to keep up with the movement of goods, some of the merchants resorted to more risky payment promises, and kite-flying took on a dangerous form.

After the peace treaty in February 1857, the discount fell, which attentive observers took as a first warning sign. In April, the dominant English economy was burdened again by the Sepoy Rebellion (Sepoy were the indigenous Indians in the British colonial army) in India. Soon after, the collapse of the Ohio Life & Trust Company in America led to the suspension of payments by 150 companies and triggered a widespread loss of confidence. The crisis spread from the US and England to their continental trading partners, particularly to Scandinavia. At the start of December, disaster was looming over Hamburg.

From one day to the next, smaller and then larger companies collapsed. Within no time at all, 11 million Mark Banco was mobilised to set up a "Garantie-Disconto-Verein", but even that was no longer of assistance; panic had gripped the stock exchange and exacerbated the situation. Requests for help sent to Leipzig and Berlin were denied. Rescue finally came from distant Austria on 12 December when the Austrian finance minister, Karl Ludwig von Bruck, sent 10 million Mark Banco in 2,825 silver bullions by railway from Vienna to Hamburg. As security, the Council pledged the state-owned securities account and approved the lending of goods and local and foreign securities at the Hamburger Bank up to a maximum amount of 12 million Mark Banco. The goal was to prevent the large companies from collapsing in an effort to limit the damage to Hamburg's entire economy.

According to Johann Heinrich Gossler's notes: "… on 17 December the main amount was deposited in the local bank. Companies which could prove that they were beyond question, or were inclined to give a security, took the necessary steps with the confidentiality commission." Johann Heinrich III, who was initially optimistic, wrote to Baring Brothers & Co. in London at the beginning of December: "Merck ruined, you may draw on us," only to realise that his company had been "unfortunately heavily impacted" and on 14 December 1857, he arranged with the confidentiality commission of the Senate a loan for 1.5 million Mark Banco to bridge the illiquidity that had resulted.

Thanks to Austrian money, the crisis ended quickly: "The effect was immediate: a wall had stopped the suspension, the expected tabula rasa that had been trumpeted to the world gloatingly was shifted to the world of fairy tales, bills of exchange were getting credit again, and when New Year's morning dawned, the balance sheets in most of Hamburg's companies were somewhat diminished, the discount had fallen suddenly to 2 percent and business was to the point of going about things as usual."

1.5 million marks to bridge a liquidity shortfall

Johann Heinrich's recollections are, of course, an elegant exaggeration because, after all, his company now had to meet government requirements: "The advance granted to Joh. Berenberg, Gossler & Co. has to be repaid on 1 June 1858 including interest of 7 percent per year from 16 December up to the repayment days of the confidentiality commission." As security, the commission had "all possessions and goods" of the owners and their portfolios. The company had to present its balance sheet from 31 December 1856 and to commit, "to provide a formal status update on their business situation every eight days", as well as to allow deputies of the commission access to their paperwork and books. Available goods could be sold "on the stock market" for constant payment and by shipment to external customers using common credit." New debts could only be made after consultation with the commission and orders could only be accepted against advance payment. Fortunately, the company was able to show in its weekly submitted status updates that it really was just a temporary liquidity shortage. The write-offs for losses, the unpaid bills of exchange, the ongoing drafts, the outstanding dues in Sweden and the delay of numerous debtors in the amount of 7,641,196 Mark Banco was juxtaposed by owner assets and fixed capital totalling 8,946,127 Mark Banco, the active

Panic broke out on 31 October 1857, resulting in the storming of the Seamen's Savings' Bank in North America

balance accounted for 1,304,931 Mark Banco. On 5 February 1858, Joh. Berenberg, Gossler & Co. submitted the last status update, and almost immediately the repayment of the advance payment began.

In his diary, Johann Heinrich Gossler III noted that the losses did not come from goods trade – there was no confidence in higher prices – "but rather from outside bankruptcies and bills of exchange that had gone bad. New York, Buenos Aires, London, Stockholm, Calcutta, Santo Domingo and Guayaquil are the main locations which cost us money." He decided to cut costs at home. His wife was not allowed to use the carriage, which apart from causing trouble in the household, was not good for much else, and from then on, Mary Elizabeth hired a public hackney carriage and responded angrily to the polite "Good day, Madame Gossler" with the words: "From now on, call me Mme. Hackney Cab."

To finally regulate the debts, realisation accounts were set up, with a transfer of a part of the profits, the balance of a reserve account and also amounts from private equity. In the following years, there were repeated losses, such as in Stockholm or New York, and the American Civil War, which started in 1861, led to a devaluation of the dollar so that funds had to be withdrawn temporarily from Boston.

A Painful Departure

The crisis of 1857 highlighted the risks which came with international interdependence. The capital basis of a private company was often not enough to weather an international economic crisis; corporations, in contrast, fared better. The "Vereinsbank", for instance, paid out 5 percent or 2 Schillings in dividends for each share and like the "Norddeutsche Bank", it wrapped up its realisation account with a credit balance in 1860.

Johann Heinrich III proved with his massive investment in the establishment of the "Vereinsbank" that he supported the necessary modernisation of banking and business. The crisis spoke clearly in favour of joint stock banks, yet also showed that a smaller company could survive if the partners were aware of the risks and operated in a flexible way. Johann Heinrich was willing to take risks and open for all things new. Although his boldness sometimes led to losses, and the excitement sapped his energy, the future proved him right.

Starting in 1860, the Port of Hamburg was comprehensively expanded to meet changing needs – including the growth of global trade, the increase in new raw materials arriving from abroad, and the considerably larger ships

His brother, Wilhelm, on the other hand, was more conservative and needed more security with everything. Influenced by the crisis which brought losses and hardships, he gave notice to terminate his contract – which had been in effect since 1836 – effective 31 December 1859, and started his own company devoted only to the goods trade. He also ended his investment involvement in the Boston-based company in 1862. Johann Heinrich III had not expected nor wanted him to leave. He was hurt and ultimately angered because Wilhelm Gossler had taken various business ties with him to the new company.

For Joh. Berenberg, Gossler & Co., the focus shifted increasingly to the banking business. In the 1870s, the goods trade accounted for merely 20 percent of all transactions, and at the end of the century, Joh. Berenberg, Gossler & Co. was, for all intents and purposes, a private bank, which was only active in the goods trade on the side.

The after effects of the crisis of 1857 were easily recognisable in the balance sheet totals: The rapid growth from 1848 to 1856 stagnated at first and it was not until 1869 that it began improving. At the start of the 1860s, Wilhelm Gossler had to be paid out; his share amounted to roughly 1 million Mark Banco.

The balance sheet sums 1860–1870

1860	7,569,725	Mark Banco	1866	8,701,249	Mark Banco
1861	8,075,401	Mark Banco	1867	11,293,278	Mark Banco
1862	8,418,944	Mark Banco	1868	10,466,508	Mark Banco
1863	8,708,783	Mark Banco	1869	11,766,656	Mark Banco
1864	10,167,863	Mark Banco	1870	12,186,463	Mark Banco
1865	9,875,153	Mark Banco			

The net profits for the same period were on average 237,000 Mark Banco, and 1864 was the only year that posted a decline. In the aftermath of bankruptcies in London and most notably in Sweden, a little over 50,000 Mark Banco was recorded, which burdened Johann Heinrich III to such an extent that he was bedridden for months with a severe nerve disorder. In 1871, the net profits climbed to almost 0.6 billion and in 1872 to 0.7 billion Mark Banco.

There was a company rule that employees who had been working for more than five years received a share of 5 percent of the profits. J. Otto Ahrens, for instance, in addition to his annual salary (1,200 to 1,800 Mark Courant) received his share of the profits between 1860 and 1872, which amounted to 69,195 Mark Banco, and, that which remained in the company, was invested at an interest rate of 4 percent.

The company's entire capital could always be maintained at a level of roughly 50 percent of the balance sheet total. The foreign capital of company employees and family members – especially of Johann Heinrich's brothers, the Senator Dr Hermann Gossler (1802–1874) and president of the lower court, Dr Ernst Gossler (1806–1889), was of little significance.

What had turned profitable was the investment in Gossler & Co. in Boston, which was untouched by the crisis of 1857; on the contrary, at the end of 1857, seeing as only a few engagements had been entered into, liquidity was high. The company in Boston used, as Johann Heinrich III wrote, "the exchange rate that had been pushed below par to pay back its European liabilities as much as possible."

The American Civil War (1861 to 1865) brought business to a temporary standstill, but at the end of the war, profits went up steadily, and a second branch was opened in New York, which was also profitable.

An office in New York

… and a New Generation

After Wilhelm Gossler left, Johann Heinrich III had around a 60 percent share in profits, but as the sole owner, he had to sustain all the losses. He increased the profit share of his son-in-law, Friedrich Wilhelm Burchard. He gave his nephew, Johann Heinrich Gossler IV, a son of his brother, Senator Hermann Gossler, one-eighth of a share and power of attorney which, however, expired on 1 March 1863, since he joined the Boston-based company as an associate. In his place came Ernst Gossler (1838–1893), another nephew with a share of 10 percent.

On 1 July 1864, Johann Heinrich's son, Johann (John) Berenberg Gossler (1839–1913), was brought into the company as a junior partner with a share of 20 percent. Friedrich Wilhelm Burchard left the company at this point and went on to run his own company very successfully.

Johann Berenberg, known as John B., was to become the formative figure in the company from 1870 to 1913. Initially, he showed little excitement for the banking business, his interests lay more in literature, painting and history. This was hardly surprising as in his family home these inclinations were shared: his father played piano exceptionally well and loved literature. His younger brother, John Henry, was an excellent violinist; the family often went to concerts and supported Hamburg's musical life through scholarships. Yet for all this enthusiasm, these activities were limited to evening leisure time, and business took precedent. John B., on the other hand, wanted to go to university, but coming from a Hamburg merchant family – Hamburg University was not founded until 1919 – his wish was met with bitter resistance.

His father was strict and repeatedly sent him abroad to gather mercantile experience in the offices of befriended trading companies. The fruits of his father's actions were initially a long time in coming: in Le Havre, John B. was bored at the bar, but was much more successful at reciting Schiller texts for the Schiller memorial celebration. In London, he had to work hard, but he was unable to stay for health reasons, and in southern Spain, he admired above all the literature and painting of the country. Next, he went to Boston, where he was able to work relatively independently for the first time, and now – at the age of 23 – business began to appeal to him. In Rio de Janeiro, Montevideo and Buenos Aires, he had such a successful track record that his father was re-

The port of Buenos Aires, Argentina

conciled and willing to make him a partner in 1864. That same year, John B. married the "cute Miss Julie Donner" from Altona, Juliane Amalie Donner (1843–1916), the daughter of the Danish fiscal councilman, who served as the Sicilian consular general, Johann Julius Donner.

During his many years abroad, John Berenberg Gossler keenly followed developments in German politics. The Hamburg version of particularism was foreign to him, and like many of his contemporaries, he was enthusiastic about Bismarck's purposeful unification policy.

The North German Confederation and the Foundation of the Empire

In October 1862, Otto von Bismarck was appointed Prussian prime minister by Wilhelm I. Bismarck was a tenacious advocate for the rights of the crown vis-à-vis the liberal and social trends of his time, and initiated a number of campaigns abroad, with which he ultimately destroyed German Confederation, ousted Austria as part of a "larger German solution", and contributed to the outbreak of the Franco-Prussian War of 1870/71.

Otto von Bismarck (1815–1898) was appointed Prussian prime minister by Wilhelm I in 1862

First Prussia and Austria fought together in 1864 against Denmark, which was intent on annexing the Duchy of Schleswig. After the Danish defeat, Schleswig-Holstein and Lauenburg were initially placed under Prussian-Austrian sovereignty; and a subsequent conflict between Prussia and Austria concerning Schleswig-Holstein was soon leveraged by Bismarck to force a decision against Austrian dominance in Germany. Building on the absolute obedience of the Prussian army in 1866, Prussia led a war against Austria and the German Confederation, a move that ran counter to public opinion in Germany and Prussia. The victory at the Battle of Königgrätz in July 1866 brought about Prussia's ultimate dominance in Germany.

John B. welcomed the war as a step towards German unification. On 10 September, he wrote to his friend, Gustav Schramm: "… I hope that at the next convenient opportunity, Prussia assimilates all of us and in this way turns us into one Germany. I can only approve and wish even if some things in Prussia's state machine are too conservative and still in an absolutist manner."

Prussia seized the opportunity. The German Confederation was dissolved, Prussia annexed Schleswig-Holstein, Hanover, Kurhesse, Nassau and Frankfurt am Main; the remaining states north of the Main River were merged with Prussia into the North German Association.

Napoleon III had asked for compensation from Prussia for its territorial expansion and called for the independence of the southern German states. But Bismarck stalled. He did not make any territorial claims with regard to the defeated southern German states; instead, he secured their allegiance in a secret defensive and offensive alliance, which was made public when France wanted to annex Luxembourg, which was under Prussian occupation law.

The confrontation with France was programmed. Napoleon III sought an alliance with Austria and Italy; Prussia countered with the claim of a Hohenzollern to the Spanish throne. The claim was soon retracted due to French

Prussian troops took on the combined forces of Austria and Saxony at the Battle of Königgrätz on 3 July 1866

protest, but it led to such immense diplomatic and national upsurges in France and Germany that Emperor Napoleon III declared war on the North German Confederation on 19 July 1870. France was isolated; the whole of Germany was involved in the conflict – except Austria, which remained neutral. At the end of the 10-month war, Paris was occupied, and on 18 January 1871, Wilhelm was proclaimed German emperor in the Hall of Mirrors at the Palace of Versailles.

The German Empire

With the incorporation of Hamburg into the German Empire, the methods and structure of the Prussian civil service gradually found their way into Hamburg's administration. The constitution of the Hanseatic city remained. Hamburg preserved its inner city character through the end of the 1880s, and every attempt to politicise the party system in Hamburg based on the model of the parties of the Reichstag, failed. The citizens of Hamburg maintained

On 18 January 1871, King Wilhelm I of Prussia was proclaimed German emperor in the hall of mirrors at the Palace of Versailles

the sense of being at home amongst themselves; political questions that caused a stir in Germany beyond the city's borders were not discussed in the city's parliament.

The End of a Hamburg Institution

Due to the financial and currency reforms in the German Empire, Hamburg – like Frankfurt am Main – gradually began losing its independent position from 1871 onwards and had to subordinate itself to the interests of Bismarck's politics.

As early as 1872, it was evident that the end of the Hamburg *Bankvaluta* was drawing near when leading banks in the city failed to get enough silver for bills of exchange, which France had drawn on the banks with their permission to settle its war debts. On 11 November 1872, the act to transform Hamburg's *Bankvaluta*, saw the Mark Reichsmünze replace the more than 250-year-old Mark Banco.

In the end, the gold standard was introduced in Germany in 1873 and in Hamburg as well. For the German Empire, the conversion from silver to gold was necessary to create a uniform and appropriate means of payment within the Empire and to not isolate itself when it came to foreign trade. Especially with regard to England, the world's leading trade and industrial power at the time, Germany ultimately needed to have a firm par of exchange; England had introduced the gold standard back in 1816.

The "Hamburger Bank" was dissolved in 1875 and became the "Reichshauptbankstelle Hamburg". The fact that Hamburg as the capital market would recede into the background in favour of the German imperial capital of Berlin was foreseeable, but at first, the "blessings" of the years of rapid industrial expansion in Germany were enjoyed.

The *Gründerzeit*

Even before the Empire had been established, open-minded Hamburg merchants had sought collaboration with Prussian partners. In Berlin, a group of private bankers endeavoured in 1869 to set up a German-overseas bank – later known as the "Deutsche Bank" (1870) – to finance foreign trade. The task had been mainly assumed by Hamburg merchant bankers up to this point; the Berlin group therefore was in contact with Hamburg companies, which included G. Godeffroy, L. Maas, C. Eggert, J. A. Schön, P. Siemssen, W. Pustau and H. C. Bock & Co.

As the negotiations for the founding of the "Deutsche Bank" were protracted, the Hamburg natives left the Berlin Group in 1870 and established along with the "Norddeutsche Bank" and the "Vereinsbank" the "Internationale Bank" in Hamburg, with a capital of 7.5 million Thaler. Other companies involved, in addition to Joh. Berenberg, Gossler & Co., included L. Behrens & Söhne, Merck & Co. and Schröder Gebr. & Co. Johann Heinrich Gossler III became the deputy on the board of directors. The group not only had a control function, but also set the business policy through an executive body, which, for the most part, was comprised of five private bankers. That same year, a branch was opened in London at the recommendation of Johann Heinrich III.

The "Internationale Bank" never overcame its initial difficulties and was liquidated in 1879. But with the establishment of the "Commerz- und Disconto-

Bank" in Hamburg in 1870 – without any investment from Joh. Berenberg, Gossler & Co. – the founding of the "Deutsche Bank" in Berlin (1870) and the "Dresdner Bank" (1872), other significant banking institutions arose apart from the joint stock banks, which had been established between 1848 and 1856.

The insight which German bankers, merchants and entrepreneurs had for the necessity of new economic structures, the cancellation of the licence requirement for stock corporations in Prussia and last, but not least, the 5 billion Gold Francs in French war reparation payments allowed the new business boom to last until 1873. Between 1871 and 1874 alone, 857 stock corporations were created in Germany with a capital totalling over 4 billion marks.

Investments

Joh. Berenberg, Gossler & Co. had invested in diverse new start-ups but there was one exception: the company did not invest in industry, but, rather, focused on expanding the company's international relations.

The company invested in the "Hamburg Südamerikanische-Dampfschiffahrts-Gesellschaft" (Hamburg South America Steamship Company) and the "Hamburg-Süd", which was founded in 1871 by eleven distinguished Hamburg companies. The chairmanship was assumed by Heinrich Amsinck, a nephew of Johann Heinrich III and partner at Johannes Schuback & Söhne. The mainlines of the company led to Brazil, Argentina and Uruguay, and the company had unloading-and-loading businesses in Buenos Aires, Patagonia and on the Brazilian coast, which allowed for quick processing of the ships.

The traditional connections to Scandinavia were expanded with various investments in Denmark and Sweden. In 1871, Johann Heinrich III, as a representative of his company, joined the foundation syndicate A. B. Stockholmer Handelsbanken (as of 1919: "Svenska Handelsbanken") and, at roughly the same time, took

Poster advertising the Hamburg South America Steamship Company of 1914

Further investments in new companies: Hamburg Süd, Stockholmer Handelsbanken, Dansk Landmansbank, Rigaer Kommerzbank, Petersburger Int. Handelsbank, Norddeutsche Versicherungsgesellschaft

on the German representation of "Sveriges Riksbank". Joh. Berenberg, Gossler & Co. were, moreover, involved as founders in the "Dansk Landmansbank" in Copenhagen, where 3,333 of the 29,851 founder shares had been purchased, each with a value of 200 "Danish Rigsdalern" (300 Mark Banco).

The contacts to Russia were solidified as a result of the cofounding of the "Rigaer Kommerzbank", in which – in addition to companies from Riga – banks from Petersburg, Moscow, Warsaw, Berlin and Königsberg were involved. Along with the Frankfurt companies "Gebrüder Bethmann" and Erlanger & Söhne, Joh. Berenberg, Gossler & Co. were also involved in the establishment of the "Petersburger Internationale Handelsbank". And in 1873, the Russian commitment was expanded by way of a credit that was granted to merchants Gustav Albers and Gustav Kunst to set up a trading company in Vladivostock. Thus, Kunst & Albers not only had the option of sourcing goods directly from Europe, but also, and more importantly, thanks to the connections of their investors, access to the London money market. In 1877, they recorded company assets of 100,000 Rubel.

Much less successful was an investment Joh. Berenberg, Gossler & Co. made together with the "Internationale Bank" and the "Norddeutsche Bank" in the "Deutsch-Brasilianische Bank" in Rio de Janeiro. It was the first German bank to be established there and was managed by a merchant from Bremen, who worked in Rio de Janeiro as a discount broker. The bank was permitted to issue banknotes in Brazil and ran a vibrant exchange business. The Hamburg board of directors initially "got a kick out of the millions of Pound Sterling Prima-London bills of exchange which they had remitted to Hamburg as cover for their drafts on Germany." This was taken from the memoirs of Max von Schinckel, a leading member of the "Norddeutsche Bank". This delight and a dividend of 13 percent in the first year obviously led to carelessness; the branch in Rio was granted too much freedom. In any case, the business dealings dropped in the years that followed, and in May 1875, the "Deutsch-Brasilianische Bank" filed for bankruptcy. Almost the entire capital had been lost. Johann Heinrich III attached a regretful note to the balance of 1875: "According to the agreement, I sustain the capital loss of the company, possibly the 4 percent interest charged up to the final liquidation of the account."

More gratifying was the investment in the "Norddeutsche Versicherungsgesellschaft". It became the successor of the "Dritten Hamburger Versicherungsgesellschaft" of 1804, and in addition to the Gosslers, the "Norddeutsche Bank", J. C. Godeffroy & Sohn, H. J. Merck & Co., August Sanders & Co. and C. M. Schröder & Co. were involved.

In 1871, Johann Heinrich III became chairman of the board of directors of the "Vereinsbank" following the death of Johann Christian Söhle.

A "Child of Fate"

The only noteworthy investment in the industrial sector, which was in the "Ilseder Hütte" smelter steelworks, got off to a strange start.

In the mid-1850s, farmers and residents around Celle drew roughly 1 million Thaler from a local banker, Carl Hostmann, for the construction of a mine and metallurgical company in the Harz region. A total of one-third of

Sole industrial holding: Ilseder Hütte steelworks

Joh. Berenberg, Gossler & Co. were one of the founders of the Ilseder Hütte steelworks

the sum had already been paid, and the attaché for the Austrian-Hungarian embassy, Max Graf Fugger, had moreover drawn 2 million Thaler, of which 270,000 Thaler had been received. When Hostmann required additional funds in 1857, Joh. Berenberg, Gossler & Co. granted him a credit in return for the Fugger shares as the matter appeared to be promising; Hostmann had assumed that the iron demand in Germany would continue growing, and expert reports, including one from Justus von Liebig, confirmed the good quality and sufficient amounts of iron ore from the Peine region. When Hostmann went bankrupt in 1857 and then committed suicide, the Gosslers assumed that the papers were fraudulent and set them aside as non-recoverable claims.

The papers were gradually forgotten until Hostmann's son-in-law, Carl Haarmann, suddenly appeared; he had founded the Ilseder Hütte. He offered new shares in return for the old ones, provided that more shares were bought for which a dividend was guaranteed. Haarmann as well as the other board members seemed to be trustworthy and the list of shareholders included in addition to L. Königswarter, O. L. Eichmann and J. C. Haller, the names of other respected Hamburg merchants. Although they were "worthless papers with just 6 percent," Johann Heinrich Gossler III accepted the offer and also assumed the papers of Conrad Hinrich Donner, whose owner did not want to deal with industrial companies. He moved onto the administrative board and devoted considerable attention to this "child of fate" in the 1870s. Carl Haarmann had arranged for the proper legal structure of the newly created ironworks, and the commercial technical management was organised by the engineer, Gerhard Lukas Meyer. Johann Heinrich III soon saw a father figure in him, and a friendship developed, which formed the foundation for a long-term relationship between the families.

The Vienna Stock Exchange Crash and the Crisis of 1873

The balance sheets during the rapid industrial expansion in Germany showed encouraging increases – from 12,186,463 Mark Banco in 1870 to 15,930,925 in 1872. After the founding of the German Empire, the mark replaced the Mark Banco. The calculation was 1 Mark Banco = 1.50 marks, which for the balance meant: 15,930,925 Mark Banco = 23,896,388 marks.

But in 1873, following the euphoria from years of rapid industrial expansion in Germany, the Vienna Stock Exchange crashed, which triggered the Great Depression, and lasted until 1879. With its myriad of bankruptcies all over Europe, which primarily led to a concentration of all the large banks and companies, the crisis shook the confidence in stock corporations and their founders. The already widespread anti-Semitism increased. Moreover, the reputation of economic liberalism in Germany suffered and a gradual transition to protectionism was introduced, which was concluded in 1879. Austria, Italy, North America, England, France, Scandinavia and Russia recovered slowly from the crisis, Germany was a little faster to do so.

Hamburg's economy was comparatively stable which meant that the international crisis did not have a devastating effect. Although the first phase of the economic crisis affected Joh. Berenberg, Gossler & Co., the balance sheets of the 1870s reflected rising net profits.

The company had stood its ground, but in 1877, there was trouble brewing "inside" it.

1870s net profits:		
1873	290,610	marks
1874	483,088	marks
1875	192,068	marks
1876	297,070	marks
1877	113,910	marks
1878	300,890	marks
1879	419,561	marks

The Boston Flop

After Albert Kingman's departure in 1862, Johann Heinrich IV, the nephew of Johann Heinrich Gossler III, took over management of the Boston-based company. Thomas M. Devens had power of attorney. Johann Heinrich IV was Hamburg's consul in Boston, before being appointed representative of the German Confederation and then, in 1871 representative of the German Empire. But on 31 December 1872, he left Gossler & Co. and went back home in 1873.

From then on, Thomas M. Devens was the only manager in Boston while the responsibility for New York was transferred to the previous authorised signatory, Georg Gravenhorst. John Henry Gossler (1849–1914), the second son of Johann Heinrich III, and Guido Wolff, who would later

The "Messrs. Exchange Visitors" had a permanent seat on the Hamburg Stock Exchange

9 May 1873: On this Black Friday, massive slumps in stock prices triggered panic sales at Vienna's stock exchange

OCTOBER 4, 1873.]   SUPPLEMENT TO FRANK LESLIE'S

FOURTH NATIONAL BANK

4 October 1873: New Yorkers stormed the Fourth National Bank

become director of the Hamburg America Line, were given power of attorney for both companies. In 1874, a third authorised signatur, Arthur Donner, was added. That same year, John Henry moved up to become a partner in Boston and New York.

For the first time since the opening of the Boston company, there were losses in 1877, and it was discovered that John Henry and Gravenhorst had speculated on their own, mainly in sugar. A total of 291,732 Reichsmark had to be written off "as a result of the irresponsible actions that went counter to our positive instructions and of the concealment of business details." This speculation also led to losses at the Decastro & Donner Sugar Refining Company in New York, in which Johann Heinrich III had personally invested 440,000 marks; the sum also had to be regarded as a total loss. In addition, there were the justified claims of third parties, which had to be fulfilled.

John Henry was called back immediately from America by his infuriated father while older brother, John B., and long-time authorised signatory, W. Barttram, packed their bags, boarded the omnibus to the landing stages and set sail for the US in an effort to save what could be saved. Poor John Henry was read the riot act back home: 839,114 Reichsmark were "debited to the future" and Johann Heinrich III ordered: "As my son, John Henry, has – as a result of his unauthorised actions in 1877 as manager in charge of my New York company, Gossler & Co., to my deep regret – had to withdraw his involvement in the same as well as in my companies in Boston and Hamburg, I revoke everything set out in Paragraph of my will as far as it applies to him positively or potentially, and I leave everything

that concerns this company as well as the ones abroad to my son, John B. ..."
And with that, John Henry was cut out of the company.

With financial support from his mother, John Henry next became an associate of the company he cofounded, Warnholtz & Gossler, and business went well. John Henry purchased a sizeable estate on Krähenberg in Blankenese – the "Gossler Haus" and "Gossler Park" are reminders of him.

An Impressive Legacy

On 10 September 1879, Johann Heinrich Gossler III died at the age of 74. "The loss is so unspeakably difficult for me," wrote John B. on 11 September to Baron Westenholz, "I was so used to leaning on him and trying to work according to his wishes that with his passing, my sphere of activity appears so bleak to me now." Contrary to earlier fears, the collaboration between father and son was harmonious and trusting, and children and grandchildren remembered Johann Heinrich III as an affectionate and loving patriarch. The father's strictness, under which the children sometimes had suffered, had disappeared in the last years, and his numerous grandchildren were allowed to do almost everything in the office.

Johann Heinrich III left behind a fortune of more than 18 million marks. In addition to his share in Joh. Berenberg, Gossler & Co. and at Gossler & Co. in Boston and New York, he had widely spread shares, mortgages and property. Apart from the shares in the "Vereinsbank", he owned diverse American securities, several railway bonds (Mecklenburg, Rhenish, Altona-Kieler, Romanian, Cuban and others), investments in industrial companies – such as the "Lauensteinische Wagenfabrik" (a manufacturer of railway cars) in the "Dampf-Zuckersiederei" of 1848, the "Ziegelei Rennberg", and bonds – such as of Nassau, Kurhessian ones, Russian ones. Moreover, he had also purchased property starting in 1869 in Wandsbek, at the Elbe levee and in Hammerbrook. Niendorf and the house on the Esplanade were also added.

In addition to presents for the Comptoir staff and his long-time coachman, Johann Heinrich Gossler had stipulated donations of 75,000 marks in his will. Money was donated to charitable institutions, including, of course, the Dutch Relief Fund for the Poor, the church in Niendorf and St Jacobi Church, the "Israelitische Stiftungsschule" of 1815, the "Israelitische Mäd-

Johann Heinrich III left a fortune worth 18 million marks

The landing stages in Hamburg, ca. 1890

chenschule" of 1789 (a Jewish school for girls), the "Talmud-Tora-Schule" (a Jewish high school) and the girls' school of the "Deutsch-Israelitische Gemeinde" (German Jewish community), and 16 schools for young children from poorer families. The "remaining fortune" was split among six children and/or their descendents.

Trends in Economic Development from 1870 to World War I

The year Johann Heinrich Gossler died, 1879, was the same year the economic depression ended. After a phase of normalisation, Germany experienced an upswing in 1885 which lasted until World War I.

During this time, Germany grew into the largest industrial power on the continent and eventually surpassed England in the production of pig iron and steel, in the chemistry and electrical industries as well as in the level of industrial organisation and technology. From 1873 to 1913, the German national product increased three-fold. The lion's share came from industry, manual skills and mining, one-third in 1873, and one-half in 1913.

Between 1850 and 1913, the chemical industry recorded average growth rates of around 4 percent, and in some areas, notably in colour synthesis, it almost gained a worldwide monopoly together with the Swiss. The industrial manufacturing method also prevailed in the textile industry between 1870 and 1913; cotton production increased continuously, the linen industry declined and wool and silk were ranked in the middle.

The number of stock corporations grew. Between 1871 and 1885, 1963 stock corporations had been founded in the German Empire with a capital of around 3.7 billion marks; between 1886 and 1912 there were 5,001 stock corporations with a capital of around 6.6 billion marks.

In 1885, an increasing number of cartels, syndicates and trusts developed, which sought better sales opportunities on the world market with jointly defined price mechanisms. In 1875, there had been just four cartels, in 1890 there were 106, in 1896, 205 and in 1905, 385.

Yet, the number of large companies was also growing. In 1907, 13.7 percent of workers were employed in companies with more than 1,000 employees. One good example of this trend towards large companies was the rapid rise of Siemens and AEG in the electrical industry.

Large companies were also created in the coal and steel industry, such as Gutehoffnungshütte, Ilseder Hütte, Krupp, Thyssen at the Ruhr, Henckel-Donnersmarck in Upper Silesia and Röchling or Stumm at the Saar. Coal mining production went from 22.3 million tonnes in 1880 to 114.2 million tonnes in 1913, and in the same time frame pig iron production jumped from 2.7 million to 19.3 million tonnes.

Germany as a Great Power

In 1882, soon after Bismarck's protectionism came into force, there were fears in Germany that a general depression could impact German industrial production. Bismarck's financial advisor, banker Gerson Bleichräder, tried to persuade the chancellor to change German trade policy. In Prussian yearbooks, the fear of an over production crisis was fueled; there was a campaign to support German export trade and open new markets.

Harbingers of economic recovery: a foundry run by Gutehoffnungshütte in Oberhausen

Bismarck adopted suggestions and gave them an anti-English bent, when in 1884, he had possessions owned by Bremen merchant Adolf Lüderitz on the coast of West Africa put under protection of the German Empire. This was the start of a colonial policy; the first German colonies German South-West Africa, Togo and Cameroon and the free trade zone set up on German insistence at the Congo increasingly came into conflict with England's colonial plans.

Germany's overseas trade had been largely dependent on the English valuta: a sample at a Hamburg bank revealed that of over 100,000 pounds of issued bills of exchange, only 2,000 pounds were issued to Germany. To ensure overseas trade credit with a view to making credit transactions abroad as independent as possible from England, and improve the German balance of payment through own interest gains, various banks, branches, commercial establishments were set up overseas in the mid 1880s with political backing.

Of the so-called four "D"-banks – the "Deutsche", "Dresdner" and "Darmstädter Bank" as well as the "Disconto-Gesellschaft", which together managed roughly 40 percent of all the money invested in Germany, the

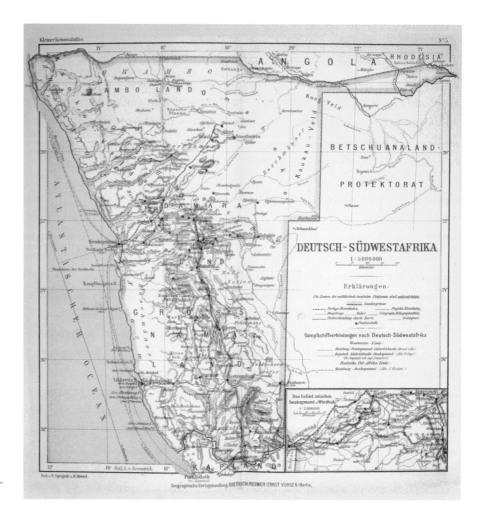

Map of German Southwest Africa, a German colony equivalent to present-day Namibia from 1884 to 1915

"Disconto-Gesellschaft" excelled particularly well at establishing overseas financial operations.

In 1887, the "Disconto-Gesellschaft" and the "Norddeutsche Bank" founded the "Brasilianische Bank für Deutschland". This successor of the "Deutsch-Brasilianische Bank" soon had branches in Rio de Janeiro, São Paulo and Santos. In 1889, again under the aegis of the "Disconto-Gesellschaft", the "Deutsch-Asiatische-Bank" was founded. In 1895, came the "Bank für Chile und Deutschland", the "Deutsche Palästina-Bank" in 1899, the "Deutsche Afrika Bank" in 1906 and several others.

Problems of Private Banks

In light of the fast growth of the joint stock banks and the industrial companies after 1880, private bankers were only partially involved in the economic development of Germany. Although they continued to play an important role in the issuing of shares and bonds, in the business of setting up companies and in the granting of credit to smaller and mid-sized companies, they gradually fell behind the rapidly growing major banks.

The middle class and small traders struggled to recover the lost business, and private bankers were also faced with fierce competition. This area was being looked after by credit cooperatives and in even greater measure by savings banks, which as of 20 April 1909, were permitted to carry out current account business. Thus, a first step to the regular bank was made. At the same time, the savings banks set up "safety deposit boxes", hijacked solid asset management business from the private and country banks, and were also able to grant higher interest rates for savings and deposits.

Assorted Stock Exchange Acts from the 1880s and 1890s brought taxation on the issuing and turnover of securities in addition to a state approval obligation and the state exchange supervisory authority. The Stock Exchange Act from 22 June 1896 prohibited futures trading of industrial and mining companies and limited futures trading in general. Forward transactions were only then valid if both parties were registered in a stock market registry, which entailed high entry and publication fees for the registering institute.

The private banker was particularly affected by the terms for the issuing business: shares of a newly-founded or transformed company were only permitted one year after it was registered in the commercial registrar. For a private banker, it was almost impossible to finance such a large payment in advance over such a long period and to wait one year to issue shares. Since these Stock Market Acts led to speculative trading abroad, in 1908 most of the limiting passages were lifted, but for many banks this decision came too late. After 1897, a concentration took place in the German banking system, with more than half of all the private banks succumbing by 1913.

Berlin was the most important banking centre in Germany, but Hamburg gained in importance at the expense of Frankfurt and Cologne. Remarkable here was the number of start-ups and the fact that only a few survived. The Hamburg merchant bankers had undoubtedly numerous advantages, especially as they could expand merchandise financing and achieve considerable success in the international syndicated business. This was especially true for M. M. Warburg, Joh. Berenberg, Gossler & Co. and L. Behrens & Söhne. But even they walked a thin line in the decades leading up to World War I. Risks had to be taken to avoid being driven out of business, and yet, the risks posed by growing financial crises were increasingly unmanageable.

John (Freiherr von) Berenberg-Gossler (1839–1913)

A Lucky Partnership

The partners' holdings:
60 % John Berenberg-Gossler
30 % Ernst Gossler
10 % W. Barttram

After the death of Johann Heinrich III, John B. and his cousin, Ernst Gossler, took over the management of the company. John B. was now officially known as Johann Berenberg-Gossler (1838–1893), which resulted from a 1880 senate resolution granting him the right to incorporate his second first name "Berenberg" into the family name.

In 1881, authorised signatory W. Barttram, who had proven himself in processing the speculative transactions of John Henry Gossler in New York, received a share of 10 percent. John Berenberg-Gossler retained 60, cousin Ernst 30 percent, and, as usual, 5 percent of the net profits were distributed in advance to deserving employees.

John B. always found the partnership with his cousin to be very fortunate. He called him "a splendid fellow", "a superb employee and helper", "a good and faithful soul" and "a gentleman in every respect." "Ernst and I get on splendidly," he wrote to Gustav Schramm on 12 August 1864, and that was never to change.

At this time, Ernst Gossler – who had apprenticed at Schuback & Söhne and had then been sent to Portugal and the US to take his mind off initially unwanted marriage plans – was the *Prokurist* at Joh. Berenberg, Gossler & Co. On 1 January 1873, he became a partner and with his calm and balanced temperament, he often had a pleasant and mod-

Johann, Baron von Berenberg-Gossler
(1839–1913), called John B., was co-owner
of the bank from 1864 to his death

erating influence on Johann Heinrich III and John B. As the long-time author-ised signatory of the company, Rudolf Sandow, reported in 1921, "since he was very impulsive," John B. used to ask Ernst Gossler, "whether he can do this business deal or that. If he said 'yes', then he did it. If Ernst said, 'John, don't touch that', then he didn't touch the business again." The good rapport be-tween the two was also evident in the following letter: "Ernst Gossler and I rub shoulders every day with the petty and narrow-minded people in Ham-burg. Overseas, life is completely different. Very sad and often very lonely, but much freer and non-committal ...," wrote John B. to Gustav Schramm. And so the cosmopolitan junior bosses were also in agreement on political issues and soon ended up in heated arguments with the majority of the merchants in Hamburg.

The Dispute over the Customs Union

Contrary to most people in Hamburg who still had a grudge against Prussia for refusing to help in 1857 and leaned more toward Austria, Johann Heinrich III, John B. and Ernst Gossler were very strongly in favour of Prussia. The particularism so prevalent in Hamburg was foreign to them and they were sup-ported in their position by acquaintances in the banking business from Ameri-ca and, above all, from England. There was hope that after the political and monetary union, a customs union would follow.

As a federal state, Hamburg was part of the German Empire, but in terms of customs, it was foreign soil. Since the establishment of the Customs Union in 1834, people in Hamburg knew how to avoid joining, much to the annoyance of the inland region, which unleashed criticism of the "un-German citizens of the Hanseatic city", the "German Barbaresken", who were said to be only interested in earning money.

In 1879, Bismarck had moved from a policy of free trade to protection-ism and was attempting to finally ease Hamburg into the Customs Union. The Gossler cousins had no doubt that Bismarck had the appropriate means at his disposal to achieve his goal. And they were also sure that the Union, given specific conditions, namely, maintaining a free port, would be advantageous for the Hanseatic city. But most of the merchants were of a different opinion. On 9 May 1879, in his capacity as president of the chamber of commerce,

Ernst Gossler addressed a letter to the organisation, in which he outlined his position and requested his own dismissal:

> "Since my views … differ significantly from those of the other members of the chamber, in that in light of the current economic circumstances in Germany I consider a principled opposition to the programme put forth by the Reich Chancellor not opportune, and, under certain circumstances, not to be discussed in detail here, I consider Hamburg's entry into the Customs Union necessary, I have abstained completely from participating in the manifestations of the chamber of commerce related to the issue.
>
> I have refrained from communicating to this body my dissenting opinion about this publically, in an effort to avoid further escalating the already opposing positions for my part, until I was recently provoked at the *Börsenhalle* and compelled to come out of my shell.
>
> After the public statement I gave to rectify facts, I left my position as chairman of the chamber of commerce to my colleagues, seeing as I no longer consider myself in a position to be in the office I held, and allow me to request the high senate my dismissal from the office of member of the chamber of commerce in a manner which is commensurate with the constitution."

The request was granted. Bismarck began using diplomacy. On 8 May, he held a speech before the Reichstag, in which he ensured in the event of accession:

> "… that the right to free ports could only end with Hamburg's approval, and that as long as I have a say in things, I would make sure that this is not restricted to smaller borders than those that are necessary so that it corresponds to its designation in a perfect and loyal way, a real, full, free port that corresponds to all developments which are to be carried out in a free port and to all uses which one expects of a free port."

But the people of Hamburg were in direct opposition, and so the "rigid Unitarian", cousin John B. made himself extremely unpopular when he approached the Imperial Chancellor directly with a submission and requested affirmation of these promises:

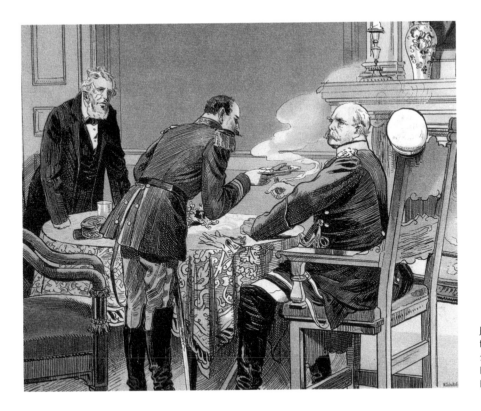

Jules Favre (left) negotiates a cease-
fire with Otto von Bismarck; on
10 May 1871 they signed the Treaty of
Frankfurt, which ended the Franco-
Prussian War

"High and Mighty Prince, Your Most Serene Highness …
The question of joining the Customs Union, or as one is entitled to call it,
the question of the appropriate limitation of this free port, is being constantly deprived of an impartial assessment; it is being made a plaything
of politics and so exposes the confusion of passions. Especially the fac-
tion which describes itself as being progressive vis-à-vis the population, is
making efforts in the heated matter which could aim at nothing else than
by virtue of the economic separation of the ports on the Elbe and Weser
from the Empire to keep up the alienation of these cities from Germany
and also in other areas of national legislation and social order even up
to expanding an every deeper gulf. Liberal secessionists are going in the
same direction. No effort was made to arouse opinions in every imagi-
nable way; the plans of the imperial government amount to an impair-
ment of the constitutional rights of the Hanseatic cities and to a stunting
of their prosperity, and the latter would be the result.

The *Hamburger Nachrichten* of
15 November 1880 published John
B.'s correspondence with Bismarck

There is hardly a need for the assurance that we for our part have been pervaded with the sympathetic intentions of the imperial government for the country to which we belong, like for all other parts of the fatherland. We add to this that with the city of Hamburg joining – keeping the free district and other appropriate facilities – we see significant advantages not only for all commercial and industrial activity, for retail trade as well as for property, but also anticipate the same for import, export and wholesale; businesses about which we feel called to pass judgement given the experience we have gathered in our lifetime posts.

This, our conviction, is shared by a very large part of the population, which in its judgement and sympathy for the fatherland did not allow itself to be distracted by incitement."

In his response to the Messrs. Joh. Berenberg, Gosser & Co., dated Friedrichsruh, 15 November 1880, the Imperial Chancellor reiterated his promise, and John B. had both his petition and Bismarck's response published in the *Hamburger Nachrichten*. But his hopes of winning over the people of Hamburg with the explanations from the Union were dashed. For one, "this, our conviction" was by no means "shared by a very large part of the population" – there were merely 31 signatories and moreover, the tone of the petition was hardly appropriate to win over the opponents to the Union. There was a storm of protest and the Amsinck cousins of Johannes Schuback & Söhne objected "vehemently opposed the action of a small number of self-proclaimed men." There were strong voices in favour of maintaining Hamburg's entire free port even if that meant redefining it, "so we expect that such a thing would only be pursued with the assistance of our legislative factors and by taking into consideration all of the interests that would be affected." Apart from that, they protested against not being as nationally inclined as the opposition party.

The quotes were taken from a document, which the "particularists" had displayed at the stock exchange. In the end, there were 1,730 signatures. From Sanders, Merck, Münchmeyer, Westphal, Lutteroth, Warburg, Tesdorpf, Pinckernelle, Möring, Hudtwalcker, de Chapeaurouge, Nottebohm, Schröder, Edye and Willink right up to stock corporations, in which Joh. Berenberg,

Gossler & Co. had shares – Hapag, "Hamburg-Süd" and the "Dampf-Zucker-Siederei of 1848" – all of the big company names in Hamburg were against John B. and Ernst Gossler and their modest following.

Nevertheless, the Gossler cousins had correctly assessed the balance of power and the economic consequences. Confidential negotiations with the Empire were taking place during the crucial phase, by May 1881 they were concluded. Hamburg joined the Customs Union but maintained a large free port area, which had just as much room for shipyards as it did for various finishing industries. The Empire contributed 40 million to the costs of the new facilities, which were estimated to be around 106 million marks. The customs authority would be under the control of Hamburg authorities. In 1882, the accession agreement was signed and construction was underway.

The changes to the cityscape were immense: the picturesque *Kehrwieder*, with its sailor pubs was torn down as was the venerable merchant

Imperial sunshine: on 29 October 1888 Wilhelm II formally opened the "warehouse city" and free port in Hamburg

quarter Am Wandrahm and Holländischer Brook. It marked the end of the most beautiful burgher houses, including *Mortzenhaus*, which had been in the possession of the Gossler family for 100 years and also served as the office. The company found new quarters at Ferdinandstraße 52, and later moved to Adolphsplatz 5.

Around 24,000 people had to be relocated during the construction of the free port; most of them found accommodation far from their work in places such as Eimsbüttel, Barmbek, Hohenfelde and Rothenburgsort, where streets of tenements popped up overnight.

On 15 October 1888, the free port was completed, and 14 days later, it was opened in the presence of the young Kaiser Wilhelm II. The customs barriers fell, which also diminished the attraction of smuggling, which many women, including Juliane Amalie Berenberg-Gossler, had developed quite a knack for on the return trip through the suburbs.

To John Berenberg-Gossler's satisfaction, the predictions whereby that after accession, only cows would populate the Jungfernstieg, proved to be wrong. Economic development grew quickly after accession. People earned well and the prevailing prosperity soon reduced the resentment towards Bismarck and his supporters in Hamburg.

A Dubious Honour?

John B. is granted an aristocratic title for guiding Hamburg's membership into the German Customs Union ...

John Berenberg-Gossler's commitment was not forgotten in Berlin. On 23 January 1889, he was acknowledged for his efforts in the accession of Hamburg to the Customs Union and granted a hereditary Prussian aristocratic title. Two months later, the Senate granted him authorisation to use the name "von Berenberg-Gossler". As a member of parliament, John B. needed the approval as nobility was excluded from performing any duties in Hamburg's government, and he would have otherwise had to resign his position.

Hamburg was disapproving. In the words of Mayor Johann Heinrich Burchard on the occasion of the ennoblement of the merchant Schröder to the rank of hereditary nobility: "A Hamburg merchant can't be honoured." John B.'s sister, Susanne, whose married name was Amsinck, is supposed to have said: "But John, our good name!," but this was to suffer another blow, because on 5 December 1910, John von Berenberg-Gossler also received the title *Frei-*

herr (baron) for himself and his successors on the Niendorf estate, which was converted to a property which always had to be in the possession of a family member, where only the earnings were at the disposal of others.

Outside of Hamburg, the new titles proved to be advantageous. They made John B.'s interaction with Berlin easier and with Karlsruhe as well after he was named consul of the Grand Duchy of Baden in 1894. When the Grand Duke was in Hamburg, he stayed at his consul general on Alsterglacis, where the lounges on the first floor offered a unique view of the Alster River with the silhouette of the city and its six towers in the background.

... and appointed consul to the Grand Duchy of Baden

Turbulent Years ...

The last two decades of the 19th century were so hard on private banks that many of them were abandoned. In 1881, out of fear for Russian competition, Bismarck blocked the German capital market from czarist Russia, which was a detrimental move in every respect. It harmed not only German partners of Russian companies, including Joh. Berenberg, Gossler & Co., but also promoted a rapprochement between France and Russia, which was now receiving capital support largely from France.

1882 began "under bad omens," as the Hamburg merchant Siegmund Robinow wrote in his diary. He noted that the goods trade was at a low point, and when it came to coffee, one of the most important goods, there was almost a "panic". Two years later, Arnold Otto Meyer noted: "1884 turned out to be a very hard year for the world in terms of finances. All of the assets suddenly fell sharply regardless of whether they were below or above ground, and some people, who had many goods, have either lost some or all of them. People are anxious about the year end and the statement of accounts."

In 1885, Joh. Berenberg, Gossler & Co. started putting 50,000 marks into a reserve account regardless of whether it was really necessary. It was a wise decision as in the years that followed, there were many precarious situations.

In 1890, there was a major stock crash in Argentina, followed by one financial crisis after the other in Portugal, Greece and, notably, in Latin America where Joh. Berenberg, Gossler & Co. had quite an interest. In 1897, several companies stopped payments in Nicaragua, meaning that Hamburg companies which had granted a blank cheque for the expected coffee harvest and

Financial crises hit banks

Hamburg's Outer Alster (front) and
Inner Alster during the 19th century

shipments were affected. Wilhelm Amsinck Sr. informed a business associate in London on 9 June that those affected included F. Gerlach; Joh. Berenberg, Gossler & Co. stood behind the latter as a sub-participant, "which has now become the norm given the sometimes very large advance payments to Central America". A similiar situation happened in Guatemala in 1899, again with F. Gerlach, and an affiliated company in Caracas went bankrupt. In Argentina as well, things were not going as planned.

In 1901, the Leipziger Bank collapsed. It was preceded by a few bankruptcies in the industrial sector, resulting in losses for Joh. Berenberg, Gossler & Co. In 1902, there were difficulties due to the insolvency of Spethmann & Hellweg in Valparaiso, and in 1907, Haller, Söhle & Co. had to close its doors, which had an impact on affiliated companies.

Joh. Berenberg, Gossler & Co., in contrast, not only weathered these times, which were hard on all private banks, but also consistently posted respectable profits with the exception of 1901. Approximately 5 percent of the net profit went as before to deserving employees; in 1880 there were eight, in 1913, there were 15. The *Herren Chefs*, as the bosses were affectionately known, were usually generous and in less profitable years contributed significant amounts out of their own pockets. Almost all of the employees took advantage of the option of leaving some or all of their bonuses in the company to earn interest. In 1913, there was an employee share of 287,637. John B.'s share in the company's assets in the same year was almost 7 million marks, smaller than the share of his father's in 1879: the son had invested the lion's share of his assets in shares and in properties.

Like his father, John B. also sat on various supervisory boards including that of the "Vereinsbank", "Ilseder Hütte", "Peiner Walzwerk", "Bank für Handel & Industrie", "Blohm & Voß" and many more. Moreover, he was a member of the regional council of the "Reichsbank".

More and more frequently, the partners took extended business trips to solidify ties and to establish new ones – and sometimes to prevent the worst. In 1890, the year of the crash in Argentina, John B.'s son, John Jr., made a successful, albeit strenuous trip to Latin America, where for weeks he took trains and wagons and rode on the backs of horses and donkeys. In addition, he also stopped off in Boston and in New York to maintain contacts.

As always, the visits to London involved a trip to Barings, to William Brandt's & Sons, where there was a long-time affiliation, and, increasingly to

1890 marked the centenary of the business partnership with the Baring Brothers

We hear by telegraph today of the reconstruction of your firm and take the liberty to congratulate you sincerely to the same. Our Senior wrote the other day to your Lord Revelstoke assuring him of our sympathy in the bereavement of your eminent house. We have had the honour to be your correspondents in Hamburg for more than 100 years and we hope that also henceforth we shall be entrusted with the interest of your firm in our place.

We should also much like to continue our intercourse, which for many years has been so pleasant and for which we have always been sincerely thankful, and we expect to hear from you after your arrangements have been entirely completed in this regard.

the London and River Plate Bank, with which Joh. Berenberg, Gossler & Co. did business together in South America. In Amsterdam, N. V. Nederlandsche Handelsmaatschappij was particularly important; Joh. Berenberg, Gossler & Co. were general agents for the company. And again, one of the partners travelled to Russia, where favourable opportunities arose after the outbreak of the Russo-Japanese War (1904–1905) as long as the necessary caution was exercised when it came to the sometimes rather odd conventions in place there. When gathering information on Russian companies, the first question was typically: "Is the bookkeeping European or Asiatic?" It was worth being well-informed when dealing with Russia, to ensure good returns on investments such as the Maikop oil operation.

Staff Shortage

The workload had become somewhat overwhelming for the partners, and management was simply too small to keep pace. Gossler & Co., closed the Boston company in 1891 despite the favourable business situation because John B. and Ernst Gossler could not find a suitable manager. The New York office was shut down in 1880 after clearing and settling John Henry's speculative transactions. On 1 January 1892, John B.'s oldest son, John Jr. (1866–1943), was made partner with a profit share of 10 percent.

On 5 July 1893, Ernst Gossler died from blood poisoning. His early death – he was just 55 – affected everyone who knew him. Uncle Wilhelm Gossler wrote to Ernst's brother: "… and if I am not mistaken, even on the stock market, where everything is so much about material things and envy is rampant, your blessed brother leaves behind no enemies." Ernst Gossler's death left a noticeable gap in the company; John von Berenberg-Gossler missed his friendship, his experience and his advice.

It wasn't until 1898 that reinforcement came at the management level when John B.'s son, Cornelius (1874–1953), became a partner. From 1903 onwards, the sons each received 25 percent and John B. 50 percent, increasingly one of his sons now did the travelling for John B.

Given the current business volume, an even broader base in company management would have been advantageous, as was the case at M. M. Warburg & Co., where several brothers with an exceptional knack for business

The partners' holdings:
50 % John v. Berenberg-Gossler
25 % John v. Berenberg-Gossler jr.
25 % Cornelius v. Berenberg-Gossler

headed up the company. However, it was not customary to take on partners who were not relatives and there was no one else in the family: John B.'s second son, Paul, was a farmer; the fifth, Herbert, became a doctor and Andreas, the fourth son, was still in training. Of the sisters, Julie, the oldest, married the civil servant Gustav Jakob Kirchenpauer; the second, Frances, married the officer, landowner and passionate ornithologist Hans Freiherr von Berlepsch, who to the delight of everyone, enriched the Niendorf estate with several bird species but provided no assistance in the company. Only the husband of Marianne, Johannes Theodor Merck, offered indirect support for a brief time. In 1894, he associated with a man from Buenos Aires from Duhnkrack & Merck, in which Joh. Berenberg, Gossler & Co. had invested as a limited partner, and the investment remained intact when Merck withdrew two years later because he was offered the job as director at Hapag.

Business or Politics

Starting in 1908, the main business responsibilities rested on the shoulders of Cornelius von Berenberg-Gossler. That year, John Jr. left the company, but not voluntarily: John B. terminated the partnership in anger because his son was elected into the senate on 20 January. For the father, politics and business were not to mix, and that was understandable to a certain extent as the duties of a senator had evolved and increased. During the swearing-in ceremony of the new senator, which was as festive as ever and took place in the imperial hall in the town hall, Mayor Johann Georg Mönckeberg outlined the most pressing issues of the Hanseatic city to the new senator.

John jr. is elected senator and resigns his position at the company

    The first challenge was the redevelopment of entire city districts, which, scandalously enough, was still not finished. The catastrophic living conditions in these city districts had remained virtually unchanged for over 300 years, and in 1892, the conditions led to a cholera epidemic. Robert Koch, who had discovered the cholera pathogen, travelled from Berlin to Hamburg and made the shameful conditions known outside of Hamburg's city limits: "I forget that I am in Europe." It was not until after this incident that the Senate drew up a redevelopment programme. While the relics of the Middle Ages were being removed in Hamburg, in other cities construction had already gotten underway on elevated railways and subways. Another task, which the mayor

In 1892 Hamburg was in the grip of a cholera epidemic: disinfection crews in action

discussed, was the transformation of Hamburg's centre to a "city", another expansion of the port and deliberating on all issues relating to the Empire, especially tax laws.

The mayor concluded his speech during the swearing-in ceremony with the words: "My honourable Herr von Berenberg-Gossler! From these brief comments, you can see how important the issues are which you will be working on and for which you will have to find solutions. You have been elected into the senate based on the confidence of your fellow citizens … You are from a family, which for several generations, has produced a number of exceptional citizens of our city and more than one richly deserved member of the senate. You have grown up in the old Hamburg tradition where the highest honour of a citizen of Hamburg is to devote time and effort to the welfare of the home city by putting aside personal preferences and interests." But unlike previous generations of the family, for whom public duties and business duties went hand-in-hand quite naturally and often complemented each other, John Jr. had to decide between business and politics.

Cornelius was very upset about John's departure, as his brother, who spoke several languages fluently, was not just a kind partner and skilful diplomat, but also an excellent banker. For years he had co-managed the company as the anticipated successor of John B. and especially in Central America had an excellent business track record. In John's place, the younger brother, Andreas, joined the company. In 1910, in addition to John B. with 60 percent, Cornelius with 25 percent and Andreas with 10 percent, a long-standing employee, G. Tiedemann, had a share of 5 percent. But Andreas' contribution was not helping the business, and John B. was no longer resilient due to his age.

In October 1912, it looked for a moment as though John would return to the company, as his career as a senator was at risk of coming to an unusual end: to better view a race in Horn, Count Königsmarck climbed on a chair at the Union Club, and after repeated requests did not bring him down, a policeman was called to remove him. Königsmarck thought his honour had been violated and challenged the chairman of the race club board to a duel, of which John Berenberg-Gossler was a member. Attempts to intervene failed on account of Königmarck's persistence, and John ultimately accepted the challenge. The exchange of fire was, fortunately, without bloodshed. It took place on 17 September 1912 in a forest near Wittenberge and had unforeseeable repercussions. Duels were forbidden according to the criminal code and as John was a reserve officer, a Prussian military court sentenced him to three months in prison. But a "delinquent" senator was unthinkable, and so the alternative was either to resign, or petition the king of Prussia for pardon. The Senate decided in favour of the latter, and the majority of the population obviously agreed, as can be inferred from contemporary press reports as John von Berenberg-Gossler was considered to be a very competent senator and was allowed to stay by the grace of Prussia and to the detriment of the company.

Cornelius was left to manage the business of the company alone. His father had withdrawn from the company's business a few years earlier and pursued his intellectual interests, particularly literature and history. And towards the end of his life, he often voiced his concern over the possibility of a war with England and France.

On the Eve of the War

After Bismarck's dismissal in 1890, German foreign policy became much less predictable. John B. was always complaining that with the abandonment of the German-Russian Reinsurance Treaty, the traditional commitment in the east had ceased while a rapprochement of France to Russia had been promoted. Moreover, he pleaded – unlike his son John – for a colonial policy that was as reserved as possible with a view to not disrupting the understanding with England. The English became disgruntled with the "Kruger Telegramme" of 1896 and the "Daily Telegraph Affair" of 1908. In addition to the conflicts of interest in the colonial policy, there was an abrupt and threatening tone in German foreign policy, which was geared primerily to the "insatiable appetite of the english." The fleet policy of the German Empire under Alfred von Tirpitz fuelled the English fear of a rivalry with Germany on the world's oceans and promoted a rapprochement between France and England. The relationship with Russia was strained by German plans for a Baghdad railway in 1911, new customs regulations which excluded Russian grain from Germany and the backing of Austria.

This foreign policy brought about such deterioration in the diplomatic position of Germany in Europe, fearing a ring of superpowers threatening to surround Germany, thoughts turned as early as 1905 to a pre-emptive war against France. Although England had shown willingness to talk – in 1912 there were negotiations regarding a halt to fleet building and in 1914, an agreement was reached on the Baghdad question – the German military was soon planning for a war on two fronts, which would emerge as the Schlieffen Plan. England had indicated that in the event of war on the continent, it would not accept Germany's hegemony. Russia's desire for the straits, its support of Serbia against Austria as well as France's goal of recapturing Alsace-Lorraine were other additional trouble spots.

The End of an Era

John B. did not live to see how accurate his pessimistic prognoses were. John Freiherr von Berenberg-Gossler Sr. died on 8 December 1913. He left behind a fortune of over 40 million marks to his children, largely in the form of widely-

Kaiser Wilhelm II's "Kruger Telegramme" of 1896 incensed the British

Ausw. Amt ... 122

n. 3t Januar 1896

Berlin den 3 Januar 1896

79

Präsident Krüger

Pretoria

Ich spreche Ihnen Meinen aufrichtigen Glückwunsch aus, daß es Ihnen ohne an die Hülfe befreundeter Mächte zu appelliren, mit Ihrem Volke gelungen ist, in eigener Thatkraft gegenüber den bewaffneten Schaaren, welche als Friedensstörer in Ihr Land eingebrochen sind, den Frieden wiederherzustellen und die Unabhängigkeit ... zu wahren.

... die Unabhängigkeit des Landes gegen Angriffe von Außen

spread shareholdings and a company which was among the most distinguished in Hamburg. Under his management, as the *Hamburgische Correspondent* wrote on 9 December, the company had developed far beyond its previous scope. And the *Hamburger Nachrichten* on the same day reasoned: "With Freiherrn von Berenberg-Gossler's death, the merchants here have lost one of their most noble representatives. The great standing of his company is based not just in cultivating old tradition, but to a large extent, on the truly exemplary way he managed the business. His refinement and business acumen are to be credited with the fact that Joh. Berenberg, Gossler & Co., even in times of bank concentrations and the advancement of large banks, was undisputedly able to maintain its distinguished rank in the echelons of Hamburg's high finance."

Schrift

On 7 September 1911, Hamburg's Elbe
Tunnel was officially opened

IN THE SHADOW OF WARS AND CRISES
CORNELIUS VON BERENBERG-GOSSLER
1874–1953

In World War I

After the death of Freiherr John von Berenberg-Gossler, management of the company passed to his sons, Cornelius (1874–1953) and Andreas (1880–1938). Their shares in 1913 were 2,637,450 and 307,996 mark respectively. To Cornelius' disappointment, the involvement in the company was similar to the figures. To put it more bluntly; the primary responsibility for the company continued to rest on his shoulders.

Cornelius von Berenberg-Gossler had enjoyed a sound merchant training at Barings in London, and thereafter, in keeping with family tradition, he had worked for a longer period at other affiliated companies abroad. When his father died, Cornelius was almost 40 years old and had been a partner for 16 years. He had a seat on the board of directors of the "Berliner Handelsgesellschaft" since 1912. As the successor of his father, he was appointed to various supervisory boards, including that of the "Vereinsbank", "Ilseder Hütte", "Peiner Walzwerk" and "Blohm & Voss". In addition, he was part of the regional committee of the "Reichsbank". In July 1907, he was appointed general consul of the Kingdom of Bavaria.

General consul of the Kingdom of Bavaria

Since 1898, Cornelius had been married to Nadia Clara von Oesterreich, a daughter of Constantin von Oesterreich and his wife Clara Dorothea (née Brandt). The families had long been acquainted with each other, both on personal and professional levels, and the same was true for the family of Nadia's mother: Joh. Berenberg, Gossler & Co. had maintained good ties with Wilhelm Brandt in Arkhangelsk and Petersburg since the founding in 1806; the successor William Brandt's Sons & Co. in London was one of the closest business associates.

Cornelius and Nadia had known each other since childhood, and their marriage, which produced six children, was a particularly happy one. Cornelius had inherited the property in Niendorf and the title of *Freiherr* (baron) which came with it, and so in accordance with old Hamburg tradition, the family lived in the city in winter on Fontenay, and spent the summer outside of Hamburg in Niendorf.

From 1 January 1913 right up to his death in 1953, Cornelius von Berenberg-Gossler kept a diary. With brief entries in point form, it provides a look into the life and attitude of a Hamburg merchant and banker, whose integrity and free thinking in the upheavals of those 40 years remained unchallenged.

Hamburg prepares for World War I: the 76th Infantry Regiment heads for the front

Cornelius Baron von Berenberg-Gossler (1874–1953) was co-owner of the bank from 1898 to his death

At heart, Cornelius was a monarchical liberal and was full of hope that reason would prevail in politics. Like his father, he complained that the Reinsurance Treaty with Russia had not been extended and that the German Empire was seeking a stronger tie with the Austrians. For a long time he thought a war was unlikely: political crises were nothing new and as for German foreign policy, which was increasingly in the hands of the military, the parliament and the general public were often only informed to an extent which suited the purposes of the army command. It was not easy to evaluate the situation.

When the Austrian heir to the throne, Franz Ferdinand, was murdered in Sarajevo on 28 June 1914 and the conflict between Serbia and Austro-Hungary, Germany's only ally, intensified, Cornelius still hoped for a diplomatic intervention. But when Austro-Hungary declared war on Serbia with Germany's backing, thus mobilising Russia, he, like the vast majority of the population, thought Germany's declaration of war on Russia was logical.

The optimism of the countless German war volunteers knew no boundaries, and in unwavering faith that the other party was to be blamed for the war, the English and the French mobilised themselves with a clear conscience.

Cornelius von Berenberg-Gossler, who was not conscripted as he had appendicitis, provided the war ministry "with provisions transported by car". Several times he drove with his heavily loaded 50 hp Mercedes to the Eastern and Western fronts and brought the soldiers goods sent by the German population to boost morale. With his friend Percy Lebenbaum, he was involved in financing a hospital train. In November 1915, as the Red Cross delegate in Kowno and Wilna, he took over "the management and supervision of the soldier's barracks to be set up on the front on Hindenburg's order."

Early on, he had assessed the situation realistically. The diary entry from 11 December 1914 read: "I have the feeling that lots of people are only talking optimistically about our situation in the war to give themselves and others courage." In the following months, he repeatedly doubted the credibility of the army reports.

War Economy

Financially, Germany was not prepared for the war. The increased *Reichs-kriegsschatz* (consisting of reparation payments made by France to the German Empire as per the Treaty of Frankfurt at the end of the Franco-Prussian war of 1871) of a nominal 240 million marks, which had been earmarked for mobilisation anyway, would have only lasted a few days gauged by the actual war costs of 165 billion marks. When the "Reichsbank" noticed that gold was being withdrawn fast and in large amounts shortly before mobilisation, it illegally lifted the gold redemption obligation on 31 July 1914. The backing of the currency was expanded considerably by "law" as a result of the possibility, to use Empire exchange and Empire treasury bonds with a term of up to three months. In this way, the Empire created unlimited access to central bank credit – a devastating move, which the inflationary development of the following years revealed. After a phase that saw the Empire take out short-term debts with the central bank, there was a "consolidation" as a result of the issuing of bonds, the main means of financing the war. The war bonds were initially viewed as a great investment; many people sold their material assets for them. Only a

Unter den Linden: Mobilisation began in Berlin on 31 July 1914

small portion had to be paid for in cash; the rest was procured by pledging bonds with the loan society of the Empire.

Just as in 1870/71, the government set up loan societies which were to act as auxiliary central banks. Cornelius von Berenberg-Gossler was appointed to the supervisory board of the newly created loan society in Hamburg, and the Hamburgische Bank von 1914, created in August, elected him to the supervisory board.

The Company during the War

After the war broke out, Cornelius von Berenberg-Gossler succeeded in recouping most of the roughly 36 million marks which the company had outstanding in acceptance credit with foreign banks. A total of 24 million marks could be secured notably through compensation transactions via Copenhagen and in connection with Hapag representatives there. Credits to Russian banks amounting to 9 million marks were lost, while 3 million marks were voluntarily paid back after the war by a South African company. Director Schwartz of the Vereinsbank sent congratulations when he learned on 22 January 1915 just how good the situation was for Joh. Berenberg, Gossler & Co.

While Cornelius was working in Wilna, the business was in the hands of his seasoned employees, with whom he was in constant contact. The authorised signatories Tiedemann, Ziem and Sandow had already worked under John B., and in 1917/1918, they celebrated their 25th anniversary as employees with powers of attorney.

Business dealings were only possible with neutral countries abroad. The most important cities were Copenhagen and Amsterdam, but also São Paulo, Buenos Aires and New York – until the Americans entered the war. On 16 July 1916, Cornelius noted in Wilna: "Ask Schulz & Rückgaber in New York via radio telegramme, whether a credit, which we [granted] last year in favour of Firma Arp & Co. in Rio de Janeiro can be increased. I'll telegraph approval to Hamburg, and from there an answer will be sent via radio telegraph to New York. Telegraphic communication with overseas is possible after all." Shortly thereafter, Cornelius requested to be dismissed from his voluntary nursing care duties because the company required his constant presence in Hamburg. Meanwhile, the economic situation in Germany had become catastrophic.

When the plight of the German military took a turn for the worse in 1916, the sale of war bonds gradually dried up. The ensuing bonds were assumed by the ministry of finance, which then printed banknotes. The mark exchange rate in neutral countries had fallen roughly one-quarter compared to 1914. The middle class lost its economic foundation, mass poverty increased. In 1917, the costs for the war reached 3 billion marks per month. The population was now starving.

Hamburg suffered more than other states. The English naval blockade, which cut off Hamburg from world trade traffic, was wreaking havoc. In 1913, Hamburg had been the third-largest port city in the world after London and New York, but towards the end of the war, the total tonnage sank to one-tenth of its pre-war level. The German commercial fleet had to be handed over in its entirety for military purposes. Maritime freight was arranged largely by foreign shipping companies; offices in Hamburg stood mostly empty during the war.

On 25 November 1916, Cornelius von Berenberg-Gossler noted another telegraph connection with Guatemala via New York. Next, the connection with North America was inevitably severed. Despite all concerns raised, Germany resumed unrestricted submarine warfare at the start of 1917; it had been interrupted in 1915 due to worldwide indignation over the sinking of the Lusitania. The hope was to break the naval blockade, to stop American supplies from reaching the entente and, in this way, to quickly end the war. But the results were all the more sobering: the US entered the war in 1917, providing the entente with unexpectedly large amounts of material and 2 million soldiers to the war effort. For centuries, the political, military and, in part, economic initiatives had emanated from Europe; the balance of power had now shifted in favour of the US.

After submarine warfare had been resumed, diplomatic relations to Latin American countries were served. Almost all of the ties Joh. Berenberg, Gossler & Co. had to the South American continent had been severed; only contact to Argentina could be maintained through Zurich.

The winter of 1917/18, the so-called *Steckrübenwinter* (turnip winter), remained etched in the collective memory as a particularly hard winter. On 17 February, Cornelius noted thankfully that authorised signatory Sandow had given him a leg of veal. In the spring, the groomed lawn in the garden at Niendorf became a potato bed, and in May of 1918, "the work to remove the confiscated copper" started on the façade of the office.

On 9 February 1918, Germany and the Ukraine agreed an end to hostilities in Brest-Litovsk

The Peace Treaty of Brest-Litovsk and the Defeat in the West

The developments in Russia were registered with relief: "Hopefully the revolution spreads further," wrote Cornelius on 15 March 1917. The hope was that Russia would withdraw from the war. On 16 April, Lenin arrived in St Petersburg from Swiss exile with official German support. A few weeks after the October Revolution, there was an armistice on 15 December, and on 3 March 1918 the Treaty of Brest-Litovsk was signed. Cornelius von Berenberg-Gossler took part in the conferences in Hamburg and Berlin, which dealt with the financial claims to Russia.

Successes were soon visible, and Hamburg merchants pinned all their hopes on business with Russia. In the conference room at Joh. Berenberg, Gossler & Co., a meeting about a Russian consortium took place on 24 April 1918. Five days later, the "Verein Hamburger Exporteure" (association of Hamburg exporters) advocated for the involvement in a company for trade with Ukraine. However, there were a number of difficulties as the English had

almost completely bought up German investments in Russian banks, and the imperial officials showed hardly any understanding for the interests of Hamburg's
foreign trade.

Cornelius now thought the war was
lost and considered every additional battle
to be a pointless sacrifice. The breakthrough
of the Allied Forces at Amiens on 8 August
1918, the "black day of the German army,"
paved the way for the defeat of the German
troops on the Western Front. A continuation of the war would be "madness", since
the peace conditions would as a consequence be even more humiliating, but,
as Cornelius wrote on 17 October: "… the lack of insight has already gotten us
into the most dreadful of positions."

Germany was not willing to accept the armistice demands of the entente, but the government had lost its authority. A sailor's revolt in Kiel spilled
over to large German cities and the Empire, with workers' and soldiers' coun-
cils being created. On 8 November, Bavaria was declared a republic, and on
9 November, the revolution reached Berlin. The emperor had to abdicate,
Philipp Scheidemann declared the republic, and the SPD chairman, Friedrich
Ebert, was named chancellor the same day. On 11 November 1918, the armistice was ultimately signed.

Philipp Scheidemann (1865–1939,
left) pronounced the end of the German Empire and, on 9 November
1918, proclaimed the Weimar Republic; the Social Democrat Friedrich
Ebert (1871–1925, right) became the
new Germany's first president

The Weimar Republic

In 1919, the Weimar Constitution was adopted. It was to guarantee a maximum of democracy, but contained a few sections that proved to be disastrous-
ly destabilising: proportional representation and the unproven possibility of
referendums and petitions for referendums were juxtaposed by far-reaching
emergency powers of the chancellor. Disputes over domestic policy rocked the
Weimar Republic right from the start, they were fought from the right and the
left, and only a few Germans were prepared to work towards establishing and
preserving democracy.

The "November Revolution" in Berlin: revolutionary soldiers at Brandenburg Gate on 9 November 1918

In Hamburg, the government was taken over by a workers' and sailors' council on 12 November 1918. The senate and parliament were dissolved, and at town hall, the red flag flew. However, after just six days, the workers' and sailors' council was forced to recognise that it was not up to the task of running a city with a million people. The famine in Hamburg endured even after the armistice. The English and French were unable to agree on Hamburg's reparation payments, the English demanded ships and the French wanted gold, which could not be used to buy food. Unemployment and hunger grew, plundering and strikes were the order of the day. On 16 March 1919, Hamburg elected a new parliament after universal and equal suffrage had been granted; for the first time, women were allowed to vote. The Social Democrats won the absolute majority, but in the new senate, they left half the seats to previous senators, including John von Berenberg Gossler, who went to Rome in 1920 as the German ambassador. For the merchants, a certain degree of continuity was maintained.

Cornelius became a member of the "Deutsche Volkspartei" (DVP), which in December 1918 – at the instigation of Gustav Stresemann – became the successor organisation to the National Liberal Party. The DVP entered the Senate Coalition of Democrats and Social Democrats in Hamburg in 1924. In the 1920 Reich election, the DVP received a 13.9 percent share of the vote, its biggest success; from 1923 to 1929 DVP member Gustav Stresemann was the foreign minister of the German Reich.

Cornelius von Berenberg-Gossler criticised the German domestic policy for not being democratic enough and for lacking a connection between the government and the people. For him, there was no question that liberal and democratic tendencies would dominate in the future and that the question of the workers would not be solved through humanitarian efforts and Christian charity. He continued to see himself as a monarchist, but made very critical comments on the memoirs of the emperor. "... how great is our fault that we let ourselves be led that way." (diary entry dated 18. November 1923)

In 1925, when Field Marshal von Hindenburg was elected president of the Reich at the age of 78, Cornelius feared that it would keep the memory of the war alive in countries outside of Germany, more importantly, he regarded the "victor from Tannenberg" to be politically inept and too old for the office. He regarded the preoccupation with the past and the discussion of responsibility for the war as pointless, "because nothing more could change the misfortune." For him, it was "far more important to look at how Germany would come out of the serious present situation."

Rioting in Hamburg during 1918

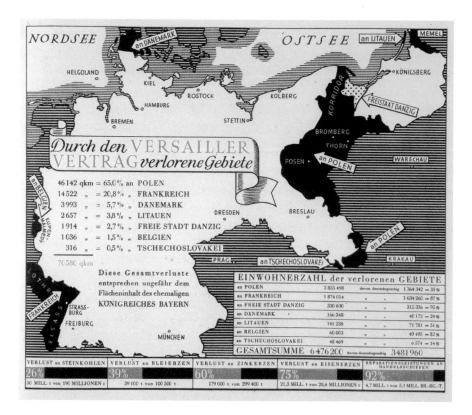

The Treaty of Versailles enforced major territorial losses for Germany

Inflation

On 22 June 1919, the German National Assembly accepted the Treaty of Versailles. Thus, it had to cede extensive territories as well as make considerable reparation payments to the victorious power, relinquish colonies to the League of Nations, lose 75 percent of the annual mining of zinc and iron ore and scale back its military to a minimal size. This treaty was perceived by many Germans as a humiliation and weighed heavily as a propaganda munition of the right on the democratic development of the Weimar Republic.

The US delegate who attended the negotiations of the treaty of Versailles – Henry Cabot Lodge – a distant relative of the Berenberg-Gosslers from Boston – criticised the treaty as being "unchristian" and was of the opinion that it would only create evil. The American Congress refused to ratify the treaty and any additional peace treaties and even returned German property it had confiscated back to Germany.

In addition to the reparation claims, the interest on the Germans' debt incurred during the war burdened the budget of the German Empire and spurred inflation. For 1918, the interest alone was 6.8 billion marks, which corresponded to 8–10 percent of the national income. The financial strains could hardly be compensated for with the rising tax revenues.

In an initial inflation phase from mid-November 1918 to March 1920, the circulation of paper money increased from 28.5 billion marks to 54.5 billion marks; the exchange rate of the mark to the dollar rose from 7.43 marks on 11 November 1919 to 103.75 marks on 9 February 1920. At Christmas 1920, the employees at Joh. Berenberg, Gossler & Co. received a package with flour, rice, fat and other food items instead of the usual cash gifts.

Travelling

Cornelius von Berenberg-Gossler travelled regularly to Berlin to participate in meetings of the board of directors the Berliner Handelsgesellschaft; there were important contacts moreover to the "Reichsbank" and to the "Darmstädter und Nationalbank". In Munich, he often paid a visit to the Bayerische Handelsbank, the Bayerische Vereinsbank, the Hypotheken- und Wechselbank, the Staatsbank and Merck, Finck & Co. August von Finck had worked as a trainee at Joh. Berenberg, Gossler & Co., and they had remain friends ever since.

Particularly pleasing were the visits to the Ilseder Hütte: The orders from the ironworks were so robust due to the large demand for steel that in 1919, dividends of 40 percent were paid out, and in 1921, the figure jumped to 60 percent.

60 percent dividend at the Ilseder Hütte steelworks

As the deputy chairman of the supervisory board, Cornelius arranged for the purchase of the coal mine *Friedrich der Große* in Herne together with Willy Meyer. Through the Ilseder Hütte, there were close contacts to VIAG (Vereinigte Industrieunternehmen AG) – an establishment of the Empire to look after companies and receivables owned by the Empire – which had a 25 percent investment in the Ilseder Hütte.

Just as the situation in Hamburg in 1919 had become somewhat consolidated, Cornelius went on his first business trip after the war. The trip took him to

Loose change during the hyper-inflation of 1923: 20,000,000,000 marks

Deutsche Waren-Treuhand established

Amsterdam and Rotterdam. The reception was friendly everywhere; however, the information, on the other hand, sobering. Paul May from Lippmann, Rosenthal & Co. said, "To start with, Germany should pay in cash and in this way raise its credit." May advised against going to London as there was still a lot of animosity toward the Germans.

In February 1920, Joh. Berenberg, Gossler & Co., M. M. Warburg & Co., Mendelssohn & Co., L. Behrens & Söhne and other companies were among the founders of the Deutschen Waren-Treuhand AG; Cornelius joined the supervisory board. It was an organisation based on trust for credits which countries abroad were willing to give to Germany.

That same year, Cornelius embarked on a second trip, this time a gratifying visit to the Netherlands, which was aimed mainly at the Nederlandschen Handelmaatschappij. In October 1920, he went to Scandinavia, where he was able to revive the good pre-war ties.

In July 1921, Cornelius travelled to England for the first time since war. His first stop was at Baring Brothers, who had been business partners and friends of the company for more than 100 years (see p. 179). It was from Kleinwort, Benson & Co. that Joh. Berenberg, Gossler & Co. received the first reimbursement credit after the war for á meta-financing of Hamburg trade. The dealings with Barings, a large acceptance business on a joint-account basis, got underway a little later. This made it possible for the company to give credit to companies in Hamburg and Magdeburg. The trip to England was a complete success, and business with South America was picking up again. However, there was little time to celebrate as inflation was rampant in Germany. When Cornelius returned from England at the start of September 1921, 130 marks had to be paid for one dollar.

The nominal value of the new republic's stamps also surged dramatically

Hyperinflation

In April 1921, a reparation commission had set the amount of German payments at 269 billion marks. In Germany, there was much quarrelling over the extent to which it should comply with the demands of the victorious powers regarding reparation payments. The Fehrenbach government resigned over the issue in May 1921. The new government under Joseph Wirth accepted the ultimatum of the victorious powers for the payment of 1 billion Goldmark within 25 days. As a result of this policy of appeasement, the devaluation of the mark "continued in a panicky way"; on 12 September, the English Pound was noted at more than 400 marks.

Four days later, Cornelius travelled to Berlin together with Rudolf von Schröder and Max Warburg at the invitation of Chancellor Wirth "to talk about economic issues", which were understood as the relinquishing of industrial assets for a bond abroad." Yet even these measures could not stop inflation.

In particular, the French government under Raymond Poincaré was unwilling to entertain the German government's appeal for a delay. On the contrary, due to an alleged stoppage in German coal deliveries, which were one component of the German reparation payments to France, French and Belgian troops occupied the Ruhr region in January 1923. The German treasury was further burdened with the lack of tax revenues from this very important region, and the financing of the passive resistance against the occupation consumed additional funds.

In the middle of May 1923, the dollar was noted at 20,000 marks. By 15 November, the exchange rate skyrocketed to 4,200,000,000,000 marks (4.2 trillion Mark). For a streetcar ride to Niendorf, Cornelius had to pay 200,000 marks on 24 August; on 13 September, one pound of butter in Hamburg cost roughly 40 million marks. In 1922 and 1923, around 135 printing houses and 35 paper mills in Germany were focused on the printing of new banknotes.

The number of employees at Joh. Berenberg, Gossler & Co., which had fluctuated before the war between 20 and 30 people and after 1918 slowly increased, now rose quickly; the rapid decline of the mark necessitated an ongoing notation of the exchanges, which were changing by the minute. At the peak of the inflation, 400 employees were busy with "writing zeros", checking and counting emergency currency, coping with the crowds at the wickets and the very time-consuming task of processing cashless clearing.

400 employees count the zeros

On 2 August 1923, 200 billion marks in paper money was flown in from Berlin, and the "Vereinigung der Hamburger Banken und Bankiers", to which Joh. Berenberg, Gossler & Co. belonged, began printing its own means of payment on 10 August valuing 200 billion marks, but without significant effect. Using various measures, such as a *Devisenabgabe* for private individuals, of which Cornelius thought nothing, Stresemann's government tried to stop the German currency from sliding further but to no avail. In Hamburg, there was unrest, but an attempt to organise a general strike failed.

There were winners during this inflation period. As a result of credit manipulations and delayed account payments given the rapid inflation, a lot of money was to be made in the shortest of time frames, and debtors soon took on the share capital of their suppliers. Hugo Stinnes, acquired until his death in April 1924 majority shareholdings in over 1,200 companies at home and abroad in every possible branch within an extremely short period of time. In "Simplicissimus", a weekly German satirical magazine, Saint Peter warned: "Stinnes is coming. So, watch out fellows, otherwise the whole business will be his in 14 days!"

As a result of a wage adjustment, workers were initially able to be compensated for inflation. The middle class, in contrast, was almost completely eliminated: small merchants and business people became welfare recipients over night. Along with the impoverishment of the middle class, grew the susceptibility for extreme political orientations, which would contribute to the failure of the Weimar Republic a few years later.

Stabilisation

On 23 October 1923, street fighting broke out in Hamburg; workers were threatening with more strikes and closures. That same day, a precedent-setting decision was made to establish "a bank in Hamburg, which issues covered methods of payment with money and foreign currency. Probably the first bank of its kind in Germany." More than any industry, it was the shipping industry that had been urging the founding of the Hamburgischen Bank von 1923 – the officers on Hapag steamships could not even pay the 5 cents for the subway in New York with their monthly salary when they wanted to visit relatives. Cornelius von Berenberg-Gossler was elected to the supervisory board of the new institute, his brother, John, the former ambassador in Rome, took over the role of chairman of the board.

Of the 120 companies involved, roughly one-third were banks and two-thirds trading and industrial companies as well as shipping companies. The capital amounted to 12 billion marks divided into 120 shares, each worth 100 million marks, for which every shareholder accepted a guarantee obligation in the amount of 100,000 Goldmark. Of this, 25 percent had to be paid in dollars (1 dollar = 4.20 Goldmark). The sum paid in dollars was invested for a short period in New York banks, and with the interest earned, the fees were paid. The customers – companies, but also the city, which had stable foreign exchange from port revenues – deposited their dollars into the bank and in return received banknotes, which bore the name *Hamburgische Verrechnungsmark*: this corresponded to the Goldmark and its parity to the dollar. Banknotes were covered up to the full amount by foreign currency, which remained the possession of the bank up until they were redeemed at the bank. Due to its stable value, the new money soon enjoyed great popularity beyond the borders of Hamburg.

Meanwhile, there were disagreements in Berlin regarding the stabilisation of the mark, which resulted in pegging the currency on material backing. On 13 October 1923, the *Verordnung über die Errichtung der deutschen Rentenbank* was announced. The new currency, the Rentenmark, was based

In October 1923 street barricades were erected in the Barmbek district of Hamburg

John jr. becomes Chairman of "Hamburgische Bank" von 1923

on gold, but did not have any legal tender. The introduction of the Renten-mark was planned for 15 November. On this day, the dollar exchange rate was noted as 4.2 billion marks. At the suggestion of the "Reichsbank", Hjalmar Schacht, the new currency commissioner, determined that

1 dollar = 4.20 billion marks = 4.20 Rentenmark

1 billion mark = 1 Rentenmark

The "Reichsbank" immediately refused to accept any emergency money. The speculation against the Rentenmark collapsed within a few days, and on 3 December, the New York exchange rate was set at 4.20 marks.

Cornelius von Berenberg-Gossler did not have much hope in the Rent-enmark, "it lacks really any real tangible base … there is only one backing for a currency and that is gold, and we don't have gold anymore." But Germany soon had gold again. The prosperous American market had found a suitable sphere for investments in the financially weak but highly sophisticated indus-trial Germany. With the Dawes Plan – named after the American lawyer and banker Charles Gates Dawes, who received the Nobel Peace Prize for his plan in 1925 – which was adopted in August 1924, not only were the German repa-ration payments redefined with new terms of payment, but there was a stream of American bonds to stabilise the German currency. The Dawes Plan was the first attempt after the Treaty of Versailles to reintegrate Germany into the global economy. The political right denounced it as an enslavement policy on account of the monitoring terms imposed on the Germans. The left saw the unloved Republic as a colony of the New York Stock Exchange. Yet, Germa-ny became a reliable debtor for the years that followed. In 1924, the return to the gold standard was possible, inflation had ended.

But the Dawes Plan was operating on the assumption that the global economy would expand and that Germany would soon have a balance of pay-ments surplus.

As neither happened, the reparation payments had to be raised in for-eign funds. Debt increased. Despite the shaky situation, prosperity developed. The violence of the political conflicts temporarily subsided, the people were relieved, and cultural life in large German cities experienced an unprecedented recovery, and the "Golden" Twenties began.

The "Golden" Twenties

The German Empire collapsed and with it, the old authority and the aristocratic canon of values. Personal interaction and customs experienced a profound change. The traditions and institutions of the past seemed to have been finally overcome or lost and there was a spirit of optimism, a liberation and challenge in which everything seemed possible: The "modern era" was heralded in.

The majority of emerging artistic and scientific movements, including Constructivism and Expressionism in painting and literature, relativistic physics, psychoanalysis and depth psychology, sociology of recognition and atonal music – had existed prior to the war, but it was not until during the Weimar Republic that they permeated public consciousness. The generous spending from the public sector in the cultural area, such as on elaborate museum buildings and exhibits, contributed to the spread of these movements.

Otto Dix (1891–1969) was the painter associated with Germany's "Golden" Twenties: his triptych "Grossstadt" (Metropolis; detail from the centre panel) was completed in 1927–28

Starting in 1925, the Bauhaus movement in Dessau spawned major new design ideas

The architects and artists of the Bauhaus, led by Walter Gropius, achieved great international acclaim. Steel, concrete and glass became the new materials for buildings. Bauhaus design and productions also included industrial design and furniture joinery.

As a result of general mechanisation, the working world and leisure time began to change radically. Diesel and electric motors revolutionised shipping and agriculture, while in offices, typewriters and accounting machines were increasingly commonplace. At the start of the 1930s, the first punch-card machine appeared. The 1920s were the golden age of German film and weekly newsreels; the first radios were produced. The enthusiasm for jazz as a dance and entertainment genre corresponded to the general acceleration of life. Major events, such as at the Berliner Sportpalast, were growing in popularity. However, many German intellectuals remained deeply sceptical of mechanisation and modernity, and when it came to the rejection of the republic, most of them were of one mind, regardless of their assorted political views.

"It is not good if mankind overexerts its intellect and tries to order things with the help of reason, which are not yet even accessible to reason. That is when ideals arise like that of the American or that of the Bolschevik, which are both extremely reasonable and yet violate and rob life in a dreadful way because they simplify so naively. The image of people, once held as a high ideal, is about to become a cliché." These are the words which German author Hermann Hesse put in the mouths of his characters in *Steppenwolf,* which was published in 1927.

The mechanisation and rationalisation tendencies were also mirrored in politics and society. Company mergers led to even larger companies; organisation and centralised management – even of the masses – were characteristic of everyday life.

And even larger German banks followed the trend of amalgamation. Increasingly, they took over country banks which were linked to them in interest groups and established an extensive branch network across Germany. As a result of their involvement in the war financing effort, savings banks and credit cooperatives had entered the securities business by way of bonds, and by doing so, had taken an important step in the direction of a universal bank. For private bankers, these developments meant a further restriction to their scope of activity and made resorting to niches imperative. In the crisis years after 1919, it became clear that the foundations of many private banks were too weak, but business continued to bloom.

The precursor of modern data processing: the punch-card machine invented by Herman Hollerith (1860–1929)

The Company from 1924–1929

For Joh. Berenberg, Gossler & Co., the period from 1924 up until the economic crisis of 1929 was a positive one; there were only upheavals right after the stabilisation. After the introduction of the Rentenmark and later the Reichsmark based on the gold standard, from April 1924 onwards the "Reichsbank" refused to grant banks further rediscounting facilities with the aim of avoiding a repeat of the catastrophic inflation. The banks now had to rely on their own funding and had to be very cautious when it came to granting credit. Some of their customers got into difficulties. Moreover, there was speculation when the French Franc began falling. Many companies, especially in the metal industry, collapsed. But Joh. Berenberg, Gossler & Co. managed to weather these difficulties without major losses.

In these years, particularly close business contacts came about with the Berliner Handelsgesellschaft, Vereinsbank in Hamburg, with Simon Hirsch-

Close cooperation

land, Merck, Finck & Co., Mendelssohn & Co., Berlin, and the old bank L. Behrens & Söhne. And with the Reichskredit-Gesellschaft, which was founded in 1925 by VIAG, friendly contacts also emerged.

Cornelius von Berenberg-Gossler ended the unproductive collaboration with his brother Andreas in 1922, but took on his nephew as partner, Heinrich Burchard, who had been with the company since 1913. In January 1923, Walter Gleich became a partner. As a former general agent of Arthur Brandt in London, Gleich brought with him many new foreign contacts. Both partners did not have any capital in the company and were only then liable if Cornelius von Berenberg Gossler dropped out. The capital of the company consisted of private assets of Cornelius von Berenberg-Gossler, which were made up of land and shares. The will of his father, John B., had been drawn up without any regard to the company, so that Cornelius was often forced to compensate family members, or to buy shares in the Ilseder Hütte to maintain the family property.

The year 1924 started with business trips for all of the partners. Burchard went to London in January, Gleich went to New York in February and Cornelius travelled to Vienna and Budapest in March. During a stay in London at the end of 1924, Gaspard Farrer, the partner at Barings, said: "It is not only friendship between our firms, but more than that: a sort of partnership. Besides Kidder, Peabody, you are the nearest to us."

Visit to New York and Boston

Kidder, Peabody & Co. had taken over from Baring, Magoon & Co., which 40 years earlier had assumed a large part of the business of Gossler & Co. in Boston. In the spring of 1925, Cornelius von Berenberg-Gossler visited numerous business acquaintances in New York and Boston, and Kidder, Peabody & Co., too, with whom a very close collaboration evolved, particularly when it came to the financing of the cotton business.

Company operations focused on the ongoing short-term business involving the financing of import and export.

In the 1920s, the company still did a considerable amount of business in commodities, notably with Brazil and Pernambuco, and the goods department was still profitable. But towards the end of the decade, there was a general decline in the goods trade. In 1929, the partners finally gave up the goods trade and sold the storage area at Sandthor Quay.

Up until 1929, the profits of the bank Joh. Berenberg, Gossler & Co. were around 300,000 to 400,000 marks, and at the start of 1929, the bank was

The Sandthor Quay in Hamburg's free port during the early 20th century. In 1929, Joh. Berenberg Gossler & Co. moved out of the warehouse located there

on it solid footing. Nevertheless, Cornelius was concerned about the future of his company.

One reason might have been the fact that the economic situation abroad had worsened, and in the early summer of 1929, a new crisis was looming on the horizon. The diary kept by Cornelius reported company collapses all over the world. The banking sector as a whole was uneasy because – despite the money that had flowed in from abroad between 1924 and 1929 – there was a lack of liquid funds. Stresemann, who at one time had been the committed supporter of the Dawes Plan, came to the realisation in 1928 that "in the recent years we have lived from pumped money in Germany … We are not only militarily disarmed, we are also financially disarmed. We no longer have any funds of our own."

The development of costs and the strengthening of capital in the interest of industrial credit supply were posing even greater difficulties for the banks.

The industrial production capacities remained largely underutilised, and the banks were forced to restructure numerous companies. In response, a range of fusion models were put forward at major banks in Berlin and Hamburg.

The two most significant fusions in 1929 were the "Commerz- und Privatbank" with the "Disconto-Gesellschaft". In the course of the latter, the "Norddeutsche Bank" in Hamburg, the "A. Schaaffhausensche Bankverein" in Cologne, the "Rheinische Kreditbank" in Mannheim and the "Süddeutsche Disconto-Gesellschaft" in Mannheim merged into a new institution, the "Deutsche Bank und Disconto-Gesellschaft"; it was the largest fusion up until that point in the history of the German banking sector.

Wall Street in New York during the stock market crash of 24 October 1929

Stock Market Crash and the Depression

The most significant fusions had just been concluded when the stock market in New York crashed: the immense industrial production in the US had led to a terrific foreign trade surplus, and the dollar bonds scattered over the world were in the possession of debtor countries that could only pay their debts with new credits. England and France had considerable war debts to the US and intended on repaying them in part with the reparation payments they received from Germany and Austria. However, Austria's reparation payments had to be waived in 1921, and Germany was only able to pay with the help of American credit.

The over-production crisis in the US economy was accompanied by unrestrained speculation. The stock prices of American companies reached incredible heights only to start crashing down on 25 October 1929, Black Friday, into a bottomless pit. Within nine days, the North American stock exchange recorded losses of 15 billion USD.

"Black Friday" – the crisis in America spreads to Europe

The American crisis – which ultimately saw many banks change hands, or cease doing business altogether, hundreds of industrial companies disappear and the collapse of farming – spread quickly to Europe. Credits were terminated, the flow of American foreign bonds began to run dry, the turnover of European goods on the American market fell drastically, and it became increasingly difficult to come up with the interest and amortisation payments owed in dollars. Germany was especially hard hit. In 1929, the Young Plan, which replaced the Dawes Plan, took effect (named after Owen D. Young, American lawyer and business consultant), and brought about the liberation of the Rhineland region, lifting the financial controls, but left the financial burden on the German economy. The instalments were to be 1.7 to 2.1 billion marks for the next several years.

Even Joh. Berenberg, Gossler & Co. endured losses, as payments were suspended primarily among coffee and fur-trade companies. But the bank itself was basically not at risk. Nevertheless, Cornelius considered ways to structure his company so that it could survive the difficult times, and he came to the conclusion that leaning on a stronger institution would offer the best guarantee for a continuation.

Cornelius von Berenberg-Gossler turned to the "Darmstädter und Nationalbank", and on 1 April 1930, an agreement was signed, which contained a

"Cooperation Agreement" with the "Darmstädter und Nationalbank"

In 1929, people protested the consequences of the global economic crisis; here in October in the United States

clause about a "close friendship". Cornelius took up a position in the regional Hamburg committee of the Danat-Bank, to take over management together with the previous chairman, Max Gutschke, who became a co-owner at Joh. Berenberg, Gossler & Co.

The *Hamburger Fremdenblatt* commented positively on the agreement by noting that Joh. Berenberg, Gossler & Co. "could look back on a glorious tradition", was regarded as "an especially solid and carefully managed institution with reputable clients, which even in the period of inflation did not succumb to the temptations of an ambitious expansion policy". It contributed "in addition to its contacts abroad, mainly in South America, England and the Netherlands, more than anything a sophisticated reimbursement and credit business" to the new arrangement. As a result of its ties to the "Danat-Bank", the private bank received "the prestigious and financial weighty ties of friendship with a major bank of the rank and significance of the Berlin-based institution." The "Danat-Bank" came into being in 1922 as a result of a merger between of the "Nationalbank für Deutschland" and the "Bank für Handel und Industrie-Darmstädter Bank" which was established in 1853 and was devoted mainly to industry financing.

The crisis persisted. The burden of debt at numerous companies, whose interest in good economic times and full employment would have been quite acceptable, now became an insurmountable hurdle. Without the prospect of repayment, the banks had to bail out struggling companies with new credits. Eventually they wrote off the debts of these companies and instead included even larger share packages in their portfolio. Their portfolio of securities and real industrial investments rose considerably from 1929 onwards. When the "Norddeutsche Wollkämmerei", the worsted yarn spinning works in Bremen, and the department store group Karstadt in Berlin eventually ran into difficulties, the situation of the banks grew increasingly worrisome.

The crisis revealed that the expectations associated with the "friendship agreement" with the Danat-Bank could not be realised. After long and hard discussions in Berlin and Hamburg, a new agreement was signed on 1 April 1931. The business dealings of Joh. Berenberg, Gossler & Co. were now transferred to the "Darmstädter Bank" and "Nationalbank". As a member of the regional committee of the Danat-Bank, Cornelius was "to be in very close contact with our institution so that the long-standing clients and rich experience of its bank are maintained even in the dealings with our branch in Hamburg." The step towards dependence was very hard for Cornelius. He found comfort in a letter from Rudolf Gossler, the son of Ernst Gossler, who at one point, together with John B., had been an owner of the company: Rudolf assured him that this step taken at the right time was most certainly in accordance with the wishes of his forefathers.

Cornelius' main concern was initially to look out for his partners and employees, not all of whom were taken on by the "Danat-Bank": Heinrich Burchard and Walter Gleich received a severance package. In 1934, Burchard transitioned to management at the "Deutsche Bank" in Hamburg; on 1 January 1933, Gleich began working for "Deutsches Kohlenkontor" in Mülheim/Ruhr. Cornelius von Berenberg-Gossler paid the pensions of the employees from his pocket. The office on Adolphsplatz was sold to the "Hamburger Sparkasse von 1827", to ensure that all obligations vis-à-vis the employees could be met.

Everyone tried to earn a crust somehow: rooms for rent in Berlin

The Bank Crisis

Shortly thereafter, the international economic crisis escalated into a German banking crisis. As a result of the reparation payments, high credit interest for foreign money and unproductive expenses – notably from the public sector – the German capital account was thrown off balance to an even greater extent. People had been living on credit and had simply not saved.

By way of an emergency decree, the Brüning government then tried to balance the budget through cuts to expenditures and tax increases, but as a result of these deflationary measures, hardships worsened: demand went down, unemployment continued to rise and the capital flight from Germany continued to grow.

In April 1931, an increasing number of American shares were sold in Europe and an immense flow of capital went from Europe to America. And while post-inflation Germany still could have raised long-term foreign bonds, the foreign capital had only been available on a short-term basis since the start of the economic crisis. Short-term foreign debt reached a high, which would not have been absorbed given a sudden withdrawal of funds.

The situation was critical. On 21 March 1931, Germany and Austria agreed on a customs union. In response, French banks declined to extend their financial acceptance credits of roughly 300 million USD, which they had granted to Austrian and German banks. The customs union had to be shut down, but disaster could no longer be avoided. On 11 May, the annual financial statement from the "Österreichische Creditanstalt" in Vienna was announced: the largest Austrian banking institution posted a loss of 140 million Schilling or 37 million Reichsmark. Following the debacle, a lot of foreign currency was withdrawn from German banks; in June 1931, the "Reichsbank" lost 1.5 billion Reichsmark in money and foreign exchange.

Everywhere, withdrawals continued to be the order of the day, even at the "Danat-Bank". Various cooperation and fusion suggestions were voiced, but they did not meet with approval from the *Reich* government, nor from the "Reichs-Kredit-Gesellschaft". On 11 July, when foreign currency withdrawals at the "Reichsbank" increased sharply and the capital flight from Germany intensified, the "Reichsbank" tightened its credit restrictions. A request by the Danat-Bank to rediscount 250 million Reichsmark financial bills was declined.

On Monday, 13 July 1931, the Danat-Bank stopped issuing funds. The following announcement was made on a notice board. … "The imperial government has authorised us to explain that it … will ensure a smooth processing of the business dealings of the Darmstädter Bank by way of a guarantee for all deposits …" But there was no calm to speak of as the run on the banks had began. The government declared the following days to be bank holidays and closed the stock exchanges until the end of the week. Yet panic endured, and almost all of the banks were essentially insolvent – their creditworthiness was reflected merely by the date of the bankruptcy.

Restructuring

On 21 July 1931, teller cages reopened the banks; however, individuals received no more than 100 Reichsmark from a bank account or 20 Reichsmark from a savings account. While the fate of major German banks and savings banks was being negotiated, a conference was held in London at the proposal of the American president, Herbert Clark Hoover, to discuss economic issues. On 25 July 1931, a committee was set up under the chairmanship of the president of the "Reichsbank", Hans Luther, which ultimately reached an agreement with England and America, whereby all short-term credits were subject to a six-month stand-still. Thus, the foundation for further agreements was created. On 14 August, stand-still negotiations began in Basel with all interested creditor countries. At the end of July there were still 23 billion Reichsmark in foreign funds in Germany, of which 8 billion Reichsmark were available on a short-term basis. On 19 August 1931, a general agreement was reached: as a result of the Basel Agreement, short-term German foreign debts of over 6.3 million Reichsmark were deferred. This stand-still agreement was extended repeatedly in the years that followed.

At the beginning of August, banking business resumed, including at the Danat-Bank, and on 3 September, the stock markets finally opened again but there was still no futures trading nor trade with ongoing quotations.

On 19 September 1931, Brüning's government ordered state supervision of banking and announced an amendment to the law on stock market companies. Shortly thereafter, reforms were introduced for to the savings banks and an effort was made to restructure major banks: the "Barmer Bankverein" merged with the "Commerz- und Privatbank", and at the start of 1932, the "Danat-Bank" merged with the "Dresdner Bank" at the instruction of the bank supervisory authority. With the merger, the fate of Joh. Berenberg, Gossler & Co. was initially unclear. But at the end of June 1932, Cornelius von Berenberg-Gossler received the sole right of disposal again for the company. The "Dresdner Bank" ensured the option of being involved up to 1 July 1937.

Cornelius rented an office for his company on Am Ness 1, but he could not – and did not want to – resume his earlier dealings as the international crisis went on, and German foreign trade continued to experience great difficulties. On 20 September 1931, the English government unexpectedly resolved to depart from the gold standard as the gold and currency stocks of the Bank of England had been fused together. The exchange rate of the pound sank rapidly as a result. The German government did not get involved with the devaluation, but rather kept the mark "stable", which had a disastrous effect particularly on the German export and shipping. Meanwhile, political developments in Germany embarked on a path which made active business dealings appear inadvisable for Cornelius.

Sole right of disposition restored to Cornelius von Berenberg-Gossler

The End of the Weimar Republic

In Hamburg, three representatives of the National Socialist German Worker's Party (NSDAP) were elected into parliament – for the first time – in 1928. The majority of the people in Hamburg saw this as a temporary phenomenon, but during the economic crisis, notably in the conflicts surrounding the Young Plan, national socialist propaganda was increasingly gaining momentum and the constitution of the Weimar Republic was losing its authority.

Section 48 of the constitution allowed the president of the *Reich*, "in order to maintain public safety and order" to override crucial basic rights and, where necessary, to intervene with the help of "armed force". At the height of the economic crisis, Hindenburg's Chancellor Brüning made full use of the emergency decree in Section 48, and not just when it came to the restructuring of banks: In July 1930, he ordered the dissolution of the Reichstag against the will of parliament.

President Paul von Hindenburg (1847–1934) dissolved the German Reichstag on 30 July 1930, with Chancellor Heinrich Brüning (1885–1970) signing the authorisation

REICHSTAG
18 JUL 30

Verordnung

des Reichspräsidenten über die Auflösung des Reichstags

vom 18. Juli 1930.

Nachdem der Reichstag heute beschlossen hat, zu verlangen, dass meine auf Grund des Artikel 48 der Reichsverfassung erlassene Verordnung, vom 16. Juli ~~über Deckungsmaßnahmen für den Reichshaushalt 1930~~ ausser Kraft gesetzt würde, löse ich auf Grund Artikel 25 der Reichsverfassung den Reichstag auf.

Berlin, den 18. Juli 1930.

Der Reichspräsident

von Hindenburg

Der Reichskanzler

Dr. Brüning

Gunfights between Communists, National Socialists and the police resulted in the death of 18 people on 17 July 1932, the so-called Bloody Sunday of Altona

Cornelius von Berenberg-Gossler wrote on 1 August 1930: "Only squabbling in the bourgeois camp, while the risks that threaten us are growing and growing." New elections in September 1930 brought a tremendous polarisation of the political spectrum at the expense of the centre and the German National People's Party (DNVP). The SPD (Social Democrat) remained the strongest party, but following right behind was the NSDAP (National Socialist) with the KPD (Communist Party) behind them. Brüning continued to govern with a minority cabinet, because the Social Democrats tolerated him. However, activities outside of parliament from both the right wing and the left wing were gaining traction.

Cornelius von Berenberg-Gossler belonged to the minority of people who had read Hitler's *Mein Kampf*. He thought Hitler's settlement plans were illusory and anti-Semitism was despicable. On 1 December 1930, he noted the following after a speech made by Hitler before the *Nationalklub* at the Hotel Atlantic in Hamburg: "He enraptured the audience, but he did not make positive suggestions for improvement." In March 1932, after a speech by Hitler at

Sagebiel, he wrote: "Phrases, but again presented very skilfully." Yet in the parliamentary elections on 24 April 1932, the NSDAP emerged as the strongest party in Hamburg. Martial parades, mass demonstrations, street fighting and violent conflicts were the order of the day. The extreme parties provoked each other in an effort to force the state to intervene. In April 1932, Brüning attempted to put a stop to the increasing National Socialist violence by banning the paramilitary organisations of the NSDAP, the *Sturmabteilung* (SA) and *Sturmstaffel* (SS), but in June he was replaced by Franz von Papen. The ban on the SA and SS was lifted, the Reichstag was dissolved once again and new elections were held, which ultimately saw the NSDAP as the strongest party with 230 mandates.

In the Third Reich

On 30 January 1933, Hindenburg appointed Adolf Hitler as chancellor and on the following day, the Reichstag was dissolved again. One saving grace for many non-Nazis was that in the coalition government under Chancellor Hitler, the important departments – foreign policy, the Reich's armed forces, finances, economics – were in the hands of the DNVP or ministers closely associated to this party. But the development to an absolute unitary state soon ran its course.

After the NSDAP's propagandist exploitation of a fire at the Reichstag on 27 February 1933, the communists became the main enemy of the state. There was a first round of arrests. The Reichstag election on 5 March brought the NSDAP 44 percent of the votes and 288 mandates – not enough for the required two-thirds majority to change the constitution. But the exclusion of the 81 communists from the Reichstag – they were regarded officially as "address unknown" – the forcible obstruction of 26 social democrats and the fear the centre parties had of a military coup by Hitler brought him the required majority and thus the adoption of the "Enabling Act." From now on, Hitler had the right to enact laws without the involvement of the Reichstag and the path was now

In the night from 27 to 28 February 1932, Berlin's Reichstag building was set alight by arsonists

WUCHER UND HEHLEREI! WAREN VON JEHER IHR PRIVILEG

VOR RASSENSCHANDE WARNTE DIE JUDENTRACHT

Visitors to the Jew-baiting exhibition "Der ewige Jude" in Munich during 1937

Cornelius von Berenberg-Gossler: "I feel ashamed at the actions taken by the Nazis against the Jews."

clear for the dissolution of the trade unions and the political parties – the elimination of all opposition and the *Gleichschaltung* (forcing into line) began.

Soon after the National Socialists had seized power, economic isolation and the persecution of the Jewish population began. The day before the first boycott of Jewish businesses on 1 April 1933, Cornelius von Berenberg-Gossler wrote in his diary in London: "I feel ashamed at the actions taken by the Nazis against the Jews". Various Jewish friends, including Paul Salomon, the branch director of the Dresdner Bank in Hamburg, explained to Cornelius that people should join the NSDAP who are not anti-Semitic. Cornelius decided to join the party, but it lasted only for a short time because a few months later he realised that any influence from the inside was illusory.

From July 1933 onwards, the NSDAP was the only legal party in Germany, all others were dissolved or forbidden, their members often persecuted, arrested or expelled. In the course of the *Gleichschaltung*, the regime also terminated the self-administration of the states, cities and communities; they were now governed and controlled directly by the Reich. In Hamburg, Karl Kaufmann was appointed governor of the Reich, and for the next twelve years, his word would be law.

"Things are governed with lies and secrecy, and that will take its toll," wrote Cornelius von Berenberg-Gossler on 22 December 1933. That same year, it became clear to him that the policies of the Nazis would end in war: after the toiling read through Alfred Rosenberg's *The Myth of the 20th Century*, he criticised the "incredible arrogance, (which) would lead to severe conflicts abroad." Not only was the training of the SA and SS "being done for the event of war", but most notably the youth "were being raised in a warlike spirit that despises other peoples." Following the murder of Austrian Chancellor Engelbert Dollfuß (on 25 July 1934) he wrote: "Violence on the inside and outside is impossible in the long run," but the events of August 1934 destroyed the hope of a speedy end. After the death of President von Hindenburg on 2 August, there was a "referendum" on the succession aiming at declaring Hitler to be the "Führer – Head of State". Cornelius regarded the referendum as a "farce": "No opposition party, no criticism, radio, movies, newspapers, everything is entirely in the hands of the Nazis. The population only hears what it is supposed to be told. And then there is the fear of the referendum, of making oneself unpopular." He voted "no" but the referendum revealed that 89.9 percent of the votes were overwhelmingly in favour of Hitler. After that, Cornelius wrote a statement where he outlined his reason for withdrawing from the party: in addition to the oppression of civil liberties and the hostility towards the church, he noted, above all, the anti-Semitism of the NSDAP as the main motivation for his decision.

The National Socialists profited from the fact that the international financial crisis was abating and from the end of the German reparation payments, which had been decided at the Lausanne Conference in 1932. Their economic strategy focused right from the start on job creation, armament and on the politics of autarky.

One major boost to the regime's authority came from the speedy reduction in unemployment. The programmes that had been created under the governments of Franz von Papen and Kurt von Schleicher through various measures, including the law on the establishment of a *Reichsautobahn* enterprise, were intensified, and by the end of 1933, the number of unemployed had sunk to 4 million compared to 6 million at the start of the year.

With Germany's departure from the League of Nations in October 1933 and the termination of its collaboration in the disarmament conference, the path was now clear to increase armament production. It also contributed to a further reduction in unemployment: in August 1934, there were just 2.4 million unemployed, in 1936 1.1 million and in 1938 just 180,000.

Hitler's autarky policy intended to make Germany independent mainly from the import of strategically important goods. Companies were subjected to a state economic programme, and for political reasons, there were considerable consolidation activity. The production of synthetic rubber, synthetic grease and fuels, all kinds of plastics and other goods mainly conducive to armament, were sponsored by the state. Companies that were active in this area or in the general area of road construction and armament, notably large ones, profited, in some cases, exceptionally, others, mostly small ones, had to give way or were merged into the larger ones.

The financing in the area of job creation was done primarily through the German Society for Public Works AG which was set up in 1930. The so-called Mefo bills covered the investment requirement of the growing armaments industry; the companies affected were allowed to draw bills of exchange on the Metallurgical Research Corporation a shell corporation in Berlin with terms of six months starting in 1939 and were discounted by the "Reichsbank". From 1934 to 1937, Mefo bills amounting to around 12 billion marks were issued.

The result of the economic policy was a continuously increasing national debt. But "complaining and bemoaning the bad state of our foreign exchange," which Economics Minister Schacht did and eventually led to his dismissal, had to give way to higher tasks. In 1936, Hitler had outlined in a secret memorandum that the German economy and the armed forces should be ready for a war in four years – Germany's victory would make all debts incurred meaningless.

Hermann Göring became the head of the Four-Year Plan, which was to conclude the economic war preparations. Göring immediately confiscated all foreign assets held by German citizens abroad and attempted to accelerate the collection of all outstanding receivables from the export business. Moreover, he passed an act to prevent mortgages and an amendment to the banking supervisory authority. In December 1938, the Act on Foreign Exchange Controls followed, which introduced various types of blocked assets.

Heinrich v. Berenberg-Gossler joins the company

In 1935, Cornelius' son, Heinrich von Berenberg-Gossler (1909–1997), joined Joh. Berenberg, Gossler & Co. as a partner, but engaging in the earlier, traditional business dealings based on foreign trade, was still out of the question as there was no free trade, import and export and all of the related foreign currency transactions were subject to strict controls, food had been rationed for a while and the quality of commodities continued to diminish. Cornelius von Berenberg-Gossler concentrated on security transactions and a few larger placement businesses. In March 1935, he was involved in a consortium which acquired the majority shareholding of the "Winterhuder Bierbrauerei" from the possession of the Engelhardt-Brauerei. In early 1939, Cornelius and his friend Rademacher sold the shares at very reasonable terms to Haake-Beck in Bremen.

He also tried to help his many Jewish friends and the Jewish community in Hamburg. For the National Socialists, the Jews were just as much representatives of the "international financial capital" as the "international Bolshevism" and were hence absolute enemies of "Germanness". As a result of the Nuremberg Law for the Protection of German Blood as well as a number of regulations, the Nazis exacerbated the economic ruin and increased persecution of the Jewish population by 1935. On 14 June 1938, the third regulation of the Reich Citizenship Law enacted. Thereafter, all operations were regarded as Jewish if one owner, one personally liable partner, one director, board member of supervisory board member was a Jew, or if Jews were significantly involved according to shares voting rights. Jewish operations were "Aryanised"; forced or asked in a coercive way by existing owners to transfer ownership to non-Jewish partners.

In the *Reichskristallnacht* from 9 to 10 November 1938, attacks on Jews heightened as the result of a pogrom which Propaganda Minister Goebbels had initiated. The government ordered the confiscation of all Jewish property in Germany and arrests and deportations began soon after.

A tragic fate met many of the Jewish private bankers, including several friends of Cornelius. As a result of the "Aryanisation", the number of private bankers in the German Reich declined from 1933 to 1939 from 1350 to 520. For the sake of foreign countries, a few large Jewish banks were still allowed on the stock market in 1938 under considerable restrictions; however, they were deprived completely of their rights. M. M. Warburg & Co. and L. Behrens & Söhne were also impacted by the move, the latter was integrated into a branch of the "Norddeutsche Kreditbank".

Heinrich von Berenberg-Gossler (1907–1997), a company partner from 1935 to 1979

View of the Port of Hamburg in 1930

Cornelius was friends with George Behrens, who was managing L. Behrens & Söhne in the fifth generation, and Cornelius had worked with Max Warburg on the regional committee of the "Reichsbank" and on the supervisory board of the public limited company for domestic and foreign enterprises. After the Nuremberg Laws had been enacted, Cornelius visited him to express his sympathy.

Interests acquired in the companies Wilhelm Rée and Erich Sülz

In April 1938, Richard Kauffmann, who worked at Wilhelm Rée, turned to Cornelius and Joh. Berenberg, Gossler & Co. to get involved at Rée as limited partners. On 27 September, the agreement was approved by the local NSDAP representative for economic matters in Hamburg. Cornelius helped Kauffmann move abroad. He accompanied him in a Danish airplane to London, recommended him to his friends there and was able to assist Kauffmann in getting some of his possession out of harm's way. The former authorised signatory, Wiesmann, now became owner, and Cornelius was given power of attorney. The company name "Rée" remained since the National Socialists were able to be convinced of the fact that it was of Huguenot origin. Rée ran a fast-selling securities operation and was an agent for Lazard Brothers in London and Lazard Frères & Cie. in Paris. It was used by the "Reichsbank" as a certified purchaser for bankers' acceptances, which were then passed on to the "Reichsbank". In September 1937, Joh. Berenberg, Gossler & Co. joined Erich Sültz in Hamburg as a silent partner. Sültz was a private banker, who mainly worked in security transactions. As a result of this activity, Cornelius joined the supervisory board of Triton Belco Werke. Sültz and Rée posted profits in the years that followed.

Otherwise, Cornelius lived with his family relatively withdrawn out in Niendorf. He stepped down from clubs, associations and the Niendorf church council, and during events Hitler repeatedly held to gather public's consent, he handed in blank pieces of paper. He did not want "even as an atom to assume responsibility for Hitler's foreign policy". After the annexation of Austria and the Sudetenland by the German Reich, he wrote on 21 October 1938, that Hitler "as result of his system has turned Germany into barracks and jails," and under the date 26 November, two weeks after the November pogrom, his diary reads: "What are all the successes and conquests of Hitler alongside these beastly acts of cruelty, which must fill all decent people in the world with disgust. Better a small and properly run state than such a big Reich … with a government of robbers and murderers."

In World War II

World War II began on 1 September 1939 with the German invasion of Poland. Cornelius commented on 16 September 1939: "If National Socialism conquers the world, then all decency is lost". He continued to support the Jewish community in Hamburg, but the number of his charges grew getting smaller and smaller. Most members of the Jewish community were "to be transported like animals to the east, never to return".

In June 1942, Cornelius' oldest son, Johann, was killed while working as a regiment doctor outside of Nowgorod. The youngest, Hellmuth, was seriously wounded. During a bombing on 25 July 1943, a large part of old Niendorf was destroyed, and the devastation the city endured after the attacks from the end of July and in early August was indescribable. Half of all the flats and work places were destroyed in World War II, 45,000 people suffocated, burned or were struck dead by the ruins. The transport network was interrupted in countless places; schools, churches and public buildings were destroyed or severely damaged. The *Comptoir* of Rée was a heap of rubble, the *Comptoir* of

Cornelius von Berenberg-Gossler: "If National Socialism conquers the world, there will be no place for decent human beings."

German troops invading Poland during September 1939, an act that triggered Word War II

The 7th British tank division entering Hamburg on 3 May 1945 via the bridges over the River Elbe

Sültz was gutted. In the phases between the air raid sirens, attempts were made to save what could be saved from the smoking ruins.

On 17 August 1943, Cornelius wrote, "that this cursed war brought about by the crimes of Hitler and his Nazis is completely lost (unfortunately not over) …," on 16 April 1945 he noted; "Hamburg resembles a city on the front." Three days later, English troops occupied Lüneburg, and on 3 May 1945, at five in the afternoon, English troops marched into Hamburg. Reichsstatthalter Karl Kaufmann handed over the administration to British Brigadier Douglas Spurling and was arrested a short time later. Two tanks took up their positions in Niendorf near the market square.

In his diary, the 71-year-old Cornelius von Berenberg-Gossler wrote on this day: "Now it is a matter of coming to terms with the consequences of the war and gradually trying to help the children build their futures."

On 8 May 1945, the Third Reich capitulated.

World War II transformed Hamburg into a wasteland

1948–1959: The Bank after the War

8 May 1945. After almost six years, the war was finally over, with more than 60 million dead, it is the worst in the history of mankind, 60 countries have been impacted by the war and its consequences.

Unlike at the end of World War I, the victors were not at the German borders – the German Reich is occupied and divided into four zones: the Russians occupy the east, the British are in the entire north right down to the Ruhr area, the French are in Saarland and parts of Rhineland Palatinate and the Americans are in parts of Hesse and in all of Baden-Württemberg and Bavaria. For a long time, most of the Germans took the end of the war to be a defeat; however, Federal President Richard von Weizsäcker emphasised in his speech on 8 May 1985: "We have to see this day as a liberation".

Cities have been destroyed, cultural and historical treasures are lost forever, there is hardly any infrastructure left.

Hamburg lay in ruins. "Operation Gomorrah" in the summer of 1943 brought the heaviest bombing of the war up until that point.

The period after the end of the war is also very hard in Hamburg. The city is a rocky desert made up of pitch black fields of debris and 43 million cubic metres of rubble, 80 percent of the port has been destroyed, 300 ships are grounded and 3,000 are damaged.

Around 900,000 people live in the ruins – happy to have survived the war, willing to experience peace – and are without work, most of them are homeless, without a regular supply of food and other everyday items. The black market is one of the few ways to exchange goods for food. The default currency is American cigarettes, five Reichsmarks for one cigarette. Like everywhere else, city dwellers travel to the countryside and trade everything the farmers accept in exchange for eggs, fat, sausage and bread. The extremely cold Hunger Winter of 1946/47 cost many hundreds of thousands of people their lives in Germany and Europe.

Slowly but surely, supply lines improve, life returns to the ruins, cinemas open and makeshift repairs are done to theatres and schools and they begin operating again, rubble is moved aside – a type of daily life blossoms amongst the ruins.

The international situation is no calmer, given the increasing conflicts between the three victorious western powers and the Soviet Union. From June

Lines of *Trümmerfrauen* clearing debris in Hamburg after the war, allowing the devastated city to be rebuilt

Large areas of dockland were also destroyed in the Port of Hamburg

1948 to May 1949, the Russians block West Berlin, this "island of freedom" (Mayor Ernst Reuter) held by the Americans. Supplying around 1.2 million people in West Berlin is only made possible through airlifts. Slowly the Iron Curtain between East and West is drawn.

From 1948 onwards, the Marshall Plan pumps around 11 billion USD through the *Kreditanstalt für Wiederaufbau* (Reconstruction Credit Institute) into the West German economy. There is only a small-scale credit industry in place. The banking system of the German Reich is dismantled, in line with the peace settlement.

The banks got off to a cold start. A contemporary eyewitness, apprentice at the Hamburger Kreditbank in Hamburg-Altona recalls: "We were all freezing. The employees sat in hats and coats and worked with gloves without fingers. My job was to heat the oven first thing in the morning. There was a pipe stuffed full with sawdust and paper in the middle." Joachim H. Wetzel, born in 1928, had to go to the Front at the age of 17; he was the youngest in his class. Released from an American prisoner of war camp, he comes to Hamburg quite by chance and gets by with casual jobs. A woman, whose son had fallen during the war, takes him in. He goes to school and right after he graduates, he starts working at the bank. "As an apprentice, I earned 50 marks a month, my first salary was 137 marks. A friend and colleague earned 80 marks more only because had had gone to university."

He takes the streetcar to work every day. He recalls: "Gee, that was a great time. You were on your own, just needed to take the future into your own hands. Those starting in the working world today have it much harder. Regardless of where you go, there is always someone already sitting there."

The days of the Reichsmark become numbered at the end of the war. The country needs a new currency, new money. Where to get it? Just for the paper alone, 3,000 tonnes of wood have to be processed, which are nowhere to be found in war-ravaged Germany. That is why the Americans take things into their own hands, print German banknotes in the US with a nominal value of roughly 5.7 billion marks, ship all of the cash assets of a future nation with the greatest secrecy in 23,000 wooden crates under the code name "Operation Bird Dog" to Bremerhaven, unload it onto 800 military lorries and eight special trains and take it discretely to the issuing centres. Lieutenant Edward A. Tenenbaum, 26, and responsible for the feat speaks proudly of the "largest logistic effort of the US Army since the invasion of Normandy."

On 20 June 1948, the currency reform signals a new beginning. For 100 Reichsmark in the account, 6.50 Deutsche Mark are credited. Wages, salaries, rents and pensions remain at the old rate of exchange and are converted one-to-one.

Just in time for the currency reform, the 71-year-old Cornelius Freiherr von Berenberg-Gossler and son Heinrich decide to re-open the bank. In 1932, the family-run company had pulled out of the active banking business and weathered the Nazi era as a holding company, in which the investments of the company were combined, including two smaller private banks, which dealt with asset management. The baron manages the company together with Heinrich, whom he added in 1935 as a partner. They are able to revive their old contacts abroad,

The currency reform: on 20 June 1948 the Deutsche Mark replaced the Reichsmark in the French, British and U.S. occupation zones

The No. 9 tram running past the ruins between the central bus station and the airport in 1949

especially to Baring Brothers & Co. in London, soon after the war. They arrange a cooperation with their friend, August Rohdewald, chairman of the "Norddeutsche Kreditbank AG" (NKB) in Bremen. The NKB was looking to expand its business dealings to Hamburg, but, according to the terms of the Allied Control Council, a bank was limited to one state in the occupied area, meaning that a Bremen-based bank was not able to establish a bank in Hamburg. Heinrich von Berenberg-Gossler and August Rohdewald became acquainted before the war at the "Reichs-Kreditgesellschaft". Because they had previously met, they are allowed to reach an agreement.

On 30 August 1948, the Joh. Berenberg, Gossler & Co. bank opens its office in the corner building Alter Wall 32, which has very impressive architecture. The Berenberg-Gossler family and the Norddeutsche Kreditbank Bremen AG each have 40 percent of the capital in the new bank; August Rohdewald has 20 percent. The managing partners are Cornelius Freiherr von Berenberg-Gossler, Heinrich von Berenberg-Gossler and August Rohdewald. The basic capital is 180,000 DM, but it is bolstered by the private assets of the Berenberg-Gossler family, mainly with shares from the Ilseder Hütte. The private bank starts with 30 employees, a capital of 250,000 DM and in its first annual balance sheet, records a transaction volume of approximately 1.5 billion DM.

The partners' holdings:
40 % Berenberg-Gossler family
40 % Norddeutsche Kreditbank
20 % August Rohdewald

Hamburg is the most important German stock exchange

Business is going well. In 1948, Hamburg's private bankers set up an association with 38 members. There are six foreign banks in Hamburg, including the Hong Kong and Shanghai Banking Corporation; the Berenbergs were among its founding shareholders back in 1865. In Bremen, the Ibero-America Bank is formed, and Berenberg assumes the representation in Hamburg.

The stock exchange is perking up. Hamburg is still the most important stock exchange of the three occupied zones, considerably ahead of Frankfurt and Munich. The Hanseatic city is an important banking centre. In addition

Berenberg opened its counters in the corner building at Alter Wall 32, Hamburg

to the private banks, the "Neue Sparcasse" von 1864, the "Hamburger Sparcasse" von 1827 and the credit cooperatives begin operations, and in the background, there is the "Hamburgische Landesbank".

The terms of the occupying forces are designed in such a way to prevent a structure similar to the banking system of the German Reich, which is why major banks get off to a slow start. In Hamburg, the "Deutsche Bank" becomes the "Norddeutsche Bank", in place of the "Dresdner Bank" the "Hamburger Kreditbank" starts doing business, both with a balance sheet total of around 200 million DM, the "Commerzbank" has to be content as the "Hansa-Bank" with 134 million DM. The major banks are not small, but they are too weak to meet the demand for very large loans. Only after tedious negotiations with the occupying powers is progress gradually made in mitigating the decentralisation by law to the extent that subsequent reorganisation to their former size is possible.

On 15 September 1949, the German Bundestag elected Konrad Adenauer (CDU) as first the chancellor of the newly formed German Federal Republic

Along with the currency reform in 1948, which saw the introduction of the Deutsche Mark in the western zones, the division of Germany is further deepened and ultimately formally concluded with the founding of two German states in 1949: On 23 May 1949, the three western zones become the Federal Republic of Germany with Bonn as the capital city and Basic Law as the new constitution. The first elections for the new Bundestag take place on 14 August. Konrad Adenauer is the first chancellor of the new republic and remains in office until 1963.

On 7 October 1949, the German Democratic Republic is established with East Berlin as its capital; the election to the People's Chamber, the rubber-stamp parliament of the GDR, is held on 15 October 1950.

A new development is looming, namely, the economic cooperation of European nation states. It began with the European Community for Coal and Steel (EGKS), the Montan Union. The idea came from the French foreign minister, Robert Schuman; Chancellor Konrad Adenauer is keen. The agreement enters into force on 23 July 1952 and is valid for 50 years. One year earlier, the Federal Republic of Germany joined the Council of Europe as its 14th member; on 28 June 1952, it became a signatory of the Bretton Woods Agreement and thus of the International Monetary Fund (IMF) and the World Bank.

ES LEBE
DIE NATIONALE FRONT
DES DEMOKRATISCHEN
DEUTSCHLAND

7 October 1949: Wilhelm Pieck
proclaims the German Democratic
Republic in the National Council

While in the West the first cornerstones are being laid for the later development of the European Union, in the East, the Council for Mutual Economic Assistance (Comecon) is formed on 25 January 1949. The divide between West and East becomes more pronounced. Comecon is the counter model of the "socialist brother states" (under the leadership of the Soviet Union) to the Marshall Plan and to the Organization for European Economic Cooperation (OEEC).

Military blocks are coming together at this time as well: In June 1955, the East counters the founding of NATO in April 1949 with its own Warsaw Pact. The division of Europe is thus completed and will endure until 1989/90.

The 1950s are years of construction and major accomplishments. On 18 August 1952, the Equalization of Burdens Act enters into force, the largest restructuring of assets in German history. War debts and pre-war debts are to be settled and compensation is to be paid to the victims of the dictatorship.

Adenauer's minister of economics, Ludwig Erhard, has a lucky hand, a healthy sense of self-confidence and proven staying power.

In June 1950, the Korean War breaks out. At first, it appears to be a war between two halves of one nation with clashing ideologies, but as a result of intervention by the Americans, Russians and Chinese, it becomes a three-year proxy war with more than 2 million deaths. Prices rise, the population starts to loot savings accounts and to hoard food. There is a lack of foreign exchange. The young Federal Republic incurs debt, just as loans within the European Payments Union climb to almost 2 billion DM. Added to the concern over the stability of the mark, is the fear the Germans have of inflation. Erhard stays on track, contradicting the theory that only a currency backed by gold can be stable. Instead of gold, hard work and the products made from it are the inner value of currency. The social market economy passes its baptism by fire.

Private banks in Hamburg are doing better and other banks soon crop up in addition to Joh. Berenberg, Gossler & Co. such as Brinckmann, Wirtz & Co., Conrad Hinrich Donner and Münchmeyer & Co. Among the top addresses are Nottebohm & Co. and Schröder Gebr., Erich Sültz, Werner & Frese, Marcard & Co. and Hesse Newman & Co. Many of them were classic merchant bankers, who are now tackling new challenges.

Joachim H. Wetzel changes employers. In 1952, he goes to Berenberg. "Heinrich von Berenberg-Gossler hired me; he was 42 at the time. I was lucky to be in the right place at the right time and doing the right thing." During his apprenticeship, Wetzel concentrated on foreign exchange trading, which is permitted from 1952 onwards; foreign exchange traders are now in demand.

The young man is getting to know the world. "Baron Heinrich sent me to Belgium. I was supposed to learn to speak French. That was not so easy at a Flemish bank. And then he sent me to London to the National Provincial Bank." The private banker knows how to motivate his employees. His bonus system was rather spontaneous and exhibited sound judgement. "Once, Baron Heinrich came to London and gave me 20 pounds. I even went to Scotland with friends and got paid."

On 1 September 1952, the *Lastenausgleichsgesetz*, which compensated citizens for losses suffered as a result of the War, came into effect; the first payments were made in cash

Joachim H. Wetzel starts at Berenberg as a foreign exchange trader

Joh. Berenberg, Gossler & Co. is increasingly active in the international arena, finances wheat, which the traditional company, Alfred C. Toepfer brings in from Australia, organises together with Stinnes the delivery of iron from the Ilseder Hütte in exchange for coal from the US and finances factory furnishings for Theodor Wille in Brazil. Old connections to Argentina are revived with a handshake, and the traditional ties to England are once again activated.

On 5 March 1953, Josef Stalin dies and on 17 June, there are strikes, demonstrations and protests in East Berlin and other cities in the GDR aimed against the SED (Socialist Unity Party of Germany) regime and the speed of the labour standards and for democratic changes. The uprising is crushed by the Red Army, hundreds disappear into GDR prisons; 17 June becomes a national holiday in commemoration of the uprising and its victims in the Federal Republic and remains one until 1990.

Cornelius Freiherr v. Berenberg-Gossler dies

On 29 September 1953, company patriarch Cornelius Freiherr v. Berenberg-Gossler dies at the age of 79. The private banker was a *homo politicus*, a liberal in spirit and full of hope that reason would prevail. The life work of the baron was to manage the family-run company with wisdom and moral integrity (through catastrophes notably inflation and hyperinflation), world economic crises, bank crises, two devastating world wars, two total collapses of the economy and state order. It required courage and skill to continually make new decisions, where the consequences were unforeseeable given that there was nothing to go on in terms of experience. The tombstone of Cornelius in Niendorf reads: "Blessed are the dead, who die in the Lord. They rest from their work, and their deeds follow them."

His death left a gap, but it did not mean a break in the course of business. Gradually, Cornelius passed on responsibility to his son, Heinrich; even while his father was still living, he was his successor. In November 1949, Heinrich von Berenberg-Gossler was elected to the supervisory board of the "Hüttenwerke Ilsede-Peine" at the wish of his father; a little later, he also received his father's seat on the supervisory board at Ilseder Hütte as well as the supervisory posts at Triton-Belco AG and the Treuhand AG. The transition from Cornelius to Heinrich was implemented smoothly and without difficulty.

After completing his A-levels at the *Schlossschule* in Plön in 1930, Heinrich von Berenberg-Gossler did an apprenticeship in his father's company and then at the "Darmstädter und Nationalbank" (DANAT). Next, he worked for a time as a trainee at Barings and the Bank of London and South America in London (May 1932 to May 1933), at Neuflize & Co. in Paris (until November 1933) and at the "Nederlandsche Handelsmaatschappij" in Amsterdam (until June 1934). Other positions were in Guatemala (until March 1935) as well as at Kidder, Peaboddy & Co. in New York and Boston (until October 1935). A stay at the Reichs-Kredit-Gesellschaft AG in Berlin (until November 1937) was followed by a trip to Buenos Aires and to the branch of the Bank of London and South America (until February 1939). Next, on behalf of the "Deutsch-Südamerikanische Bank AG", Berlin, he went first to Lisbon and then to Milan and Genoa, after a planned stay in Buenos Aires was prevented by the beginning of the war. There was a brief time as a soldier, where he worked mainly as a translator due to his acquired language skills. The work at the "Reichsbank" – also as a translator – is a brief transitional solution until the opportunity arose in November 1945 to begin working at the "Ilseder Hütte",

A labour dispute escalates into to a popular uprising: on 17 June 1953 Russian tanks patrolled the border of Berlin's Russian sector on Friedrich-strasse

as authorised signatory. After his family's company was re-opened in Hamburg, he resigned and left his job in Peine. There, he met Irmela von Consbruch (née Meyer), the daughter of councilor of commerce Gerhard Meyer, the long-time director of the "Ilseder Hütte" and the "Peiner Walzwerk". Their wedding was in 1949. Her son from her first marriage, Joachim von Berenberg-Consbruch, would later become a personally liable partner.

The people of Hamburg are still developing their city; each year they build 20,000 new apartments, the economy is gathering speed. Industry, petroleum industry, shipyards and shipping companies are springing up. The bank is focussing on the acceptance business and overdraft facilities, the financing of the import and export business is picking up. "We quickly gained a foothold in international business," recalls Joachim H. Wetzel. "The reason was that Hamburg's banks traditionally worked internationally and thus had experience. More confidence was placed in us". Among the customers of the bank are top names in big industry: Siemens, AEG, Thyssen, Mannesmann, Klöckner, Krupp, BASF and VAW. International connections to Scandinavia and Western Europe and a carefully woven network of international correspondent banks promote business.

At the end of 1955, there are 120 banks registered in Hamburg with 360 branches, with banks from other federal territories accounting for another 35 branches and foreign banks are represented with seven branches. The equity was just under 240 million DM, the sum of the commercial loan 2 billion DM, import and export are financed with 481 million DM.

In 1956, an advisory board was installed to support the personally liable partners. Members of the board include respectable representatives from industry and trade such as Dr hc Karl Blessing, later president of the "Deutsche Bundesbank" (German Federal Bank); Clemens von Velsen, board chairman of "Salzdetfurth AG" and Ernst Wolf Mommsen, board chairman of "Fried. Krupp AG".

There is no peace in the East. On 23 October 1956, thousands of students demonstrate at Budapest University for democratic changes in Hungary. In the evening, the government orders its own people to be shot, the peaceful demonstration becomes an armed rebellion, which is victorious to begin with: In the days that follow, the communist one-party government is dissolved, Hungary leaves the Warsaw Pact, declares its neutrality, and urges the Soviet army to leave the country.

Berenberg appoints a board of directors

Karl Blessing, president of the German Federal Bank from 1958 to 1969, also sat on the advisory board at Berenberg Bank

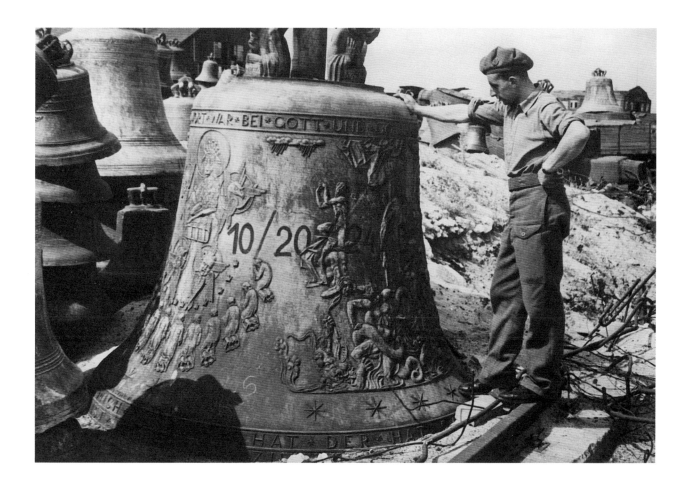

A bell graveyard in Hamburg-Veddel: the 75,000 church bells had been destined for recasting into military hardware

But once again, the Red Army marches into a "fraternal country", on 4 November the democratic dream is over. The Soviets install a new pro-communist government, with hundreds of the insurgents executed and thousands fleeing to the West. After 1989, 23 October is a national holiday in Hungary.

Finally, on 24 December 1956, the successor institutions of the old major banks are permitted to join forces again. The *Großbankengesetz* (Big Bank Law), which dates back to 1952, is lifted. And Germany expands its territory; on 1 January 1957 the Saarland is added as the tenth federal state. The foundations of the welfare state are laid. The *Bundestag* passes a law on pension reform and introduces the indexed pension. The IG Metall union achieves the 45-hour week with complete wage and salary compensation.

Europe is coming together. On 25 March 1957, representatives from the Benelux states, France, Italy and the Federal Republic sign the Treaty of Rome on the founding of a European Economic Community (EEC) and of the European Atomic Energy Community (EURATOM).

Signing of the Treaty of Rome on 25 March 1957: West Germany was represented by its chancellor, Konrad Adenauer (centre)

On 1 August 1957, the "Deutsche Bundesbank" becomes the central bank of the Federal Republic and West Berlin. Erhard's politics made the Germans rich. The mark is one of the strongest currencies in the world. The constant flow of foreign currencies from abroad makes it possible for the currency reserves of German state banks to swell in just seven years from 700 million DM to just under 18 billion DM. Meanwhile, the share of gold in the currency reserve climbs from under 10 percent to 60 percent.

A golden age begins in Germany. The construction industry is booming, the economy is posting double-digit growth rates, the turnover in retail sales increases by 35 percent, the export figure by 37 percent. The FAZ stock index (the DAX is introduced in 1988) skyrockets from the end of 1958 to the end of 1959 from 100 to 175.5 points. The first people's shares are issued. The Preussag shares marks the beginning of privatisation of industrial federal property. And an army of millions of young small shareholders rejuvenates economic life.

All signs point to the future. Outer space approaches. On 4 October 1957, the USSR launches its *Sputnik*, the first satellite. It is only 58 cm in diameter, weighs 83 kg, is equipped with a thermometer and a short-wave transmitter, circles the Earth, sends signals for 21 days from space before it burns up, and thus "proves" Soviet superiority in technology and ideology – next, the US establishes NASA in 1958, the space race gathers speed.

In Garching, near Munich, a research reactor is the first federal German nuclear power plant to start operation. The first German USSR Trade Treaty concluded in 1958, and for the next three years provides for a goods exchange valuing 3.15 billion DM. And in Strasbourg in 1957 the European Parliament is created as a joint organ of the European Coal and Steel Community, the EEC and of the European Atom Energy Community.

1960–1969: In the *Wirtschaftswunderland*

What do the 1960s have in store? Colour TV, party financing and paid holidays, the pill, the German Council of Economic Experts, value added tax, the Eurocheque card, *numerus clausus*, sick pay and the subject of computer science.

Europe continues to grow into a single entity. In January 1960, Norway, Sweden, Denmark, Great Britain, Portugal, Austria and Switzerland establish the European Free Trade Association (EFTA) as the counterpart to the EEC. And the petroleum exporting countries establish OPEC in Bagdad. In 1960, the Foreign Trade Law of the Federal Republic of Germany takes effect. Foreign exchange control and state control of commercial trade with countries abroad cease. One year later, the first market regulations of the European agricultural market are passed. In 1963, the Federal Republic of Germany signs the Elysee Agreement with France as an act of reconciliation and signs a trade agreement with Poland. US President John F. Kennedy makes his legendary visit to West Berlin.

National wealth is growing. There is the first issuance of Volkswagen shares on the regulated open market. Meanwhile, major banks are also turning to private client banking. And as companies begin paying wages and salaries without using cash, business with private clients is becoming more interesting for major banks. Due to the fact that clients are not yet familiar with cashless transactions, many initially withdraw all their entire wages or monthly salary; they are used to finding their entire salary in their pay envelope.

4 October 1957: the USSR launches its first satellite *Sputnik* and sends the dog Laika into orbit

illion

It runs and runs and runs: on 5 August 1955 Volkswagen celebrated its millionth *Beetle* in Wolfsburg

Christmas shopping in a Frankfurt department store at the start of the 1960s

Change of owners at Berenberg: August Rohdewald departs, Heinz Lessing is his successor

The world of work is changing. The tariff partners in the metal industry agree on the gradual introduction of the 40-hour week, and in the banking sector, the five-day week is introduced; from now on, banks are closed on Saturdays. The *Bundestag* passes legislation to promote the capital formation of employees, "312 mark act" and another act granting child benefits. In December 1962, the Bundestag sets the minimum holiday entitlement to 15 days.

In 1961, there is a change of owners at Joh. Berenberg, Gossler & Co. August Rohdewald departs as personally liable partner. To the regret of Heinrich von Berenberg, he transfers to the board of the "Kreditanstalt für Wiederaufbau" in Frankfurt. Difficulties with the Norddeutsche Kreditbank in Bremen forced him to make the move. In general, the collaboration with the NKB had become less smooth as time passed. The generation which formed the board in Bremen in 1948, had been replaced by another, and the old harmony could no longer be maintained.

In August 1961, the former chief representative, Heinz A. Lessing, who like Heinrich Freiherr von Berenberg-Gossler was born in 1909, became a personally liable partner. When he joined, he already had a diverse professional career. After graduating from Schloss Salem grammar school, where he later worked as a treasurer for many years, Lessing did his apprenticeship at M. M. Warburg & Co. in Hamburg and built on this knowledge in New York at the International Acceptance Bank, at the Bank of the Manhattan Company as well as at international auditing firm Price, Waterhouse & Co. In 1936, he assumed the commercial management of the organising committee for the XI Olympic Games in Berlin. Other posts followed, such as working abroad for the Hamburg-Amerika-Linie and as the general agent of "Alsen'sche Portland Cementfabriken KG" in Hamburg until he joined Joh. Berenberg, Gossler & Co. in 1959. Colleagues attest to Lessing's entrepreneurial spirit, versatility, wealth of ideas, sociability and an unbiased attitude on current issues and those of the future. Other plus points include his international connections and the fact that his advice is sought, something which is documented by the numerous positions he held on supervisory boards and in other offices.

Another personally liable partner was hired in 1964, namely, Karl Theodor Lindemann, a son of the chairman of the supervisory board at the Norddeutsche Kreditbank AG. However, he left on his own accord in 1972 to work abroad.

Karl Theodor-Lindemann becomes a personally liable partner

World politics is characterised by competing systems. The USSR sends the first person into space; on 12 April 1961, cosmonaut Juri Gagarin goes around the Earth in 106 minutes and returns safe and sound.

In the summer of 1962, the Russians start positioning rockets in Cuba. The Cuban Missile Crisis results and brings the world to the brink of a third world war. Nuclear missiles in Cuba that are aimed at American cities is not acceptable for the US. There is a naval blockade of Cuba by the Americans; both sides have already considered a pre-emptive nuclear attack. At the last minute, US President Kennedy and Kremlin chief Khrushchev reach an agreement and the missiles are withdrawn.

In divided Germany, the political climate drops below the freezing point. On 13 August 1961, armed GDR police start to build a wall across Berlin.

Over the night of 16–17 February 1962, northern Germany experiences the worst flooding in over 100 years; 330 people die. Dikes are broken, and

13 August 1961:
the birth of the Berlin Wall

Claus-G. Budelmann begins his
apprenticeship at Berenberg

many parts of the city are under water. Yet, Hamburg's developmental efforts to become an international port and international economic centre are not hampered. The turnover of goods transported by sea reaches 31.23 million tonnes, the highest amount ever in the history of the city.

In 1965, Claus-Günther Budelmann a 20-year-old Hamburg native, who is full of energy and initiative, joins Berenberg. His father is a family doctor and close friend of the Berenberg family. He recalls: "My father thought it was good for me to learn to get up at eight in the morning and to have stable employment. I recall his words: I can give you two things: a good education and a good name."

In addition, as the banker noted, there was a great deal of luck. "Baron Heinrich was like a second father to me. Educated, interested in music and very well read. If he found a book interesting, he gave it to me with the words, "You have to read this, my boy!" Budelmann describes his patron and promoter as a charismatic personality: "The baron liked to be among people. He liked getting in touch with people, nurtured many contacts and as a partner was something of a foreign minister for the bank."

His partner, Heinz Lessing, had quite a different temperament – Prussian, highly disciplined. "I learned a lot from him because I sat in when he received visitors and file notes. He responded willingly to all my questions." Budelmann takes the bank assistant test, and is sent to England early on. "We have to make you less German first," says the baron, something which proved to be an easy exercise for young Budelmann. "I had English friends, was enthusiastic about Wimbledon and polo. For the first time, I was all alone in a cosmopolitan city, got to know girls who took their toothbrushes when they left the house in the evenings – a new world."

The staff at the Berenberg Bank had doubled since 1948. "Back then, it had around 100 people. I was placed in the partner office where the specialised business dealings, industry and overseas affairs were handled. The motto was: do business and process transactions in a hands-on way. We were a young team, close to the bosses. We travelled a lot. It was mainly about foreign trade. We set up a department for foreign business, and soon we were 45 people in processing and 25 looked after the shipping business. We granted loans mainly to import and export companies and were in Paris, Brussels and Switzerland. We exchanged transactions, processed transactions and created the securities business. It grew out of the commercial banking business,

Flooding in Hamburg: in the night from 16 to 17 February 1962, sections of the North German city – seen here the district of Wilhelmsburg – were inundated

1 December 1966: Kurt Georg Kiesinger (CDU) becomes West Germany's chancellor and Willy Brandt (SPD) its foreign minister and vice-chancellor

like foreign exchange trade. We proceeded systematically and visited banks. They gave us limits within which we were able to operate freely. A great time."

But there were clouds on the horizon. In March 1964, the German federal government announces the introduction of a coupon tax meaning 25 percent on the profits of fixed income securities in the possession of "non-residents", a move which leads to an uproar in Germany and abroad. Ludwig Erhard, who succeeds Konrad Adenauer as chancellor is having less success than in his years as economics minister. The father of Germany's post-war economic miracle is fighting for votes and promises to reduce taxes while taking out new loans, which burdens the budget with 5 billion DM. Twenty years after the end of the war, the economy of the Federal Republic of Germany, which had been growing steadily up until that point, shows signs of weakness. For the first time, the national economy feels the threat of a recession. Within one year, the number of unemployed grows from roughly 100,000 to 400,000. The crisis is taking on an explosive character. The construction industry complains about declining investments. The industry lacks capital. Order intake is getting worse, cheap oil replaces expensive coal, mining suffers, the steel industry is wavering, and the state is going into debt.

In the dispute over tax increases, the Bonn Coalition consisting of CDU and FDP falls apart on 27 October 1966. On 1 December, Kurt Georg Kiesinger becomes chancellor of a Grand Coalition consisting of CDU/CSU and SPD. The Social Democrat, Willy Brandt, becomes the vice chancellor and foreign minister. The recession becomes the main topic of the government. The mismatched pair of Franz Josef Strauß (CSU) as the finance minister and the economics professor Karl Schiller (SPD) takes over the reins and embarks on a course that reflects the highly modern ideas of the economics philosopher John Maynard Keynes (1883–1946). A confident state creates the parameters for economic development and intervenes with control measures. The spin-off from this is that the Bundesbank loses its influence. Schiller invites representatives from employee and trade associations, economists and government experts to informal talks. The concerted action proves to be a success. In May 1967, Schiller's Stability and Growth Pact takes effect. It calls for a strong infusion of investment and capital. The name of the cure becomes a dictum, *Aufschwung nach Maß*. The crisis is over for the time being. And the German Federal Bank gives the banks more room to breathe. On 1 April 1967, the *Zinsverordnung*, dating back to 1936, is lifted. Banks and savings banks are now free to set interest rates on their own.

A shuffling of positions at Berenberg. In 1968, the bank expands its management. Joachim H. Wetzel becomes a personally liable partner. "Back then, I sold my townhouse for around 125,000 DM to have enough for the deposit," he later explains. "The balance sheet total at that time was 3 million DM. Back then, that was still a small amount."

Wetzel joined Berenberg in 1952 after completing an apprenticeship and working for several years at the Dresdner Bank. At first, his job was in the international department, with occasional stays in London and Brussels. In 1958, he took over management of the stock market and securities department. In 1962, he was appointed to management where he was responsible for expanding national and international major transactions and industry business. He also represented the bank on supervisory and administrative bodies of both German and foreign companies and banks, worked on the committee for the capital market of the Federal Association of German Banks, and in his capac-

Joachim Wetzel becomes personally liable partner

Philadelphia National Bank and
the Bank of Montreal become
limited partners

Shares in the bank:
30 % v. Berenberg-Gossler family
      und PhG
50 % Norddeutsche Kreditbank
10 % Philadelphia National Bank
10 % Bank of Montreal

ity as a member of the Committee for Private Bankers, he represented issues relevant to Hamburg in this federal association.

The question of further development arises. Bremen's "Nordkredit-bank" still has a 50-percent share. Should the bank look for other partners? "There were discussions about merging the bank with Marcard, Schröder and Münchmeyer. But that would have meant too many chiefs and hardly any braves." Instead, Joh. Berenberg, Gossler & Co. finds two prominent insti-tutes, the Philadelphia National Bank and the Bank of Montreal, and each goes in for 10 percent.

Unlike the balance sheet totals of both the new long-standing partners, the business volume at Berenberg is rather modest. But the investment of the important international partners facilitates access to world trade. The interests of the Berenberg Bank have traditionally been in foreign business, mainly in Scandinavia and Western Europe. In North and Central America, there is a lot that can be initiated. "That brought new impetus for international busi-ness," recalls Wetzel. "Philadelphia was particularly interesting, a port city like Hamburg." That was a trend-setting decision. The bank focuses on the lend-ing business as it relates to foreign trade, the trade with securities and tradi-tional asset management.

For Joachim H. Wetzel, it is an exciting time. "It was a fascinating task to start as a young partner and shape things, meaning from receiving a task to developing it to accompanying it right to the end. I was the third man besides Heinrich von Berenberg-Gossler and Heinz Lessing. They let me do things. It was a trusting relationship. That is a gift which I was always aware of. Some-thing like that is very rare. But there were also absolute patriarchal traits." The banker talks about earlier times: "When I wanted to marry, I had to introduce my future wife, Margit. An interest was shown in the relationships a partner had. My wife went into the office of the baron. The door closed behind her, and I never learned what they talked about. I only know that afterwards Bar-on Heinrich said to me: "You can marry her as long as you are aware that you will have nothing to say in the marriage."

The trusting relationship remains and deepens in the decades of work-ing together. "Later, when he no longer took an active part in day-to-day busi-ness, Heinrich von Berenberg-Gossler looked in on my office every morning and asked: 'Hey, anything new?' and before I could give him an answer, he was already gone."

Joh. Berenberg, Gossler & Co. was on the up and up with 15 million DM in capital, a balance sheet total of 259 million DM in solid assets. Meanwhile, the private banks "Münchmeyer & Co." and "Schröder Gebr. & Co." reached an agreement on merging with the Offenbach-based bank "Friedrich Hengst & Co." On 1 January 1969, the business starts operating under the name "Schröder, Münchmeyer, Hengst & Co." And the major banks activate a new line of business and decide in future to also grant clients overdraft credits if they have a chequing account.

Mergers ensure the future and 23 mining companies, which account for roughly 85 percent of the entire coal mining in the Ruhr area, make up the "Ruhrkohle AG" (RAG). The Federal Republic of Germany and the state of North Rhine-Westphalia in return, provide surety for the debts of the old companies.

While Western Europe moves closer together and the Customs Union of the EEC enters into force on 1 July 1968, Eastern Europe is forced to remain

End of the "Prague Spring": on 20–21 August 1968, demonstrations on Wenceslas Square were halted by Soviet tanks

unified under the leadership of the USSR and democratic efforts are once again suppressed. Warsaw Pact forces occupy Czechoslovakia in August 1968 in a move against the democratic movement known as the Prague Spring.

The stimulus packages in Germany are having an impact. The export surplus doubles in just two years and with around 17 billion DM, breaks all records. But in the fall of 1968, there is conflict. For the "Bundesbank", things are moving too fast and it calls for a halt to growth. The foreign exchange markets react nervously. Reluctantly, Economics Minister Schiller agrees to increase the value of the mark, while France lowers the value of the franc by 11.1 percent. The economy is strained. The Central Bank Council of the Deutsche Bundesbank resolves on 18 April 1969 to increase the bank rate from 3 to 4 percent, and two months later, from 4 to 5 percent due to the "very high interest rates abroad."

Joh. Berenberg, Gossler & Co. focuses increasingly on the stock market and on the stock and shares business in addition to foreign business. In 1968, the private bank takes part in a total of 112 German and foreign share issues, some in consortiums and in international sales groups. And for investment funds, a market is also evident in Germany. In 1968, Berenberg is among the founding partners of the "Universal-Investment Gesellschaft" in Frankfurt, which is one of the most successful German capital depositaries today. One year later, Berenberg opens a branch in Frankfurt, which focuses on stock exchange transactions and the international securities business. Investment consultancy and asset management become more important; the lending business for the short-term financing of import and export is going very well.

The Deutsche Bundesbank ends its intervention in foreign currency markets and lets the exchange rate of the mark float. On 1 and 2 December, the conference of the heads of state and government in the European Community (EC) in The Hague reaches an agreement on a common market. France agrees to an expansion of the EC.

An eventful decade draws to a close. It brought not only a wall right through Germany, the moon landing on 21 July 1969, and the open air festival in Woodstock, but also the Beatles and the Rolling Stones, student movements and civil unrest. In October 1969, the first social-liberal coalition forms with SPD and FDP, led by Willy Brandt and Walter Scheel.

Founding of the Universal-Investment Gesellschaft

Berenberg opens the first branch in Frankfurt

1970–1980: The Seventies – Europe Expands

After decades of the Cold War, the social-liberal government initiates a gradual rapprochement to the leaders of the communist hemisphere and with it, a new eastern policy is born. Willy Brandt kneels down at the memorial to the victims of the Warsaw Ghetto, a move which goes down in history. In 1971, he is awarded the Noble Peace Prize. However, on the German-German border, there is no normalisation to speak of. The SED regime has more than 2 million mines and over 80,000 kilometres of barbed wire installed. Finally, the Four Powers Agreement on Berlin involving representatives from the US, Great Britain, France and the USSR achieves a breakthrough; the Transit Agreement is followed by the Basic Treaty between both German states, which specifies mutual acceptance and underscores a joint effort to strive for good neighbourly relations.

At Joh. Berenberg, Gossler & Co. business is slowly getting cramped. The bank building on Alter Wall does not have enough room for the growing company, which moves to Neuer Jungfernstieg 20, where next to the *Übersee-Club* and not far from *Hotel Vier Jahreszeiten*, Hamburg architects Schramm + Pempelfort had built a high-rise building for the "Nordstern Lebensversicherung" (today part of AXA) – the highest building on the Alster River. The Berenberg Bank leases five of the ten floors.

In 1971, Joachim von Berenberg-Consbruch joins the bank. Born in Vienna in 1940, he grows up with his mother and grandparents. His father, Dietrich von Consbruch, died in 1941. His mother, Irmela Meyer, daughter of steel entrepreneur Meyer from Peine (Ilseder Hütte), marries her second husband, Baron Heinrich von Berenberg-Gossler, who adopts his wife's son. Their marriage produces two children, Clarita and Johann Heinrich. The latter was, according to the intentions of his father, to become his successor at the bank. But his interests lie in the humanities and in music. He abandons his bank apprenticeship and works in various publishing companies as an editor and translator. Today, he owns the well-known *Berenberg Verlag* in Berlin. Clarita studies Germanic philology. Thus, Joachim becomes the prime candidate for succession in the bank.

A prayer for forgiveness: on 7 December 1970, Chancellor Willy Brandt knelt down before the monument to the victims of the Warsaw Ghetto uprising

Joachim von Berenberg-Consbruch starts work

Excavations for the new Berenberg headquarters at Neuer Jungfernstieg 20 in Hamburg

Joachim von Berenberg-Consbruch recalls his childhood: "My stepfather, and later adoptive father, had a range of interests; he was enthusiastic about history and literature and had an exceptional talent for languages. I am not interested in music, and, in this respect, I was the black sheep of the family," he says with a smile. "I was interested in mathematics and the natural sciences." After graduating from grammar school and completing a bank apprenticeship at the "Deutsche Bank", he studied law in Lausanne and Hamburg. "I liked the logic and precise nature of law. It is what keeps our world together; law shapes our life. Contracts create order in our coexistence. At the age of 30, I was finished, that was in 1971. Then I held various posts at the bank." When the head of the accounting and tax department dies suddenly, he takes on the position. "On a Monday morning, I sat in his chair, just before the end of the month. It was a major challenge. What helped me is that I used to work with balance sheets, taxes and controlling, but now I was also responsible for electronic data processing. We had only had EDP for three years. At that time, the focus was on the normal lending business, the traditional relationship between client and bank. The banking sector only changed later on. The Industrial Revolution had taken place in all economic sectors, not just in the banks. It did not change until the transition from manual data processing to electronic processing of information. The demands made on the banker changed dramatically. At the same time, the mathematics of financing was evolving. This altered many things." Joachim von Berenberg-Consbruch holds the position for two years, before taking over the lending business.

The expansion continues. In 1972, Berenberg is one of the first German banks (with the "Norddeutsche Landesbank" in Hanover) to set up a branch in Luxembourg. The Berenberg Bank International is equipped with a converted sum of 7 million DM and focuses on international transactions, which begin to emerge in the decades to come in Luxembourg. On 1 February 1972, the Berenberg Universal Fund was established in the Frankfurt branch, which ensures a flexible investment policy for the smaller depots, whose number had increased considerably. By the end of April, the capital had grown to 8 million DM. Next were the "Berenberg Universal Rentenfonds" (bond fund) with German and international bonds.

At the start of the 1970s, the ownership structure changes at Joh. Berenberg, Gossler & Co. The relationship with the "Norddeutsche Kreditbank" (NKB) in Bremen, which still had a 50-percent share in the bank, was no longer good. Ultimately, the NKB (which in the meantime had been taken over by the "Allgemeine Deutsche Creditanstalt ADCA") ran into difficulties and had to be supported by the Nord/LB. In the meantime, the Nord/LB assumed 40 percent of the shares. Both foreign banks now assumed 5 percent more, thereby increasing their capital share to 15 percent. As a result, no other bank had a 50-percent share and was also not a personally liable partner. Thus, management in Hamburg became more independent. In addition, the bank now had a large and capable bank at its side.

The Norddeutsche Landesbank becomes a limited partner

Later, the Nord/LB reduced its share to 25 percent. Each year, Berenberg increased the share capital proportional to the growing business volume; in 1977, it was 45 million DM. It was and remains important to pay close attention to liquidity. This was ensured in two ways. Firstly, short-term transactions were mainly done with applicable congruent refinancing. Secondly, the shareholders, the "Norddeutsche Landesbank", the Bank of Montreal and the Philadelphia National Bank offered considerable refinancing capabilities.

Shares in the bank 1973:
30 % v. Berenberg-Gossler family and Managing Partners
40 % Norddeutsche Landesbank
15 % Philadelphia National Bank
15 % Bank of Montreal

1 September 1970: Norddeutsche Lloyd and the Hamburg shipping line Hapag merge into Hapag-Lloyd AG

The merger trend continues. "Bremen's Norddeutscher Lloyd" and Hamburg's Hapag merge to form Hapag-Lloyd AG. The Berenbergs were founding shareholders for both companies. The "Hamburger Sparcasse" von 1827 merges with the "Neue Sparcasse" von 1864 and the "Vereinsbank" in Hamburg with the "Westbank AG" Hamburg/Husum. In 1976, the Karstadt Group takes over the large mail order company Neckermann.

And Europe is growing as well. In 1972, Great Britain, Norway, Denmark and Ireland sign the instrument of accession to the EEC. The economic policies of industrialised countries demonstrate conflicting goals. The carefully aligned balance of growth and monetary stability runs counter to the monetary worldview of the US economist Milton Friedman, which pushes back the influence of the state and places trust in the powers of the market. The US introduce a change of course when it announces on 15 August 1971 that it is no longer going to convert the dollar to gold. The finance ministers and heads of the central banks of the ten largest Western industrialised countries are forced to stabilise the dollar as the leading currency with massive support purchases. With the "Deutsche Bundesbank" having to purchase around 5.8 billion USD within a few days to support the US currency, the federal government shuts down the foreign exchange markets.

The system of fixed exchange rates adopted in 1944 by the Allied Forces in Bretton Woods collapses on 19 March 1973 when Germany floats the exchange rate of the DM vis-à-vis the USD. The Europeans go their own way and now form a European Monetary Block with the DM as the new lead currency. Outside of the block, EC currencies can float "freely."

A new global player is in the game. In June 1973, the Organization of Petroleum Exporting Countries (OPEC) increases crude oil prices by 11.9 percent. When attacks by Egyptian and Syrian forces on Israel trigger the Yom Kippur War, the situation heightens. The petroleum exporting Arab states increase the price of crude oil again, and ultimately proclaim an oil embargo against states which take a pro-Israeli stance. The US and the Netherlands are no longer supplied with crude oil; other western countries such as the Federal Republic of Germany only receive 75 percent of previous amounts. Germany's government introduces Sunday driving bans and speed limits.

The oil crisis of 1973 closed petrol stations and brought a ban on Sunday driving

The war ends after 18 days, but the oil crisis persists. In 1973/74, the oil states gradually quadruple the price of crude oil. The Bundesbank embarks on an extremely restrictive course, but the oil shock annihilates all efforts of state intervention. Germany learns to cope as the inflation rate climbs to 7 percent at the start of 1973.

Turbulent times. The market gets going. The fixed pricing for brand products is lifted. Manufacturers transition to recommended retail prices. Purchasing power increases. Wages and salaries in the public service increase by 11 percent. On 6 May 1974, Willy Brandt resigns in a surprise move after his aide, Günter Guillaume, is revealed to be an East-German spy. Helmut Schmidt is the next Chancellor.

In June 1974, the collapse of the Cologne-based bank Iwan D. Herstatt rocks Germany. There are tremendous losses in foreign exchange trading and fraudulent activities carried out by executives come to light. Foreign exchange dealer Dany Dattel becomes famous. The biggest collapse of a bank since 1929

27 June 1974: Hans-Hermann Gerloff (with megaphone), a director of the Herstatt Bank, makes a statement to the assembled depositors

leads to a crisis in confidence. Joh. Berenberg, Gossler & Co., which, at the time, was also a big name in foreign exchange trading, is not directly affected. Twenty banks had provided surety for the losses. An emergency fund set up by German banks, in which Joh. Berenberg, Gossler & Co. participated, protects the money of 35,000 people who had made savings deposits. Joachim H. Wetzel recalls: "The banks were all sitting in the same boat. Regardless of whether we were a reputable bank or not, we were treated as if we were just like Dattel. I was sitting in Heinz Lessing's office when one of our business partners from the Bank of Montreal called. It was a very short conversation. The Canadian asked: 'Are you ok?' And Lessing responded: 'We are ok.' And with that the matter was settled. The Bank of Montreal was willing to manage our US Dollar clearing smoothly. That was sensational!"

Berenberg had free reign. "We pre-financed loans for Swedish and Finnish paper production," explains Wetzel. "And as security, we had the claims against the German importer. At the time, we were not globalised, not even Europeanised. But we organised a loan of more than 40 million DM for one company. Five million came from us, with 35 million coming from secondary foreign partners. That was great fun. Heinz Lessing arranged it. He was the strategist, he had an amazing knack. He just didn't enjoy life enough."

The baron, on the other hand, was a self-confessed epicurean. "He was very hard when necessary, but also very sensitive," recalls Claus G. Budelmann. "He was educated, international and down-to-earth all at once. And he was very sociable." Between the patriarch and his young confidante, there was a typical Hamburg version of closeness and distance. "At the start, he addressed me in the familiar form. Then he called me 'Claus' and addressed me formally. And I said: Baron Gossler."

By the middle of the 1970s, the windows of the financial world were opening towards the East. The GDR gave western banks its approval to set up branches in East Berlin. France re-enters the European monetary union. The oil crisis seems to be over, but it highlighted how dependent affluent societies are on oil imports. In Germany, a recovery is emerging. The export country is standing its ground in light of growing competition on the world market.

The bank expands its management. In 1976, Peter Freiherr von Kapherr becomes a personally liable partner (until 1999). Two years later, Joachim von Berenberg-Consbruch joins the other partners as a personally liable partner. "I was something like the finance minister. My job was to keep things together. Caution ranked higher than the notion of profit. That sets us apart from most of the other banks. We have a different continuity in service, a lower fluctuation. Continuity creates trust."

But he always had the world in view. The Federal Republic of Germany had been receiving natural gas from the Soviet Union since 1973. The economic relations to Eastern Bloc countries are still in the early stages. At Joh. Berenberg, Gossler & Co., Joachim C. Wetzel sees the tremendous potential behind the Iron Curtain. "I looked after business with Russia at a time when nobody took it seriously. But that was not just my doing. Opportunity only comes when you reach out to it. Russia approached us. The Russian fishing fleet has to bunker oil; Russia only has its own in summer because the ports are free of ice then. Russia needed someone to pre-finance it. We organised that. They founded a company and wanted to celebrate the launch. I had a problem though as my daughter, Patrizia, was turning 18 that same day. I had arranged a boat tour for her and her friends and just took the Russian business

Peter Freiherr von Kap-herr and Joachim von Berenberg-Consbruch become personally liable partners

Business with Russia and China

December 1979: U.S. President Jimmy Carter and Britain's Iron Lady and Prime Minister Margaret Thatcher

partners along. Patrizia learned a few words of Russian and greeted the guests in Russian. That was the breakthrough. Ever since then, we have been friends."

This cosmopolitan outlook has tradition. Berenberg has maintained ties to China for more than 200 years and steadily makes new contacts. In 1979, together with the Norddeutschen Landesbank International Luxemburg, Berenberg succeeded in concluding the first 50 million USD credit with the Bank of China. "It was pretty strange," recalls Joachim H. Wetzel. "They came to us because they wanted to know what they had to do to buy German Leopard tanks. It goes without saying that that was not going to work, but should we have sent them away? We suggested that they buy something else such as continuous track vehicles without canons. Those were conspiratorial meetings. I spoke of reconstruction and explained to the Chinese what the middle class is. And then they invited me to China. There, we signed the agreements, financed imports, pre-financed exports."

The year 1979 is an eventful one in world politics. The Shah of Iran flees to Egypt, the Iranian Shiite leader, Ayatollah Khomeini, returns to Iran from Paris after living in exile for 15 years. Margaret Thatcher becomes the first female prime minister of Great Britain. On 27 December 1979, Soviet troops cross the border into Afghanistan and capture the capital city of Kabul. At the end of the year, OPEC increases the price of crude oil by an average of 10 percent triggering a new oil crisis. However, this time the countries impacted react in a calmer way. There are no Sunday driving bans. But the confidence in the dollar as the lead currency has declined considerably. In an effort to get exchange rates back on an even keel, Chancellor Helmut Schmidt and French President Valery Giscard d'Estaing take a historic step when they set up the European Monetary System (EMS).

In the international arena, eastern policy, which entails "change through rapprochement" is gradually showing signs of success. The German-Soviet trade agreement is followed by the Basic Treaty of 1972 with the GDR, there is the inclusion of both German states in the UNO, and the following year, there are "permanent representations" in Bonn and East Berlin.

1980–1990: From the Oil Crisis to Reunification

In 1980, there is a change of owners at Joh. Berenberg, Gossler & Co. With the Bank of Montreal heavily invested in financial services provider ADCA, a competitor of Berenberg, there is a break in relations. The Canadians depart, and Gertrud Reemtsma, the widow of the deceased Hamburg tobacco giant and arts patron Philipp Reemtsma, who died in 1959, takes over the available capital share.

For the first time, the annual balance sheet records more than 200 employees. The bank is involved in the global securities business. "Slowly, the international private banking business was gaining our interest," recalls Claus-G. Budelmann, "that also resulted from the growing prosperity. The success of a bank is measured, among other things, by whether it succeeds in building up client trust over the long term because the bank has to have insight into client affairs in order to be able to offer advice and intervene in a helpful way. As a bank, we were always transparent. And we always understood ourselves as being service providers – unlike many other banks."

German politics is still struggling with the fallout of the oil crisis – adhering to strict austerity measures. The Bundestag passes laws to revamp the federal budget in 1982. The coalition experiences a crisis. Chancellor Helmut Schmidt asks for a vote of confidence, dissolves the coalition with the FDP and proposes early elections. However, the CDU/CSU have other plans in mind and begin coalition talks which lead to the overthrow of Schmidt on 1 October 1982 in a constructive no-confidence vote. The Bundestag elects Helmut Kohl as the sixth German chancellor. He will govern the country for the next 16 years.

The new government has to economise. The child benefit is reduced, co-payments for hospital stays and reconvalescence treatments are upped as are contributions to pension plans and unemployment insurance. Unemployment climbs to a record high of 9.3 percent despite the mid-80s recovery and in 1989, it is still at 7.9 percent.

Joh. Berenberg, Gossler & Co. has enjoyed continued success and is growing its operations. A contemporary recalls: "Back then, a lot could be done in conversations, there were short distances. The salary accounts were managed in main accounts. There was no Human Resources department. Agreements were prepared by hand, often only using a few sentences."

Reemtsma family takes over the capital share of the Bank of Montreal

Shares in the bank:
30 % v. Berenberg-Gossler family and PhG
40 % Norddeutsche Landesbank
15 % Philadelphia National Bank
15 % Reemtsma family

1 October 1982: the newly elected chancellor Helmut Kohl (CDU) takes his oath of office

Electronic data processing gains in importance. From small beginnings, a mainframe computer is developed at the bank with six megabytes of main memory, seven hard disc stations and 90 monitors. Given that there are 90 monitors connected to the central computer system in 1984 (and 200 employees), there is a terminal for each employee who requires information from current business activities. The intended goal of having more information for the employees and management is achieved.

Berenberg Bank's full-service palette would not have been possible without the consistently outstanding work and collaboration of its employees. Naming a few people here would inevitably be an injustice to the others. But there is one extraordinary case: Johann Mosler, who had been acquainted with the von Berenberg-Gossler family since prior to World War I, came into the office on Neuer Jungfernstieg every day right up to the age of 92. It not only says something about Mr Mosler, but also about the way the bank treated its employees.

In politics, the powers are playing the same games of pressure and counter pressure. At the World Economic Summit in June 1982, participants urge the US to change its fiscal policy and reduce the high interest rate – but to no avail. In tedious negotiations with Japan in 1983, the European Community pushes through a three-year limitation on Japanese exports to EC countries. Japan announces it will voluntarily limit the export of video recorders, colour picture tubes and other products.

In Germany, spectacular bankruptcies rock the country. In 1982, AEG-Telefunken, the country's second-largest electronics company, was forced to launch insolvency proceedings in what was the largest company collapse in the history of post-war Germany. In November 1983, the imminent collapse of the renowned bank Schröder, Münchmeyer, Hengst & Co. (SMH) set off alarm bells throughout the financial world. SMH boss Ferdinand Graf von Galen went against all reason and common sense and loaned almost 900 million DM – eight times the bank's capital – to one single client, Horst-Dieter Esch, the boss of the Mainz-based construction equipment manufacturer IBH. And he filed for bankruptcy. The move put 10,000 jobs on the line. The deposit protection funds of the banking association and 38 institutes are involved in rescuing the financially strapped bank. Count Galen is sentenced to prison. SMH is sold to Lloyds Bank International, and in 2005, merges with Swiss major UBS.

How can it be that one individual can lead a renowned private bank to the brink of destruction? If the boss defrauds his partners, things can get dicey. Joachim von Berenberg-Consbruch talks about the human element: "We used to make many decisions based on gut feelings. When someone sat across from us, we asked ourselves: Is this person ok? Electronics have changed a lot of things. Deceitfulness can be perfected."

In the annual balance sheet for 1983, the bank records its first ever total volume in excess of 2 billion DM. Hamburg had long since emerged as the second-biggest banking centre behind Frankfurt am Main.

Europe's politicians meanwhile are holding their course. In 1983, government heads of the ten EC member states sign the 'Solemn Declaration on European Union' in Stuttgart. On 15 June 1985, France, Belgium, the Nether-

The balance sheet surpasses 2 billion DM

1981: employees from the electrical company AEG attending a company meeting in Berlin-Wedding

1970: Data processing becomes the
standard in offices – photo of a French
computer centre

Also 1970: People also made the most of the new video disc system at home – developed by a consortium of firms including AEG-Telefunken, Teldec and Decca

1984: Staff form a guard of honour
as Freiherr von Berenberg-Gossler
celebrates his 75th birthday

The Fürstenberg family acquires
an interest

lands, Luxembourg, and Germany meet in Schengen, Luxembourg and agree to gradually reduce identity checks at the borders. In 1986, Portugal and Spain join the European Community, pushing the number of memberstates to 12. In 1987, the Deutsche Bundesbank resolves to allow the private use of ECU in the Federal Republic of Germany.

In May 1987, Joachim Fürst zu Fürstenberg, Donaueschingen, took over shares from the Norddeutsche Landesbank, which reduced its participation from 40 to 25 percent.

Berenberg expands further, albeit carefully and opens a branch in Switzerland. "It was one floor. Gartenstraße 17. I still remember the neon sign on the building: Elektro Meyer", explains Joachim H. Wetzel. "We actually wanted to buy a bank, but we were unable to muster up 20 percent anywhere, and we wouldn't have known if there were any skeletons in the closet. So we created our own bank." Today, the Berenberg Bank (Schweiz) AG is a real bank in a respectable five-storey building situated directly on Lake Zurich with a branch in Geneva.

In a symbolic act on 27 June 1989, the Hungarian foreign minister, Gyula Horn, and his Austrian colleague, Alois Mock, cut through the border fence between the two countries. From now on, there is no turning back on what soon happens. A steady stream of vacationers and refugees exit the GDR to Hungary and from there, over the unmanned border to Austria. GDR citizens seek refuge in the permanent representative of the Federal Republic of Germany in East Berlin and in the embassies in Budapest and Prague. On 30 September 1989, Foreign Minister Hans-Dietrich Genscher announces from the balcony of the German embassy in Prague that all GDR refugees at the German embassies in Prague and Warsaw are allowed to leave the country.

Although the GDR still celebrates the 40th anniversary of its founding with the usual military marches and parades, on 7 October 1989, the Soviet state and party leader Mikhail Gorbachev makes calls for reforms in East Berlin before the assembled world press: "Life punishes those who lag behind." The appeal of the Monday demonstrators in Leipzig is unmistakable: "We are the people – no violence." The Peaceful Revolution from below topples the

November 1989: Masses of East German citizens seek refuge in the West German embassy in Prague

communist system and tears down the Iron Curtain. On 9 November 1989, Günter Schabowski, the SED politburo member, announces without fanfare the decision of the council of ministers, which permits citizens of his state to take "private trips abroad", "immediately, without delay." In the evening, the first turnpikes along the Berlin Wall open – the Berlin Wall has finally fallen.

The historic impact of the 1980s is remarkable. The decade brought the collapse of a world order that had been embedded in concrete for decades. The balance of terror is history. The 1980s are not just the decade of German reunification, but also a decade of powerful mergers. In 1986, the Federal Cartel Office approves the takeover of AEG by the Daimler-Benz group, which was the biggest merger in the history of Germany until three years later when the federal Economics Minister Helmut Haussmann issues a ministerial decree authorising the merger of Daimler-Benz AG with the aerospace group "Messerschmitt-Bölkow-Blohm" (MBB). Thus, the largest corporate merger in the history of the Federal Republic of Germany is concluded.

November 1989: An endless line of East German "Trabis" inches across the opened border – and is greeted by West German applause

An adventure begins. The monetary union emerges from one day to the next with the smooth integration of two diametrically opposed economic systems into one. Freedom instead of socialism. The social market economy is up and running overnight with all its consequences for 16 million people. German Marks for everyone. On 1 January 1990, the DM exchange rate at banks in the GDR is set at three to one – five to one on the black market. Karl Otto Pöhl, president of the Bundesbank, maintains that the quick introduction of the mark in the GDR is a mistake, but goes along with the decision. Wages, salaries and rents are converted one-to-one. The Federal Republic of Germany assumes all pension entitlements of the new states. Savings accounts are exchanged, graduated by age up to a limit of 6,000 DM.

"The Bundesbank" brings 28 billion DM to 10,000 distribution locations, the largest money transport of all time. The state-owned bank of the GDR transfers its functions as a commercial bank to the newly created "Deutsche Kreditbank AG" and to the "Berliner Stadtbank AG". On 1 July, the Monetary, Economic and Social Union takes effect.

Baron v. Berenberg-Gossler in conversation with Swiss banker Hans J. Bär and Morris Dorrance, CEO of the Philadelphia National Bank (from right) during the celebrations. For many years Bär und Dorrance were on Berenberg's advisory board.

On 18 September 1990, Joh. Berenberg, Gossler & Co. celebrate its 400th anniversary. Hamburg's mayor, Henning Voscherau, extends invitations to the celebration in the Hamburg town hall; Karl Otto Pöhl, president of the Bundesbank, delivers the keynote speech. In addition to clients, many associated bankers from Germany and abroad are in attendance. In the evening, there is a magnificent celebration in the *Staatsoper*.

To commemorate the anniversary, the partners set up the "Berenberg Bank Foundation of 1990" with the goal of fostering young artists in the Hanseatic city. "Berenberg has always cultivated the arts and culture," notes Claus-G. Budelmann, "we were like the English merchant banks in that respect. They have the same origin and emerged from trade. The Berenbergs, as you know, were successful cloth merchants in Antwerp before they came to Hamburg."

During the anniversary year, another subsidiary is founded, Berenberg Real Estate Services GmbH. Specialised services in addition to traditional banking offerings are becoming more important. In past years, other subsidiaries have been set up, including Berenberg Consult GmbH (mergers & acquisitions, company valuations, market analyses) and "Berenberg Treuhand GmbH" as well as the "Berenberg Vermögenstreuhand GmbH". Companies added later include "Berenberg Finanzanlagen GmbH", which mainly analyses and develops investment offers, Berenberg Private Equity GmbH and Berenberg Lux Invest S.A. to realise investment funds.

In July 1990, Hendrik Riehmer, who was born in 1968, joins the bank. His father, a lawyer, is unable to instil any enthusiasm in him for law. Even occasional visits to his office are to no avail. For Riehmer's professional future, it turns out, his grandfather Louis Rodenstein is key. Back in the 1960s, he rebuilt the South American business for "Deutsche Bank", and after his retirement, he managed his entire fortune on the stock market – much to the worry of the family. The young Riehmer was so intrigued, that he listened to the stories of his grandfather almost every weekend and talked to him about the latest share purchases. He recalls: "The possibility of building up wealth by selecting the right stocks has fascinated me ever since, and when I was going to school, I spent more time with investment advisors, than I did doing my homework."

After graduating from school in Hamburg, he begins a banking apprenticeship in 1988 at "Hamburger Sparkasse". However, as he immediately opens

The Berenberg Culture Prize, with its DM 25,000 stipend, is awarded for the first time on 26 March 1992 to the mezzo-soprano Christiane Iven; stipends of DM 15,000 each are presented to the film director and screenplay author Max Färberböck and the pianist Sebastian Knauer, with whom the bank continues to partner on annual projects to this day

Hendrik Riehmer joins Berenberg

a securities account and then directly arranges share purchases with traders in Frankfurt, his days at the bank appear to be numbered after just four weeks; his bosses are overwhelmed by the pace of the apprentice. His father's profession proves to be a stroke of luck. He makes sure that Riehmer is allowed to continue his bank apprenticeship.

Riehmer already knows that he wants to work either in share trading, or in investment banking. However, as the "Hamburger Sparkasse" required one year's work in a branch – completely unnecessary in the eyes of the young apprentice – he decides to keep his eyes peeled for other options. His favourite hobby proves to be beneficial. Riehmer had begun playing hockey when he was six. As a youth, he was in the Hamburg draft along with future national team players such as Christian "Büdi" Blunck and Frederik Ness. While Riehmer plays for *Groß Flottbek*, Blunck laces up for *Harvestehuder THC* and Ness for the *Club an der Alster*. Blunck, who would go on to become one of the best German hockey players of all time, makes quite an impression on him. His only goal is to make it to the national team like Blunck. But after the tryouts, Riehmer is not invited to camps, and at the age of 17, he realises that he hasn't got what it takes for a career on the national team. He still plays for *Groß Flottbek* for a few years in the national league, and then his interest in hockey wanes in favour of his enthusiasm for the stock market. At the age of 22, Riehmer puts his stick away for good.

Whenever hockey and banking are mentioned in Hamburg at this time, the name "Claus-G. Budelmann" comes up. The then new personally liable partner is an excellent hockey player at the *Club an der Alster* and has put together a hockey team at Berenberg that always plays against the "Vereins- und Westbank".

In 1990, a hockey friend asks Riehmer if he would like to come to Berenberg as his assistant. The small unit looks after foreign institutional clients who buy German shares – a dream job for Riehmer, who thinks studying is an unnecessary waste of time.

"By hiring me, Claus Budelmann no doubt hoped to give his hockey team a strategic boost," says Riehmer with a twinkle in his eye. In terms of mixing hockey with banking, he will later prove to be a big disappointment for Budelmann. After ending his hockey career, he never plays hock-

The Berenberg hockey team

ey again, not even for his bosses. Riehmer had long since turned his attention to a new hobby: every minute he can, he spends at the golf course.

A new Germany. The Berlin Wall is a thing of the past and is being torn down. The GDR Council of Ministers resolves on 1 March 1990 to transform all combined and state-owned companies into stock corporations and to set up a trust agency or *Treuhand*. It is launched in 1990. A total of 8,500 companies are impacted with around 45,000 operations and 4 million employees, the collective fortune of the state security, state pharmacies and the organised popular masses. Thousands of apartments are sold along with 2.4 million hectares of land.

But how does one go about transforming that which even under the careful conditions of "real existing socialism" was bankrupt and totally outdated? The operations sense the icy wind of competition. In the end, 14,600 companies are transformed. Of the over 4 million employees, only 1.24 million have a job two years later in *Treuhand* operations, with the downward trend expected to continue. The unemployment rate jumps to 14.2 percent. On 31 December 1994, the work of the trust agency has recorded proceeds of around 60 billion DM and expenses of 300 billion; a mountain of debt of 200 billion DM are put over to legacy redemption funds.

On the day of the renaming, the head of the *Treuhand*, Birgit Breuel, comments: "If you recall that in four-and-a-half years, an entire economy has been transformed, which can, for the most part, stand its ground, the market economy has been introduced here in an unbelievably short period of time."

There has never been a privatisation of this scale, and certainly not at this pace. The national wealth drifts westwards. Only six percent of the company acquisitions are handled by East Germans.

The reunification is subject to approval. Mikhail Gorbachev and US President George Bush agree to let the Germans decide which alliance they want to belong to in future. Chancellor Helmut Kohl returns home from his state visit to the Soviet Union with this promise. Unified Germany receives full sovereignty and a de facto peace treaty. Allied sovereign rights end on 3 October 1990 – after 45 years. And Germany gets its Day of German Unity. The GDR comes under the jurisdiction of Basic Law and ceases to exist. Confiscated property in the GDR has to be returned to former owners. The first free, all-German elections in 58 years result in an overwhelming victory for

German President Richard von Weizsäcker signs the Treaty of Unification in Bonn on 24 September 1990, putting an end to the division of Germany

the "Chancellor of Unity". In its first session, the Bundestag adopts the solidarity surcharge to strengthen the new states.

The move towards a unified Europe and to the monetary union is going like clockwork. There is a schedule as well. The state and government heads of the 12 EC countries resolve in Maastricht to create the European Union and to introduce a European Currency (ECU) by 1999 at the latest. This seals the scheduled end to 12 European currencies, making them and the DM discontinued models.

Around two-thirds of Germans are against a single European currency. There is scepticism in German companies as well, and it is not just a German phenomenon. The British and the Italians jump ship, the British Pound and the Italian Lira leave the EMS exchange rate system in favour of single-handed sailing in the free markets. In 1993, Europe's finance ministers and heads of national banks expand the fluctuation margin of the exchange rates in an effort to stabilise the turbulence hitting the financial markets thereby practically annihilating the European Monetary System.

In 1993, the state and government heads vote for Frankfurt am Main to be the location of the European Monetary Institute, the precursor to the European Central Bank. On 1 January 1994, the terms of the European Economic Area (EEA) come into force. Thus, the world's largest market emerges for the free movement of goods, services and capital with around 375 million consumers.

Berenberg continues to travel internationally, company units bundle the unique expertise in corporate client business to trade in nations and regions like Scandinavia, Chile, Ecuador, China, New Zealand and Australia, and "by cultivating contacts and travelling, the bank's country and regional representatives have fostered our international business ties and developed new ones," as it states in the 1994 annual report.

The banking business is undergoing changes. Joachim H. Wetzel, as a personally liable partner responsible for the path of the bank and always in contact with colleagues from other banks such as Warburg and Metzler, sensed that something was amiss. "All of a sudden, everyone was doing securities transactions, yet it seemed that everyone had basically a different idea of what was meant".

In Frankfurt, Dr Hans-Walter Peters knew what was meant. In 1994, he was still working at "Frankfurter Volksbank", but was looking for his own entrepreneurial challenge.

Peters was born in 1955 in Soltau. At the age of 34, his father, Walter, was the town director and thus the top man in the community of Schneverdingen in the *Heidekreis* district, which currently numbers just under 20,000 citizens. Even as a young boy, he accompanied his father, saw ministers and other politicians and witnessed his father's knack for gathering people together at events and creating an atmosphere of comfort. "My father was an authority, he was also a very loving person; we were very close," he says full of admiration for him. "I definitely recognised the value of long-term relationships and internalised that."

Very early on, he developed a love of animals, especially of horses and dogs. For almost 20 years, he passionately pursues his hobby of dressage, riding both at home and during his studies, which first take him to Dortmund, where he studies statistics and economics. After completing his degree, he is drawn back to the north, but to Kiel on the coast. After just four weeks, he realises: "You can't learn much more, you can only give." The time spent un-

Dr Hans-Walter Peters joins Berenberg

The personally liable partners of the Berenberg Bank in 1992 (from left): Peter Baron von Kap-herr, Joachim H. Wetzel, Claus-G. Budelmann and Joachim von Berenberg-Consbruch in front of the portrait of Johann Heinrich Gossler (1805–1879)

der his PhD supervisor, Professor Manfred Wilms, was nonetheless defining, "it gave me tremendous self-confidence." After a day of work at the university, he liked going to the North Sea. "Back then, I had a Suzuki Jeep, the surfboard was always strapped to it, and I liked to surf best in a force six wind off Römö." On the side, he writes his 175-page PhD thesis. The topic covers capital market theory and stock market analysis.

After earning his PhD and deciding to embark on a career in banking, Peters moves to Frankfurt in 1987 to a subsidiary of "Dresdner Bank" specialising in American clients. "It was there that I learned what it means to work for international clients and which standards apply." Later, as head of portfolio strategy at the "DG Bank", he builds up their equity and bond research. At the end of 1990, Peters transfers to the "Frankfurter Volksbank" and becomes division manager for the securities business – "the extensive responsibility, the good salary and the first company car were enticing".

During his time at the "DG Bank", Peters recognised the tremendous potential of insurance companies. As institutional investors with high investment needs, they are the ideal partner for his business. He sets up a working group for insurance companies that allows participants to exchange views on the oppurtunities and problems of capital investment. Peters moderates the work group, extends invitations and knows how to attract insurance company board members. The working group still exists today – after 30 years. "I went through my entire career with the participants. It is a close connection which means a lot to me personally."

Wetzel and Peters become acquainted in 1993. Peters decides on a future at Berenberg – a decision which would later shape the traditional bank.

"I wouldn't say that he laughed at me," recalls Wetzel later, "But he first explained to me what *I* actually wanted from *him*. I hired him, and I am very happy about that."

Peters sums up: "What appealed to me about Berenberg was that this long-standing bank was an institution focussed on commercial banking activities yet was still relationship orientated. The securities business was still in its early stages. I am very thankful to Joachim Wetzel and my later partners, Joachim v. Berenberg-Consbruch and Claus-G. Budelmann, for giving me leeway and their trust to virtually rebuild the business completely."

Dr Hans-Walter Peters becomes director at Berenberg in 1994 and managing director at Berenberg Capital Management GmbH. In response to the question posed by friend Claus. H. Blänkner, who is responsible for investment management at the "Württembergische Versicherung", as to whether he has confirmation from Berenberg that he will become a partner, he answers dryly: "I don't have it, but my success will convince them!"

Peters' office is currently located on the ninth floor of the bank with an unobstructed view over the Binnenalster, one of those offices that is filled with the brightness of the Alster on nice, clear days. "Joachim Wetzel gave me free reign early on," explains the banker. "He never put obstacles in my way, on the contrary, he removed them. I had brought several large institutional clients, insurance companies, which, back then, quickly became the bank's largest clients. It was a milestone in the development of Berenberg as it meant entry into our large-volume equities business and, ultimately, the possibility of using the profits to professionally set up new areas such as asset management, private banking and investment banking". Just a few years after Peters joined the bank, asset management with his special funds launched for insurance companies in the working group accounted for a large part of the bank's profit.

Moving away from the lending business to security business

What sounds like a move in a new direction was basically a radical about-turn. Not everyone at the time had registered the already visible crisis in the lending business. "When I joined, the business model was geared to the lending business; there was virtually no securities business." The traditional foundation of many private banks had not yet started to falter, but those who looked closer, saw the first hairline cracks. "Back then, we started to completely change the bank's profile by moving away from the lending business towards the securities business. That was the first cornerstone for today's success," says Peters.

A good client of the bank and witness to the whole process notes just how dynamic the process was. Dr Wolfgang Peiner is a tax consultant and auditor, who was the chairman of "Gothaer Versicherungen" in Cologne in the 1990s and the Hamburg finance senator from 2001 to 2006. Thereafter, he was the chairman of the supervisory board of "HSH Nordbank AG" and he currently sits on various top-level supervisory boards. From his home on Warburgstraße, it is just a few steps to Berenberg on Neuer Jungfernstieg. "I have known Berenberg for a long time, because together with the Gothaer, we were one of the first clients when Peters began restructuring the bank. The new idea was to approach insurance companies and wholesale investors with whom one could accumulate capital and help them invest their money. Peters was the right man for the job. The institutional business is harder than the one with private clients. Professional investors have a completely different culture. Professionals sit across from you who know exactly what the situation is. And in this business, it can easily be about 50, 100 million or more. At this stage, sympathy is no longer key, but rather ideas and performance".

In business, there are some significant mergers. "Deutsche Bundesbahn" and "Deutsche Reichsbahn" are privatised and on 1 January 1994, they merge to form the "Deutsche Bahn AG", Tchibo takes over Eduscho, in 1997 the steel group Krupp-Hoesch prepares for a friendly takeover of Thyssen AG, but then an agreement is reached and the subsequent establishment of a combined steel company. In 1998, Daimler-Benz joins forces with the third-largest US car manufacturer, Chrysler; at the time, it was the largest industrial merger in history. In 1999, "Deutsche Bank" and the US investment bank Bankers Trust become the largest banking institution in the world. Daimler-Chrysler Aerospace AG (Dasa), Aérospatiale-Matra S.A. and Construcciones Aeronáuticas S.A. form the European Aeronautic, Defense and Space Company (EADS), to become the world's third-largest aerospace company.

Companies are becoming bigger and so are the bankruptcies. Jürgen Schneider AG files for bankruptcy. The balance sheets of the construction giant show a deficit of over 5 billion DM, around 50 creditor banks are impacted. In 1995, charges are laid for fraud, credit fraud and document fraud, which bring him a prison sentence of six years and nine months. In October 1996, the history of AEG, a company with a tradition spanning 113 years, comes to an end. Parts of the company are sold; parts continue to be managed by the parent company, Daimler-Benz. That same year, the largest German shipbuilding company, "Bremer Vulkan Verbund AG", goes bankrupt.

"There isn't a credit business without any losses," explains a long-time employee, "even Berenberg has been burned during its history. We had a problem with a Hamburg mineral oil dealer who had falsified his balance sheets for years to get new credit. He was making losses but recording profits. When he was exposed, we had to bear the loss. It was still manageable as many other banks were involved. We filed for sequestration with the bankruptcy court as we had noticed irregularities during an external audit. The total damage was in the double-digit millions. The dealer had to go to prison."

And then there was a honey dealer, who proceeded in an especially devious manner and had taken out credit with several banks. "Most of all, he was a gifted forklift driver," recalls Joachim H. Wetzel. Whenever a bank wanted to see if his information about the goods warehouse was correct, he would drive the goods to the appropriate spot over night. It was always the same pile of goods which was used as security for one bank and then made available for another bank to view. "In the banking business, there are always failures," attests Joachim von Berenberg-Consbruch. "They cause many sleepless nights and you remember them even decades later. Successes are easier to forget."

In 1995, the EU becomes a community of 15 countries as a result of the accession of Austria, Finland and Sweden. The transition to a single currency on 1 January 1999 is a done deal. After another summit meeting, the currency has a name: the future European currency unit is to be called the euro.

On 17 May 1997, Heinrich Freiherr von Berenberg-Gossler dies at the age of 88. He joined his father's company in 1935 as a personally liable partner and managed the private bank Joh. Berenberg, Gossler & Co. up until 1978. Afterwards, he was the chairman of the advisory board and as of 1991, honorary chairman of the same board. The baron was an exceptional banker personality, led the company through difficult times all the while exhibiting

Heinrich Freiherr von Berenberg-Gossler dies

sound judgment, wisdom and insight into human nature and shaping the style of the company in a suave and sophisticated way. Heinrich von Berenberg-Gossler, CBE, Commander of the Order of the British Empire, was also chairman of the Anglo-German Club for 23 years, an institution in Hamburg. "The ties the Berenberg Bank have to the United Kingdom have been traditionally close," said Claus-G. Budelmann, who, in 2014, was also recognised by the Queen for his efforts to promote German-British relations and awarded the Honorary Officer of the Most Excellent Order of the British Empire (OBE). He follows in the footsteps of the baron as chairman of the Anglo-German Club and when the consulate general in Hamburg is closed in 2006, he assumes the office of the British Honorary Consul. The representation of the United Kingdom in Hamburg was located in the Berenberg Bank on Neuer Jungfernstieg until Budelmann gave up this consular position at the start of 2015.

In Berlin, construction starts on the chancellor's office, a ballet of cranes dances on Potsdamer Platz. And Europe is rumbling towards unity. England's Chancellor of the Exchequer, Gordon Brown, slams on the brakes; Great Britain does not want to be among the first participants of the new European Monetary Union and wants to introduce the euro at the earliest by 2002. In 1998, a large majority in the Bundestag is in favour of Germany's involvement in the European Monetary Union. The euro is to be introduced on 1 January 1999 in 11 of the 15 member states. As a result of the 1985 Schengen Agreement, there will be no more border controls between Germany, Austria and Italy as of 1998. Europe becomes the Schengen area.

In 1998, Berenberg has a new personally liable partner in Dr Andreas M. Odefey; but he leaves the bank three years later and manages the activities of Berenberg Private Equity GmbH under his own name.

For Joachim H. Wetzel, a stage of his life comes to an end. "In 1998 I retired after 30 years as a personally liable partner. "I had begun thinking about my successor early on; that was not simple to solve, but the others let me do it. I had learned how important it is to find someone who is trustworthy. We tasked a headhunter with the job of finding the right man. But then when I was thinking about things in the car on the Elbchaussee, it came to me: We have the right man in our own company: Dr Hans-Walter Peters. It was not hard to convince the partners. I am happy to have identified the right man."

Joachim H. Wetzel departs, Dr Hans-Walter Peters becomes personally liable partner

Cranes have dominated Berlin's skyline since German reunification

Asked about what the golden rules for a banker are, Joachim H. Wetzel says. "They don't exist. What applies are the normal standards people have when dealing with each other. We are service providers. We listen. We focus on what people want from us. We know each other. You develop a relationship based on trust. And the normal rules of decency and discretion apply."

Peters develops the company further, and, in particular, the securities sector becomes more important. Asset management and advisory services are created and developed. The advantages of a private bank, namely, proximity to clients, independence, discretion and continuity, were reflected in annual growth rates of 15 to 20 percent, sometimes even 40 percent. Peters even accelerated the business with institutional clients. In so, doing the basis is direct business dealings with insurance companies. And the sales volume with foreign clients was increased considerably in the mid 1990s. The volume of special funds quadrupled during this time; once these funds were acquired, they led to longer business relations. "With the launching of the European Monetary Union, pronounced changes in the institutional securities business began to emerge in 1997," recalls Peters. For insurance companies and pension funds, there is a general increase of the share quota and a stronger tendency to equity investment in the future euro region. In institutional business, Berenberg succeeds in increasing the volume of funds administered and in repositioning asset management for European shares. In 1997 alone, the volume held in special funds more than doubled.

In the equities business, there were also dealings with foreign investors that had been under the auspices of partner Claus-G. Budelmann since 1985, but which had been expanded by Hendrik Riehmer. Berenberg was not a big name in this segment; the business was small-scale. Thanks to Dr Peters' ties to the insurance industry, the new German business quickly grew in significant orders reaching a large volume. The logical outcome came in 1997 when both areas were merged; Peters was looking for someone who could implement it and in Hendrik Riehmer, he found a young, talented employee for the task.

Berenberg extends invitations to the first investor conference

And the activities in equity research and sales were developed. Company presentations and the first investor conference in 1998 ensure that Berenberg is visible in the sector; the company participated in capital increases and in the placement of bonds. "We weren't a big player in investment banking back then, and there were the established investor conferences held by the major investment banks. And yet, they all came to our conference at the *Hotel Vier Jahreszeiten* in Hamburg: The CFOs of DAX-listed companies, from Adidas to Daimler and Telekom right up to SAP and Volkswagen. The reason was that we geared the conference to a single target group, namely, to that of the insurance companies looked after by Dr Peters," says Riehmer in retrospect. "Everyone was jealous. It marked an important point in our history because whereas earlier we were commissioned by other banks and only filled orders, we now suddenly had our own clients with the insurance companies."

Changes in private banking

Peters also structures private banking. He knew that he could attract clients and that he had to reach a certain volume to establish premium service quality. "When I joined in 1994, there were two or three consultants and two special funds with a volume of 20 million DM each". As with Riehmer in investment banking, he was looking for a young talent to further develop private banking. In 1996, he recruits Michael Schramm from Marcard, Stein & Co. to head up private banking acquisition. He knew how to translate client needs into products and to acquire them for the bank. Peters organised appearances on n-tv und other TV stations; Schramm quickly became the face of Berenberg. In 2006, he transfers as personally liable partner to Hauck & Aufhäuser in Frankfurt and later becomes head of the private bank.

Regional expansion

Around the turn of the current century, Berenberg starts expanding geographically. To begin with, Berenberg could not resist the temptation and opens an office in Berlin in 1998. After Frankfurt, Zurich and Luxembourg, it is the fourth location outside Hamburg. The strategy of regional proximity was to become an important growth driver in the future of private banking. Yet in hindsight, the Berlin office did not do the company any great favour. There was hardly any "old money" to be had, and new money was not easy to come by. Perhaps it was because the mentalities did not match. After four years, the Berlin office closes its doors. In 1999, private banking activities get underway in the Frankfurt office on Börsenplatz; the office has been around since 1969; that same year, an office is set up in Bremen to acquire and look after local private clients.

The end of the 1990s is marked by changing parameters, especially by the eurozone, but also by the more professional nature which various areas of the bank take on. The fund business is expanded, with Berenberg issuing the first open Greek country fund as well as the Hungarian country fund.

A change of government in Bonn. For the first time in the history of the Federal Republic of Germany, the incumbent government is replaced in the federal election. Together with Alli-

In 1999 Berenberg opened a branch at Hollerallee 77 in Bremen

27 October 1998: Joschka Fischer (centre) is handed his letter of appointment as foreign minister by German President Roman Herzog; Chancellor Gerhard Schröder offers his congratulations

ance 90 / The Greens, the SPD achieves the absolute mandate majority in 1998. Chancellor Kohl is voted out of office after 16 years and Gerhard Schröder becomes the new chancellor with Joschka Fischer (Greens) as the vice chancellor and foreign minister.

On 1 January 1999, the euro is introduced in 11 member states of the EU, initially just as an accounting currency. The European Monetary Union enters into force. In foreign exchange, the euro starts with an exchange rate of 1.18 USD and sinks by the end of the year to just below the dollar exchange rate.

Achievements of the 1990s: Nelson Mandela is elected the first black president of South Africa. The World Trade Organization (WTO) emerges. Europe agrees on a stability pact. And Germany experiences longer opening hours for retail businesses, the Sunday baking ban is lifted and the state postal monopoly comes to an end. Those who want to make a phone call can choose freely from among several providers. Nursing care insurance is adopted. However, sadly, another legacy of the 1990s was the catastrophic employment fig-ures. In January 1998, the unemployment rate is at 12.6 percent.

Back in 1994, the personally liable partners wrote something that still applies 20 years later: "The role technology plays in banks is becoming ever more comprehensive; the contact at the counter is being replaced by ma-chines." But also: "As a result, the private banker has a manageable and dis-cerning client base, which now more than ever values personal service from a banker who knows individual wishes and requirements."

The personally liable partners have set the course for the turn of the century. The bank has a broad base: The securities sector, heavily developed over the last several years, is now complemented by the traditional commer-cial banking business as well as by a wide range of subsidiaries.

2000–2010: The New Century

Berenberg kicks off the new century with lots of momentum. The annual surplus increases by 72.3 percent from 44.3 to 76.3 million DM. The number of employees is 358. The economy and the business are spurred on by global growth; in the annual report, the chief economist talks of the best year since reunification. The bank expands its activities in private banking, and in its capacity as a service provider manages the very large private assets of new clients. The strategy includes asset structuring and holistic investment consulting, the bank supports foundations, has a family office and offers multi-depot controlling. Consultancy teams are set up by client groups with specialist know-how for the interests and concerns of entrepreneurs, private individuals, athletes and artists. It is always accompanied by responsible and rigorous risk management. Investments are also made in asset management, investment consultancy and in investment banking. Equity research is expanded, DAX companies introduce themselves at Berenberg investor conferences, the bank organises road shows, arranges block trades of share packages. In 2000 alone, the bank takes part in five large stock issues, including as co-manager during the IPO of T-Online International, "Deutsche Telekom" and AWD. "In the IPO of Telekom small player and newcomer Berenberg, gave the largest single order. An insurance company bought the shares through us. It created quite a sensation and disturbance for the syndicate banks," recalls Peters.

These "specialised transactions" are the extra something along with the core business and ensure that awareness grows of the emerging private bank. "Berenberg was successful because it concentrated on a segment which the major banks had neglected. They focused mainly on very large companies. Peters knew that they couldn't compete with "Deutsche Bank" or with Goldman Sachs, so they focused on research and on mid-caps, on the medium-sized corporations which are not on the radar of large international investment banks – the second and third tiers of the European capital companies. Initially, research costs more than it is worth, but the analytical competence is ultimately indispensable as the basis for serious work. Now they could say to their clients: We have analysed them, they are good and you can buy them. As a result of their research, they determined which companies needed capital, which ones are growing and want to make it to the stock exchange," says

Focus on mid caps

Since 1970, the headquarters of Berenberg have been located on Neuer Jungfernstieg in Hamburg

Dr Wolfgang Peiner, the former Hamburg finance senator and insurance company boss.

The global trend of mega-mergers persists. Internet provider America Online (AOL) and US media group Time Warner merge to become the world's largest media company. Mannesmann is taken over by Vodafone for 160 billion DM. The broadcasting groups Sat 1 and Pro Sieben merge to become the largest German television group. But "Deutsche Bank" failed in its attempt to integrate "Dresdner Bank".

The new century introduces the Germans to the Riester Pension, and the law governing discounts is revoked. The government and the energy sector agree on withdrawing from nuclear energy within 32 years, and the finance minister collects an unexpected windfall: The auction of the UMTS mobile phone licences brings tax authorities record proceeds to the tune of 98.8 billion DM.

11 September 2001: 3,000 die in the terror attack on the World Trade Centre in New York

On 11 September 2001, Islamic terrorists pilot two hijacked passenger airplanes into the towers of the World Trade Center in New York and a third one into the Pentagon. The Twin Towers in Manhattan collapse and over 3,000 people lose their lives. The US put its forces on high alert. The UN headquarters and the New York Stock Exchange are closed. The shock is deep and grips the world's financial markets.

The era of the DM is over. The euro becomes a tangible reality. Banks and savings institutions sell starter kits with euro coins valued at 20 marks. On 1 January 2002, the euro is introduced as cash. Over half of Germans object to the introduction of a single European currency, but now it has arrived. Consumers react with caution to the perceived price increases as a result of the introduction of the euro. The retail industry has the worst year since the end of World War II and "Teuro" – "the expensive euro" – becomes the buzz word of the year.

The world economy experiences a global standstill with serious repurcussions. In the first years of the new century, IT companies collapse the world over.

A shock wave hits most of the young companies as well as the financial world. The stock market bubble bursts in the industrialised countries and leaves its mark. And Berenberg's annual report for 2002 speaks "of a year of profound mistrust, of extremes and of crises." Avoiding risks is the order of the day.

For the first time, Berenberg's research is praised in international rankings, which, together with the intensive acquisition and support of institutional clients, reflects positively on the amount of the processed order volumes.

Berenberg is expanding its community involvement. In addition to promoting art and culture, lecture series are now initiated, top-level speakers visit the bank and give lectures to clients; in 2001, the bank extends the first-ever invitations to the Berenberg Polo Derby at the Hamburg Polo Club in Klein Flottbek; ten years later, six tournaments will have been held under the Berenberg name throughout Germany, Switzerland and England. In addition, there are the various activities at branch locations. "We are not only doing this to attract new clients, but also to increase the loyalty of our clients." says Peters. "Advisors and clients understand each other better if they spend the odd afternoon together and talk about other things besides money and investments." Marketing is successful and the number of clients increases. But the "hard facts" also add up as Berenberg receives numerous awards.

In 2002, Hamburg's mayor, Ole von Beust, opens Berenberg's new office in Shanghai as the bank's long-standing relationship with China strengthens; as early as the 18th century, the Berenbergs, together with other families, sent the first merchant ship from Hamburg to China. "Around the turn of the century, a number of Chinese companies in Hamburg were among Berenberg's clients; our China desk, which was staffed with Chinese employees, fostered the necessary proximity to the clients and cultural understanding," recalls Budelmann.

The bank continues to grow. In 2004, the assets managed surpass the 10 billion euro mark; four years later, that amount is over 20 billion. The geographical reach expands as well. In 2001, the subsidiary in Switzerland begins offering the full range of banking services. In 2003, an office is opened in London, and now Berenberg and its investment banking are represented in the most important European financial centre. "A decision that has far-reaching consequences, which later becomes apparent, and that is the foundation for the strong growth of Berenberg in the years to come," says Hendrik Riehmer. There are also locations in important national European markets: investment

Customer events foster exchanges between the bank and its clients

Berenberg in Shanghai

Berenberg goes to London

Berenberg has been represented in London since 2003; twelve years later nearly 250 employees work at its offices on Threadneedle Street

Joachim von Berenberg-Consbruch retires

The Fuchs-Report ranks Berenberg in 2003, 2004 and 2007 first in its report "Top-Adressen für Ihr Geld" (Top addresses for your money): "Berenberg masters all aspects of the craft. When it comes to approach, communication and professional review, Berenberg knows how to put the icing on the cake in all matters," says the jury.

banking opens offices in Zurich (2004), Paris (2005) and Milan (2006–2009) and asset management in Edinburgh (2004–2008). During these years, Berenberg concentrates on small and mid-sized listed companies and offers a high added value. At the Berenberg investor conference in London in 2004, 20 companies present themselves to around 100 investors.

Private banking is also entering new markets. Since 2003, clients in North Rhine-Westphalia have been acquired and looked after by the office on Cecilienallee in Düsseldorf. The bank has been extending into southern Germany from the office in Munich, which opened in 2005. One office followed the next with locations in Stuttgart (2006), Bielefeld (2005), Wiesbaden (2006–2012) and Salzburg (2009–2012).

In 2003, Guido M. Sollors joins Berenberg as a new personally liable partner. He comes from Deutsche Bank, where he was chief operating officer and head of marketing and sales of the corporate client division for Germany. He looks after mid-sized corporate clients, the lending business and the financial sector. Five years later, he leaves the bank to establish his own consultancy and participation company.

At the end of 2004, Joachim von Berenberg-Consbruch retires after 35 years as a personally liable partner. However, he remains in the company as a limited partner and member of the advisory board. That same year, an enlarged management board is introduced. Its members include the fully authorised representatives Graeme Davies, Hendrik Riehmer, Wilfried Schnoor and Michael Schramm. After the departure of Schramm, Andreas Brodtmann becomes a fully authorised representative and a member of the expanded management board in April 2006.

In 2005, the number of employees surpasses 500, and continues to grow. For the third time running, Berenberg appears in the ranking of the *Wirtschaftswoche* magazine as one of the top 100 companies that create the most jobs in Germany.

Meanwhile, Berenberg's expertise is made available from other sources as distribution channels are expanded and the bank cooperates with savings banks and other banks as well as with independent investment managers and financial service providers, who benefit from the expertise in Hamburg when they are advising their clients.

The economic climate is clouded by events. The war in Iraq burdens the markets, there is fear of war and deflation, and Germany, France and Italy slip into a recession for the second time within three years. The central banks lower their prime rates, the mood remains sombre. The DAX falls to 2,188 points; Germany, France and Portugal are criticised because they are not complying with the guidelines of the Maastricht Treaty.

Catastrophes rock the world including the tsunami on 26 December 2004, whose tidal waves struck eight Asian countries and took the lives of more than 230,000 people; Hurricane Katrina flooded New Orleans in August 2005 and also washed away the confidence of US citizens in a caring state. During these years, oil prices doubled. Practiced control mechanisms failed and veered out of control, the weakness of the state became visible and bank managers were continually faced with new challenges.

Berenberg focuses on its business model and on its own strengths – four business areas are defined and determine the strategy and style of the bank: private banking, investment banking, asset management and corporate banking.

In April 2006, Joachim Wetzel steps down from the bank's advisory board. After working as a personally liable partner (1968–1998), he had sat on the board until his final departure from the company. Prof Dr Harald Wiedmann now assumes the role of chairman. As the former board spokesman of "KPMG Deutsche Treuhandgesellschaft", he has decades of experience working with banks.

In the 2007 financial statement, it reads: "Although we are always very innovative when it comes to developing interesting investment models, if we are offered 'trendy products', which we do not understand, we steer clear of them and also encourage our clients to do the same." The stance is appreciated by the clients as shown by the fact that the financial statements increase even in uncertain market times. Berenberg ended 2008, the year the financial crisis broke out, with a balance sheet total of 4.3 billion EUR. It is an increase of over 18 percent compared to the previous year. The reason for the climb in

And the report *Die Elite der Vermögensverwalter* has given Berenberg the best accolade of summa cum laude since 2005.

In 2005, *Börsen-Zeitung* voted Berenberg as the "Analyst bank of the year" for German shares, and a survey by Thomson Financial of thousands of fund management companies in Europe ranks the bank first in equity research and sales for German small and mid caps.

2006
Prof Dr Harald Wiedmann is the new chairman of the advisory board

Record deposits during the financial crisis

2006: "Germany a Summer Fairytale":
the World Cup in Germany sparks a mood
of euphoria – although Italy ultimately
lifts the trophy

An iconic new landmark is taking shape on the banks of the River Elbe in Hamburg: the architectonically prestigious concert hall Elbphilharmonie

revenues is not because the demand for credit was particularly high. Instead, it is due to the fact that the confidence level private and corporate clients have in the bank is so high that they entrust their money to Berenberg. The Hamburg branch of a major German bank reports 500 million EUR in new deposits in four weeks. "We had 500 million EUR in one week. The problems we were presented with were not inconsiderable," says Peters in retrospect. "It was a time when even the banks didn't trust each other because they were all afraid that after Lehman Brothers, another bank would have to cease its operations. In March 2008, I heard initial rumours about how bad things were for the bank. At this time, we had far-reaching business ties, and as part of our private banking business, we also sold Lehman certificates, they were among the best on the market. Upon hearing this, I had all of the Lehman risks reduced and despite the numerous connections, it was completed by the start of July – the positions were almost all at zero." Unlike the competition, Berenberg did not have any Lehman "problems".

During these years, the deposits at Berenberg are roughly four times higher than the loans issued and so the investment of the excess liquidity is handled – even today – in a very conservative way in a well-diversified portfolio, which mostly contains securities from German public issuers and securities with a guarantee from Germany or from a German state.

Claus-G. Budelmann retires in 2008 after being affiliated with the bank for 43 years, 20 of them as a personally liable partner. Andreas Brodtmann and Hendrik Riehmer become new personally liable partners. At this point, Brodtmann had been working for Berenberg for 16 years and had managed the Berenberg Bank (Schweiz) AG. In 18 years, Riehmer has mainly been responsible for overseeing and expanding investment banking at Berenberg, which he continues to lead today in addition to being responsible for IT. The latter has always played a big role at Berenberg as the bank relies on inhouse solutions to ensure the greatest possible flexibility. For the first time, the personally liable partners now have a spokesperson at Berenberg. That person is Dr Hans-Walter Peters. The following year, he is elected to the board of the "Bundesverband deutscher Banken" (BdB; Association of German Banks) and since 2013, he has also been one of the three committee members. The BdB represents 220 private banks with 160,000 employees.

When presenting the financial statement for 2008, Peters says that Berenberg has "a functioning business model geared to continuity and services" and that the partners will advance business with sound judgment and common sense. "We prefer to double-check things before investing." Proof of this is that the long-standing conservative risk strategy did not have to be adapted even during the financial crisis.

Due to the bail outs of ailing major banks, national debt rises dramatically, and because of impending insolvency, a few countries in the eurozone are dependent upon assistance loads. The European Union, the countries in the eurozone and the IMF put together the amazing sum of 750 billion EUR into a credit package; the European Central Bank promises to buy up government bonds of defaulting euro countries.

On 15 September 2008, American investment bank Lehman Brothers is declared bankrupt – CEO Richard S. Fuld shown leaving the Capitol in Washington

Claus-G. Budelmann retires, Hendrik Riehmer and Andreas Brodtmann become personally liable partners

In Europe "poison cabinets losses" are looming to the tune of 1.2 trillion USD, Japanese securities are in the red by about 150 billion USD, an estimate that the IMF corrects after just three months. In reality, the losses are probably three times as much. Stock prices are in a tailspin before taking a nosedive. The commodity markets record price drops, sales of automobile manufacturers collapse, within one year the industrial production in the eurozone falls by 20 percent, and comparisons with the Great Depression of the 1930s emerge. The UN Food and Agriculture Organization (FAO) estimates the number of people who are starving grows by 100 million in 2009 as a result of the world economic crisis. In Europe, the unemployment rate is at 9.5 percent, which is the highest level in ten years.

State assistance for banks – record result at Berenberg

But in the spring of 2009, the automotive and construction industries pick up pace again. Stimulus packages are having a positive effect. To stabilise the banking system, bad banks (clearing banks) are introduced to hold "toxic" assets and bad loans to give the banks room to breathe. Europe's banks receive around 4 trillion EUR in government aid, of which, three-quarters are in the form of state guarantees.

Berenberg, however, concludes 2009 with a record result of 65.1 million EUR, which is 38 percent more than the previous year, and which provides a welcome opportunity to increase the liable equity from 177 to 212 million EUR.

In Düsseldorf, Frankfurt and Zurich, the offices are becoming too small. At the start of 2008, the Düsseldorf branch moves a few buildings down into what used to be the prestigious office mansion of the president of the higher regional court situated on Cecilienallee. The area of 1,000 square meters is now spacious enough to hold events in the same building. In Frankfurt, the bank moves to the Bockenheimer Anlage into a new, spacious office mansion in the autumn of 2009. Three years later, the location is once again too small and another move is in the works. On its 20th anniversary, the Berenberg Bank (Schweiz) AG also moves into a new building in close proximity to the opera house and with a view of Lake Zurich. In the anniversary year, it numbers 60 employees and manages 2.7 billion CHF.

The expansion of regional offices also results in an increased profile for the bank. Local involvement is an integral part of the perception and marketing of Berenberg.

The "scrapping bonus" is a newly coined phrase, which refers to a tax advantage launched in 2009 toward the purchase of a new car. In the real economy, the sharpest drop in economic activity since the end of World War II is recorded as a result of the financial crisis, which threatened the entire system. Germany lost just under 5 percent of its wealth. In a climate of major uncertainty, most of the companies are hardly willing to make new investments and invest in new products. Yet, employment remains surprisingly stable. At the end of 2009, there are 3.27 million unemployed, which means that only 175,000 more people are without a livelihood than 12 months earlier.

Equity analysts at Berenberg have been located in regional offices but are now to work centrally in London. "It gives us the opportunity to design our research product even more efficiently and recruit the best talent for us," explains Hendrik Riehmer. Following the Lehman crisis, many banks reduced the size of their research departments and some German banks even withdrew from London. "We were able to recruit top people and retain them," recalls Riehmer. And the bank made a name for itself. For the first time, Berenberg took top spot in the important 2009 Thomson Extel Survey, where 7,400 fund managers, analysts and financial experts select the most significant consultants. The result showed that 16.4 percent of those surveyed turn to Berenberg first when they want advice on European stocks. Within a year, the team in London doubles to 40 and the analysts cover around 300 European stocks. "We set up our research by sectors to better meet our clients' needs," says Riehmer. London offers the ideal environment to do this. "The city is very dynamic, and you have to be Champions League calibre to play the game. That was our goal."

With the first pan-European investment conference in 2009, the European orientation becomes clear. The conference in Pennyhill Park, near London, replaces what used to be the country conferences. A total of 125 institutional investors take advantage of the opportunity during the opening event to meet 41 company representatives.

In addition to expanding into the area of equities, the focus at the end of the decade is also on the fixed income segment. Berenberg is persuasive with its high level of competence, neutral consultation and promptness in communication and trade. The expansion of a good client base is followed by the opening of fixed income units in Vienna and Düsseldorf, which now offer these services in addition to Hamburg.

In general, it is a difficult time for the banking world. Chancellor Angela Merkel and her finance minister, Peer Steinbrück, make an important state-

Focus on share research in London

Berenberg hosts the first pan-European investor conference

At the renowned Global Private Banking Awards organised by the FT Magazine's "Professional Wealth Management" and "The Banker" Berenberg is honoured as being one of the five most innovative banks in the world. And institutional asset management wins accolades; for the first time it is acknowledged in 2009 as being the best asset manager in Germany.

Speakers at a Pan-European investors' conference organised by Berenberg

Dr Hans-Walter Peters and Hendrik Riehmer acquire 21 % of Berenberg and strengthen the position as an owner-run private bank

ment: "To the savers, we say that your deposits are secure." The bank bailout fund SoFFin is created. "Dresdner Bank" is taken over in 2008/2009 by "Commerzbank", which shortly thereafter has to be bailed out by the state during the bank crisis. There are bailouts of Hypo Real Estate to IKB and the establishment of bad banks at the state banks. At the end of 2006, Sal. Oppenheim has 3,500 employees, making it the largest independent private bank in Europe, yet it has to take cover under "Deutsche Bank".

"Norddeutsche Landesbank", which has been a limited partner of Joh. Berenberg, Gossler & Co. KG since 1973, and which is impressed by the good returns of the Hamburg investment, makes an attempt in 2008 to gain significant influence at Berenberg. However, both the aggressive approach taken by the then CEO of Nord/LB as well as the circumstance itself leads to resentment at Berenberg. The relationship cools off noticeably. Peters knows from this moment forward that there will only be peace when the partnership with Nord/LB is terminated. A few months later, this is exactly what happened. To fulfil the exacting equity requirements, it is mainly the state banks that have to create equity, and they start reducing investments and closing risky positions. Fortunately, there was a change in command at the state bank in Hanover. The new CEO, Dr Gunter Dunkel, assured Peters that the bank would sell the shares only in cooperation with Berenberg.

Both personally liable partners Dr Hans-Walter Peters and Hendrik Riehmer quickly seize the opportunity. After working together for 16 years, a friendship developed between the two, and they went from being employees to partners. "Dr Peters told me early on that he sees the partner in me with whom he wants to realign the bank. At the time, I did not take this at face value, as things turned out, but we are a really good team and complement each other perfectly. Dr Peters developed the structure and the strategy," as Riehmer describes the relationship. And Peters says of Riehmer: "He is full of energy. Once we have set the course, he does everything he can to reach the goal quickly. It shaped the restructuring of the bank and benefits us time and again in client business".

For the first time in recent history, personally liable partners are on the verge of acquiring larger shares in the bank. "We wanted to further expand Berenberg's position as an owner-run private bank," says Peters. They reach an agreement with the family and the other limited partners, Joachim von Berenberg-Consbruch, in particular, quickly realises the stabilising effect of having company partners acquire shares. At the start of 2010, Peters and Riehmer assume 21 percent in the limited partnership through their PetRie Beteiligungsgesellschaft; the von Berenberg family purchases the other 4 percent. After 37 years, Nord/LB is no longer a partner. "This all transpired with tremendous respect and on good terms on the part of both companies so that today our associations with Nord/LB are once again very cordial," says Peters. "Without this change to the ownership structure, the development that took place in recent years at the bank would not have happened," adds Riehmer.

Former senator Wolfgang Peiner has been watching the development of the private bank through the years with a critical eye and sees a decisive advantage in the company structure: "With the private bankers, there is personal continuity. They know each other. If you go to a major bank, you don't know if your contact person – even if it is a director – is going to be there in a year. But because you are dealing with personally liable partners at private banks, you can be sure that when things go south, they also have to bear the brunt." Real private banks with personally liable partners cannot be compared to private banks that only bear the name and have long since sought cover as a subsidiary with a major bank. Peiner notes: "Berenberg accomplished the feat of balancing success in its institutional business while maintaining high levels of service in the sophisticated area of private clients. A bank which can create volume with 40 major insurance companies also needs to retain an appeal for its private clients. In the long run, you cannot convince the wealthy widow of a businessman with smart young banker types who only speak in a foreign language and are at home in global markets."

The former finance senator is convinced: "For the international significance of Hamburg as a financial centre, Berenberg is currently the most important bank. One thing is for sure and that is that Peters has elevated the bank to an international level. His word has value."

Shares in the bank :
30.4 % v. Berenberg family
25.6 % PetRie Beteiligungsgesellschaft mbH (Dr Hans-Walter Peters, managing director, and Hendrik Riehmer)
2 % Andreas Brodtmann and former liable partners
15 % Christian Erbprinz zu Fürstenberg
15 % Jan Philipp Reemtsma
12 % Compagnie du Bois Sauvage S.A.

A charity golf tournament marked the opening of the bank's Salzburg branch; Dr Hans-Walter Peters donated 120,000 EUR to the Franz Beckenbauer Foundation

In the "Private Banking Survey" done by the renowned magazine, Euromoney, Berenberg is acknowledged as the 'Best Private Bank in Germany' and replaces Deutsche Bank (2009) and Sal. Oppenheim (2008)

At the 2010 Global Private Banking Awards of Professional Wealth Management and The Banker (Financial Times Group) the first-ever 'Best Private Bank in Germany' award goes to Berenberg ahead of the Deutsche Bank. Berenberg does not relinquish the title for four straight years

Two years after the global economic crisis, Germany advances to become an important pillar for the global economy. In 2010, its economic output grows by 3.6 percent, which was the best result since reunification.

Berenberg concludes the first decade of the new century with the second-best result in its history. There is an annual surplus totalling 61.5 million EUR and a core capital ratio in the group of 15.1 percent. Both figures are a testament to profitability and the solid business model. The focus on the service business is also apparent in the high percentage of commission income. The ratio of commission surplus to ongoing interest surplus in 2010 is 82:18. Even corporate client business has been restructured in such a way that most of the proceeds are in the commission segment: advice is given on the design and implementation of optimal financing structures and credit is only granted to them if another business is tied in.

"Our superior expertise is an important competitive factor for our clients," says Hendrik Riehmer. He continues to expand equity research at the London office. The know-how for German small and mid caps is confirmed again in the Thomson Reuters Extel Survey with the accolade "best analysis bank". There are 55 analysts, at the end of 2010, who now start evaluating large listed companies in addition to small and mid caps. "The research is particularly important in a capital market business." If you can persuade with your analysis then you get on the broker lists of large institutional investors. The "currency" with which the research is "paid", are orders behalf of investment companies and others to buy or sell. Berenberg's research is among the best, the market share of the Hamburg-based private bank increases from year to year. This does not simply happen automatically. The analysts tour the world with company directors. There are 150 road shows with 1,200 individual meetings in 2010 alone.

This is also the right time to take IPO consultations and capital increases to a new level.

SOCIAL COMMITMENT ...

... has always been an important element at Berenberg. For the family and the personally liable partners, it has always been important to contribute to the greater good of society, but also to cultural, sporting or scientific initiatives.

In 2006, employees in the London branch launched an initiative, **Berenberg Kids**, to promote underprivileged children. In various activities, employees collect donations, climb mountains in England, bike across the country or measure their performance in a fun and athletic pentathlon or in beach volleyball. To participate, a registration fee is required. At the end of 2009, the sustained success of the initiative led to the transformation of the flexible association into a foundation. By the end of 2014, almost 1 million EUR had been raised for good causes.

However, it is not just about collecting donations. Offering hands-on help is also big at Berenberg. And in this vein, employees hold city rallies, organise a visit to the zoo, paint classrooms and nursery schools, clean playgrounds or give Christmas presents to primary school children in socially disadvantaged parts of the city.

Top: Andreas Brodtmann with Sandra Völker, Nina Bott and Mirja du Mont (from left) at the Berenberg Kids Beach Volleyball event; below: players at the 2014 tournament

Hamburg is a stronghold of the oldest and probably fastest team sport in the world: **Polo**. The Berenberg Polo Derby in Hamburg Klein-Flottbek marks the start to a season of premier competition and is a social event. Involvement is being expanded to include other cities; international polo aces now meet in five tournaments of the highest calibre. Berenberg is one of the biggest sponsors of polo in Germany. Apart from the derby in Hamburg, the Berenberg High Goal Cup in Düsseldorf and the Berenberg German Polo Masters on the island of Sylt are also social highlights of the season in an exclusive and yet familiar atmosphere. In addition, the bank also plays host to international match-ups such as the Berenberg Snow Polo in the Swiss ski resort Klosters or at top tournaments in England.

Dr Hans-Walter Peters with the 100-year-old Irmela Baroness von Berenberg-Gossler at the Berenberg Polo Derby in 2014

Above: Golf stars with Dr Hans-Walter Peters (third from left) at the Berenberg Gary Player Invitational in Wentworth: Fred Couples, Martin Kaymer, Gary Player, Rickie Fowler and Colin Montgomerie; Below: golfing legend Gary Player is a brand ambassador for Berenberg

The Berenberg Bank Classics have captured the public imagination with matches between global **tennis** legends: John McEnroe, Andre Agassi, Mats Wilander and Stefan Edberg have all competed in the prestigious event, which is held during Germany's leading professional tournaments in Hamburg (Rothenbaum) and Stuttgart (Porsche Arena).

Berenberg is active in equestrian sports and donates silver trophies for the most lucrative **horse race** held at the Hamburg-Horn Racecourse, or at the *Großen Woche* in Baden-Baden Iffezheim. With the *Club an der Alster*, it sponsors one of the most successful **hockey** clubs in Germany, not to mention the repeat winner of the German championship title and the European Cup.

John McEnroe at the Berenberg Classics in Stuttgart

The bank's participation in **golf** is growing. Since 2010, the bank has been involved in professional golf, organising the Berenberg Masters, one of the biggest events in the European Senior Tour. Golf idols Gary Player and Bernhard Langer are tournament ambassadors and up to 15,000 visitors flock to the tournaments, which in 2010 were held in Fancourt (South Africa), in the time-honoured Golf- und Land-Club Köln (2011 and 2013) and at the Golfclub Wörthsee (2012). In 2014, the event moved to the renowned Wentworth Golf Club where the bank went ahead with another concept: The Berenberg Gary Player Invitational 2014 brought together top international stars such as Martin Kaymer, Tom Watson, Colin Montgomerie, Fred Couples and Lee Westwood. The tournament becomes the European counterpart of the Gary Player Invitational Series with charity tournaments being held in South Africa, the US and China. With 60 million USD in donations over the last 30 years, it is the world's most successful charity golf tournament series. In 2015, the Berenberg Gary Player Invitational expanded to the US.

Berenberg is also on the right track when it comes to **classic cars**: it sponsors famous events around the world such as the Concorso d'Eleganza Villa d'Este, and – with its clients – participates in displays such as the Kitzbühel Alpine Rally and the Schloss Bensberg Classics.

Prize winners past and present gathered to commemorate the 25th anniversary of the Berenberg Bank Foundation of 1990, with Hamburg's senator for culture, Barbara Kisseler, Dr Hans-Walter Peters and the Foundation's board of trustees

The Berenberg Foundation of 1990 has become an institution in Hamburg's cultural life and has invested well over half a million EUR in support of young artists. To date, the Berenberg Foundation has promoted 100 artists. The bank funds projects at the *Hochschule für Musik und Theater*, the *Internationale Opernstudio*, the *Hamburger Symphoniker* and at the *Ballettzentrum John Neumeier*. It allows students from the Shanghai Conservatory to stay in Hamburg for studies and concerts, and with the Art School Alliance, it co-initiated an affiliation of six of the world's most significant art colleges. "Cultural diversity and an active intellectual life are indispensible as major factors of a lively city." In 2011, the bank was awarded with the *Kulturmerkur* from the Hamburg Senate and the Hamburg Chamber of Commerce for its successful sponsoring activities.

With the series "Wort trifft Musik" (Word meets Music), created by Sebastian Knauer, who is the first Berenberg scholarship recipient from 1990 and currently a world-class pianist, the bank promotes the interplay of literature and music and organises concert evenings with readings in which prominent German actors such as Hannelore Elsner, Gudrun Landgrebe and Martina Gedeck read texts alternating with selected piano pieces. The evenings are recorded and turned into a discerning CD series.

And the bank is also active in **science** and supports the Hamburg Institute of World Economics (HWWI). As a long-term strategic partner of the HWWI, the private bank initiated together with the institute the research series Strategy 2030 – Assets and Life in the Next Generation and a ranking of the 30 major cities in Germany.

In 2006, the **Berenberg Magazin** debuts, a discerning publication on politics, culture and sports. Dr Werner Funk, long-time editor-in-chief of *Manager Magazin*, *Spiegel*, *Stern* and Berenberg's head of communications, Karsten Wehmeier are the men behind it. The tremendous acceptance the magazine enjoys in political and business circles is documented by the number of high-ranking individuals who were available for an exclusive interview, including former Federal Presidents Roman Herzog and Christian Wulff, the vice chancellors and federal cabinet ministers Guido Westerwelle and Sigmar Gabriel and as well as Peer Steinbrück and Wolfgang Schäuble.

President of the Hamburg Chamber of Commerce Fritz-Horst Melsheimer and the city's senator for Culture Barbara Kisseler present the Kultur-merkur (Culture Mercury) to Karsten Wehmeier; last year's recipient Albert Darboven adds his congratulations

2011–2014: Looking to the Future with Expertise and Accountability

Over 1,000 employees

The second decade of the century is marred by the euro crisis, which poses great challenges to politics and the economy. Berenberg succeeds in continually growing despite the turbulent environment; internationalisation is a big theme. "As a result, we become more independent from individual markets," says Peters. In 2011, the number of employees climbs by 14 percent to 1,110. Market pressure, lack of client interest in complicated financial products and regulatory requirements with the associated costs lead to a drop in margins across the private banking sector. In addition, private German investors are typically more price sensitive than their foreign counterparts. "We are set up in a very diversified way with our four business divisions and are well able to compensate for more difficult market phases in some areas with other divisions," comments Dr Hans-Walter Peters. Investment banking is turning out to be very successful. In addition to research and brokerage, the focus turns increasingly to consulting during IPOs and capital increases, and by 2011, the

2011: Demonstration against cuts in Germany's social services outside the chancellor's office in Berlin

bank is involved in all major IPOs in Germany and provides advice on mergers and acquisitions. Berenberg is the only financial advisor to Tognum AG during its 3.6 billion EUR acquisition by Daimler and Rolls Royce.

Fixed income research is expanded, the number of equity analysts continues to grow and 400 European share values are covered. The American market shifts into focus. In Boston, where Berenberg had a branch between 1828 and 1902, a new subsidiary, Berenberg Capital Markets LLC, opens in 2011. It markets the research prepared in London to American institutional investors. And in Switzerland, Berenberg is now represented at the Geneva financial centre by a branch of Berenberg Bank (Schweiz) AG.

In 2011, efforts are underway to set up a private banking unit in London to look after English clients. In England, long-standing private bankers were integrated into international financial groups over the years meaning that there are good business opportunities for an independent, owner-run private bank with know-how and experience in consulting discerning private clients.

The image of banks suffered tremendously during the public debate on the financial crisis. There was a focus on the complicated and hardly manageable financial products of banks which found themselves in serious difficulty and had to be rescued by tax payers and of the sale of unsuitable financial investments to small investors. The phrase "cultural change" is rampant. Banks come up with slogans such as "We have understood" or "We will not rest". "Today it is more important than ever before for banks to gear their business models to the needs of their clients," says Peters. "The branch is called upon to show clients and society that banks are an important pillar in our daily economic life".

Germany is moving from being the once "sick man" to the engine in the euro region. Foreign investor interest in German companies is growing. Together with the American investment bank, Berenberg extends invitations in September 2012 to the first Berenberg / Goldman Sachs German Corporate Conference in Munich. It was a complete success. Around 750 participants from 25 countries were in attendance. Executives from roughly 100 German companies introduce themselves, including two-thirds from DAX-30 com-

Berenberg and Goldman Sachs jointly organized the German Corporate Conference

Berenberg crosses the Atlantic

panies. "We wanted to create a forum for the exchange of views between German companies and international investors," says Riehmer.

Lead role in Talanx IPO

Berenberg experiences a breakthrough in 2012 in its equity capital market business when it is given responsibility for two of the five major IPOs in Europe. Together with "Deutsche Bank", Berenberg receives a surprise leading role in the high-profile IPO of the insurance company Talanx AG (517 million EUR). Similarly, Berenberg has a leading role in the largest Swiss IPO of DKSH Holding (903 million CHF). Having now been involved in seven primary market transactions, Berenberg ranks among the top three banks in German-speaking Europe (Germany, Austria, Switzerland).

Berenberg increases its interest in Universal-Investment to 50 percent

Dr Peters continues to expand Berenberg's position in the Frankfurt Universal-Investment. In April 2012, he buys shares from Hauck & Aufhäuser, in August from the "Landesbank Baden-Württemberg".

Record results

Berenberg and Bankhaus Lampe now each hold 50 percent of the shares. Both private banks have been involved in Universal-Investment for decades and have gradually increased their shares in recent years. Universal-Investment is the largest independent investment company in the German-speaking region. With around 550 employees, it has more than 1,000 investment mandates with a volume of 214 billion EUR (January 2015).

At the end of 2012, the Frankfurt branch moves into a new building on Bockenheimer Landstraße 25. The bank is now situated in a representative building in the most important German financial centre and offers room to grow. In addition to the private banking unit, the building also houses equity capital markets, M&A, equity sales and fixed income units. In September 2013, the new chief investment office is added, which looks after the capital market view and asset management.

The year 2013 ended for Berenberg with another record result. The gross income hits 309 million EUR and the year-end annual surplus is 66.1 million EUR, almost 10 percent more than the previous year. Managed assets grow and surpass the 30 billion EUR mark. A total of 1,147 people are now employed.

The Berenberg Bank building at Bockenheimer Landstrasse 25

New York's Times Square illuminated in Berenberg's colours to mark its Nasdaq membership; Hendrik Riehmer with bank staff

"For our now international business, it is very important to be represented in the major financial centres," explains Hendrik Riehmer. It was an emotional moment for him when Berenberg was launched on the New York Stock Exchange. "Even as a young person, American shares always interested me the most. And when the NASDAQ invited us to an event to celebrate the newly received stock exchange membership – it was obviously a great occasion. At the time, we had just finished creating a new logo for the bank. It was supposed to be officially introduced two weeks later, but the 'preview' was in Times Square in New York."

With a new, confident and modern logo, Berenberg left out the "bank" – "by now, we are much more namely, an internationally operating consultancy," says Peters.

In August 2014, Berenberg opens its third office on American soil in San Francisco. "We see enormous potential in the US for further growth and are marketing our European research product there," says Hendrik Riehmer.

At the start of 2014, asset management begins managing the largest influx of new money in the history of the bank. The British Aerion Fund Management, one of the largest in-house pension fund managers in Great Britain, commissions Berenberg with the currency hedging of its investments. The volume is pegged at 3.5 billion GBP. About 50 percent of the assets managed now come from international investors. Thus, the division decides – in addition to the activities at its London location – to set up its own company with locations in New York and Chicago promoting and selling its 'Made in Germany' products and services.

At the end of 2014, a cooperative venture with Bayern LB was finalised with the goal of further improving business opportunities in investment banking. Since bridge financing is necessary in many transactions and is something that Berenberg is unable to offer because of its loan credit facilities, it entered into a strategic cooperation with Bayern LB. The Munich bank has excellent ties to almost all DAX companies and is one of the largest credit banks in Germany. However, since it is not active on the equity capital markets, Berenberg is able to jump in with its know-how. It translates into a win-win situation for both partners as well as for German companies as the dependence upon major American and European banks is reduced.

Investments in successful business model

The year 2014 is a year of investments. The bank adds 100 new employees. There are now 1,250 people working for Berenberg at 19 locations in Europe, the US and in Asia. The partners agree that "the most important aspect is the business model." It has to be right and then investments can be made in growth and in long-term success. Though high investments in 2014 did not make for a record year as in the previous one, it is the foundation for Berenberg's continued future success as the oldest private bank in Germany and the second-oldest in the world.

The bank's personally liable partners:
Hendrik Riehmer, Dr Hans-Walter Peters
and Andreas Brodtmann (from left)

"The trend towards high-level independent consultancy remains strong.
Berenberg will profit in the future from this aim with its concentration
on providing services. We are the second-oldest bank in the world and also
one of the most dynamic in Europe, a fact which shows that we move
between two poles: the continuity of tradition and the flexibility of modern
times. Courage and the willingness to embrace change are decisive as the
thought of the future must always be just as important to us as the memory
of our forefathers."

The foyer of Berenberg
in Hamburg

COMPANY GENEALOGY

1590–1626	Hans Berenberg
1590–1645	Paul Berenberg (II)
1626–1640	Hans Berenberg (II)
1645–1699	Johann Berenberg
1645–1672	Rudolf Berenberg
1660–1711	Cornelius Berenberg
1715–1749	Johann Berenberg (II)
1715–1746	Senator Rudolf Berenberg (II)
1739–1761	Rudolf Berenberg (III)
1749–1768	Senator Paul Berenberg (IV)
1749–1772	Johann Berenberg (III)
1769–1790	Johann Hinrich Gossler
1788–1836	Ludwig Erdwin Seyler
1790–1800	Elisabeth Gossler
1777–1820	Franz Friedrich Kruckenberg
1798–1842	Senator Johann Heinrich Gossler (II)
1830–1879	Johann Heinrich Gossler (III)
1836–1858	Wilhelm Gossler
1864–1913	Johann (John) Freiherr v. Berenberg-Gossler
1873–1893	Ernst Gossler
1892–1908	Senator John v. Berenberg-Gossler (II)
1898–1953	Cornelius Freiherr v. Berenberg-Gossler (III)
1908–1923	Andreas v. Berenberg-Gossler
1920–1930	Dr Heinrich Burchard
1923–1930	Walter Gleich
1935–1979	Heinrich Freiherr v. Berenberg-Gossler
1948–1961	August Rohdewald
1961–1979	Heinz A. Lessing
1964–1972	Karl-Theodor Lindemann
1968–1998	Joachim H. Wetzel
1976–1999	Peter Freiherr v. Kap-herr
1998–2000	Dr Andreas Odefey
1978–2005	Joachim v. Berenberg-Consbruch
1988–2008	Claus-G. Budelmann
2004–2008	Guido M. Sollors
seit 2000	Dr Hans-Walter Peters
seit 2009	Andreas Brodtmann
seit 2009	Hendrik Riehmer

The dates reflect the duration of the partnership.

REGISTER

IMAGERY AND COPYRIGHT HOLDERS

© 2015 Joh. Berenberg, Gossler & Co. KG
Neuer Jungfernstieg 20
20354 Hamburg
www.berenberg.de

Published by Carl Hanser Verlag, Munich

Journalism and picture selection: Karsten Wehmeier, Rainer Groothuis, Imke Borchers
Documentation: Reinhard Helling
Design, layout and production: Groothuis. Gesellschaft der Ideen und Passionen mbH,
Hamburg | www.groothuis.de; Miriam Kunisch, Carolin Beck, Janine Lattich
Lithography: Frische Grafik, Hamburg
Printing and binding: gutenberg beuys, Feindruckerei, Langenhagen

ISBN 978-1-56990-601-9
Printed in Germany